THE RELEVANT HISTORY OF MANKIND

The absence of romance in my history will, I fear, detract somewhat from its interest; but I shall be content if it is judged useful by those inquirers who desire an exact knowledge of the past as an aid to the interpretation of the future, which in the course of human things must resemble if it does not reflect it.

Thucydides, The History of the Peloponnesian War

Whoso neglects learning in his youth,
Loses the past and is dead for the future.

Euripides

For Erga

The Relevant History
of Mankind

Nathan Schur

Alpha
THE
PRESS

2 4 6 8 10 9 7 5 3 1

First published 1997 in Great Britain by
THE ALPHA PRESS
PO Box 2950
Brighton BN2 5SP

and in the United States of America by
THE ALPHA PRESS
c/o International Specialized Book Services, Inc.
5804 N.E. Hassalo St.
Portland, Oregon 97213-3644

Library of Congress Cataloging-in-Publication Data
Schur, Nathan.
   The relevant history of mankind / Nathan Schur.
      p.   cm.
   Includes index.
   ISBN 1–898595–21–6 (pbk : alk. paper)
   1. Civilization—History.   2. World history.   I. Title.
CB69.S38   1997   97–27209
909—dc21   CIP

British Library Cataloguing in Publication Data
A CIP catalogue record for this book is available from the British Library.

Cover picture: "Marco Polo Leaving Venice" – MS Bodl. 264, fol. 218R,
reproduced by courtesy The Bodleian Library, University of Oxford.

Printed and bound by Biddles Ltd, King's Lynn and Guildford

Contents

What is Relevant?

What is relevant in history? Are really all, or most of the names, dates and other details which fill the thousands of pages of many-volumed histories of the world relevant? If a good fairy would grant us a completely retentive memory should we really wish to remember all the minutiae of history?

I do not believe so. Most details are completely trivial, except to a small group of dedicated specialists in each field. This does not mean, however, that all of history is trivial. Far from it. History is both fascinating and important. There is no other way to understand who we are and how we came to be where we are now.

The way history is usually taught and written is, however, rarely of much help. Specialization in this field, as in so many others, has proceeded to such a point that most historians know more and more about less and less. They are used to handling only the small details of their specialist fields and are suspicious of all generalizations and analogies. Yet what the general reader should be looking for are these very generalizations – the forest and not the trees.

In this volume I have tried to limit the text mostly to conclusions and to mention only what is really worth remembering. The use of names, too, both of people and of places, has been severely curtailed on purpose. Nothing is easier than mentioning the name of still another king, another battle, another poet and another building. But the result would be that the reader is swamped with much more information than he or she can absorb. I have tried therefore to ration the use of names and mention only those who have real relevance.

But this approach does not mean that this book follows tamely, if concisely, in the footsteps of generally accepted historiography. The writing of history is undergoing a profound revolution. It is no longer sufficient to linger mainly on political history – to describe only the doings of kings and the outcomes of battles. Economic, social, and cultural developments are regarded now as even more important. Indeed, some schools of history have downgraded the role of the individual and believe mainly in general trends. It is possible, however, that some of these tendencies have gone too far. Theories might be interesting, but they are also dangerous. When actually describing historical events it might be best for the historian to leave his other preconceived ideas behind and to decide on the merits of the case, without too much reference to the latest philosophy of history.

There has also occurred a great change in our geographical conceptions of history. In the past, history books have tended to explain the rise of Greek, Roman, and modern Western Civilization as their main theme and to downgrade other civilizations. This is no longer possible. In a world from which European colonial empires have disappeared, in which Japan and other nations of the Pacific Rim are pushing successfully ahead in the economic sphere, in which the Islamic civilization is taking a very different road from that of all other civilizations, in which the black nations of Africa are struggling to find their identity, it is necessary to rewrite history completely. The past is becoming thus more complex and a greater number of different strands of development have to be examined. It is clear now that very different influences have created the mosaic of the present. East and West, South and North have cross-pollinated each other.

The more complicated the picture really proves to be, the more reason there is to keep its description simple. In order to deal with the complication of a multiplicity of civilizations and their mutual influences, it is the more necessary to stress only the really *relevant* developments.

Part I

Beginnings

Historians used to draw a clear line between history and prehistory. The existence of written records was the touchstone if one was dealing with "history." As writing was invented around 3300 BC in Mesopotamia, all earlier developments were regarded as "prehistory." This differentiation has lost much of its significance. Archeology and its auxiliary sciences and techniques have progressed to the point where much can be discovered about an ancient civilization even without written records.

Radiocarbon dating, for instance, is based on the decay of the isotope Carbon 14, at the rate of halving every 5730 years. When burned charcoal or the bones of an animal are found in an excavation, the age of that level can be ascertained. At first there was much uncertainty about this system, as some results were clearly unreliable. On further investigation it turned out that the reason was the past fluctuation in cosmic ray activity. This can now be overcome with the help of dendrochronology (tree-ring dating) by a special calibrating process. Further, objects made of fired clay, such as pottery, can now be dated with the help of thermoluminescence. This is done by reheating the artifact in order to measure the light emitted by electrons which were freed by radioactivity, but remained trapped in the clay. By these and other methods amazing results have been obtained in the dating of ancient remains. As a result, events which took place many thousands or even millions of years ago can now be dated. Questions such as when did man first appear and where? When did people emigrate to Europe, America and Australia? When did they first turn to hunting and to agriculture? can be answered with some confidence, just as if we had written evidence of these events.

Not only can archeology give the date of a site or an event in the development of man, but it can supply details also of the culture, customs, and religion of ancient cities and civilizations. The technology of excavation has been refined very much, both by exact stratigraphy (the relation of objects to the layers of deposits in which they are found) and by typology (the classification of objects according to types and their comparison with one another, in order to determine chronological, geographical, and technical relationships). Such related sciences as underwater archeology (equipped with scuba diving gear and sometimes with the help of miniature submarines), the analysis of food remains and textiles, the diagnosis of disease, or the interpretation of burial customs, have opened up new avenues of research.

Our knowledge of what used to be termed as prehistoric cultures and events has advanced in recent years by leaps and bounds, and we are able to give in the following chapters a much fuller description of early man than would have been possible only a few years ago.

1   Mother Earth

We shall discuss in this book the happenings on one of the smaller planets among the myriad galaxies and star clusters of the universe, moving around one of the less spectacular stars near the edge of one of the spiralling arms of the Milky Way Galaxy. We call this star "Sun" and the planet "Earth." The history of the Earth is believed to go back some 4.6 billion years, but except for the opening chapters we shall discuss only a very short ten thousand years out of this lengthy period. This is a mere eye twinkle by the standards of the universe. Yet it is all the human race has had so far and it is far from certain how much more it will have in future.

The crust of the earth is made up of enormous rigid plates, which rest on a mantle around the molten core of the planet. The continents are carried on these plates. Oceans are formed as the plates move apart. Lava spills into the new sea-bed, thus filling in the resulting scars. Most of the plates have been identified and named. There is a Pacific Plate, but not an Atlantic one. The reason is that originally most of the continents formed one huge land mass. Some 180 million years ago, America began to separate from Africa and Europe, slowly opening the Atlantic Ocean in between. The final link-up between the central and southern Atlantic was established some 90 million years ago. This ocean is therefore bisected by a North American and a South American Plate, reaching into its western part, and a Eurasian and African Plate reaching into its eastern part. Some 160 million years ago Antarctica, Australia, and India started to separate from Africa, thus beginning to open up the Indian Ocean. Most of this ocean, and also India and Australia, are indeed riding on one Indo-Australian Plate. Australia separated from Antarctica some 45 million years ago. Sometime earlier, about 85 million years ago, Greenland broke away from Canada and some 50 million years ago also from Europe. Arabia is moving away from Africa, India is moving northwards into Asia. This continental drift has thrown up the high mountains of this planet – the Rockies and Andes, as the Americas moved westward, the Himalayas and Alps, as India and Italy were pressing northwards.

Since the crust of the Earth first solidified, new rock has been added from below. This molten rock may remain deep in the crust, cooling slowly, or it may erupt as lava, forming volcanoes. There are different types of volcanoes and many of them arise along the fault lines where the tectonic plates meet. Some volcanoes build up without eruption. Though this is usually a slow process, Capelinhos island in the Azores has grown since 1957 from sea level to over 3300 ft (1000 m).

Other volcanoes erupt violently. In 1833, Krakatoa in Java sent a dust cloud right around the world, causing huge tidal waves and killing some 36 000 people. Nearby, the Tambora volcano had erupted in 1815, with even worse results. As against the 18 cubic kilometers of material released by Krakatoa, Tambora evicted 30 cubic kilometers, masking the sun sufficiently to cool the Earth in the process. In far-away Europe, the following year was called the "year without summer." An even grander eruption occurred in 1783 on Iceland. Lava poured out continuously for eight months. Some 154 million tons of volcanic gases were released, crops withered, livestock perished, and Iceland's population was reduced by one-fifth.

These events took place far from the great centers of civilization; but in 1450 BC the volcano on the island of Thera, in the southern Aegean, erupted with such violence that a tidal wave rose up, which smothered the northern coast of Crete and with it much of the Minoan civilization. Of Thera only parts of a huge crater remain – much larger than that of Krakatoa.

If, in the following chapters, we shall find human history often a rather violent process, one has to remember that it is being played out against the background of our often violent planet.

2   Early Man

About 1000 million years after the formation of the Earth the first living cells must have put in their appearance. Early life evolved everywhere in the water. For three billion years there were mainly algae, bacteria and plankton. Only in the Cambrian period, some 530 million years ago, did there evolve the trilobites, brachiopods, bivalves (such as oysters), mollusks, corals, insects, and vertebrates, such as fishes and amphibians. Some of the insects and amphibians developed the ability to live on land. New types of life evolved there. The earliest reptiles appeared some 300 million years ago. Huge dinosaurs roamed the earth for some 120 million years, but disappeared completely some 65 million years ago. They were replaced by birds and mammals. The latter were at first quite small, but grew in size and developed into the many different species known today. The earliest primates appeared some 60 million years ago, slowly developing into monkeys, apes and humans.

All early remains of man indicate Africa as his original home.

His ancestors may have diverged from the African apes between eight and five million years ago. They started to walk upright when they moved out of the forests and adapted to savannah life, according to one theory because of the climatic conditions of an early Ice Age, which had locked up so much water in the form of ice, that rainfall dwindled, forests shrank, and grassland expanded at the expense of the forests. Thus many of the previous inhabitants of the forests were forced to adapt their lifestyle to a new existence in savannah country and among them were the early ancestors of man. Hominid footprints, some 3.8 million years old, have been discovered in Tanzania, showing that these man apes were already walking upright.

The early man apes (australopiths) were a good deal smaller than modern man. Parts of a female skeleton, some 3.4 million years old, have been found in Ethiopia and have been nicknamed "Lucy," which sounds less formidable than her scientific appelation *Australopithecus afarensis*. She had a small body, slimmer hips and longer arms than those of a modern woman, and clearly used to walk upright. Adults of this type were only some 3–4 ft (1–1.3 m) tall and weighed some 65 lb (30 kg). Their brain was apparently too small for speech. Later types, with different scientific appelations (*Australopithecus africanus*, – *robustus*, – *boisei*), grew slowly larger and so did their brains.

Around 2.5 million years ago we are probably on safe ground in speaking of an early type of "man" (*homo habilis*) and no longer of "man apes." His remains have been found in eastern and southern Africa. His height was about 4–5 ft (1.2–1.5 m), his weight about 110 lb (50 kg) and his brain of some 650–800 cc (as against 1400 cc for modern man). His face looked already much more human. He may have had already the ability of rudimentary speech.

If we want to define humans, we can probably do no better than say that they are able to fashion tools. And indeed, around 2.5 million years ago the oldest stone tools were prepared. From now on we can speak about an "Early Stone Age," though actually early man is sure to have utilized much more wood, reeds, bark or hides than stones. These tools made up for his modest size and enabled him to defend himself against large carnivors. His upright stance freed his hands to use these tools and to fashion them, giving him a unique advantage.

Homo habilis seems to have lived in groups from an early period onwards, as indicated by camp sites of some 2 million years ago, discovered in Tanzania. Remains some 1.8 million years old indicate that members of such groups were already constructing rough shelters, or even huts.

By 1.7 million years ago a larger, stronger type of man had appeared, with a bigger brain. Prehistorians call him *Homo erectus* – upright man. His tools were becoming more sophisticated and some of them can be described as hand-axes. He seems to have been enabled, as a result, to advance from mere scavenging to active hunting. Fire was known at least one million years ago and perhaps much earlier.

His unique advantages enabled *Homo erectus* to leave Africa, his original habitat, pass through the Middle East and then spread out over Europe and Asia. South of Lake Genezareth, at 'Ubeidya, stone flakes, chopping tools and other remains have been found, of about 1.5 million years ago – the oldest site outside Africa found so far. He traversed Asia fairly quickly. On Java, remains some 1.3 million years old have been found and in southwest China perhaps even older ones. Other remains, from northern China, are later – some 450 000–350 000 years old. From one site burnt blackberries have been recovered – a rare reminder that early man was sure to have utilized plants more than meat as food. Some sites in Thailand are apparently some 600 000 years old.

Early tools indicate that man may have reached Europe between one million and 700 000 years ago. Later tools, from between 700 000 and 400 000 years, have been unearthed all over Europe. Also parts of human skulls have survived, the earliest ones from about 500 000 and 400 000 years ago. In southern France remains of wooden huts have been uncovered. In Spain, early man hunted elephants, deer, horses, wild cattle, and rhinoceroses, apparently using wooden spears. It must have been a hazardous undertaking – many of the skulls of *Homo erectus* show signs of having been fractured by the large animals he hunted.

More advanced types of man appeared: Neanderthal man around 120 000 years ago (but some prehistorians would date him already much earlier), and modern man (called, reassuringly, *Homo sapiens sapiens* – "wise, wise man"), from about 100 000 years ago. While Neanderthaler remains have so far been found mainly in Europe and in southwestern Asia, it seems certain that modern man originated in Africa. The Neanderthalers are distinguished by their heavy frames and may have adapted to the rigors of the glacial periods in central Europe. Most of their remains are from the first part of the last (Würm) glaciation, 70 000–30 000 years ago. But around the end of this period they disappear – wiped out or absorbed by modern man, who had come via the Levant land-bridge (where he lived for long periods side by side with Neanderthals in some of the Mount Carmel [northern Israel] caves).

Homo sapiens sapiens is the ancestor of all races at present existent. Coming from Africa he reached Europe and Asia, and from there America and Australia – the latter some 50 000 years ago and America apparently even later. Skin color appears to be a later adjustment to constant strong sunshine or to a moderate climate.

Neanderthal man must have had already some sort of religious feelings, hence his careful burials. He also practiced cannibalism – but perhaps with the ulterior motives to gain the strength or ability of those whose brains and marrow he had eaten. Early *Homo sapiens sapiens*, too, must have had some religious ideas, as indicated by the impressive cave paintings he produced. They are assumed to have played a part in rituals, involving hunting magic and the initiation of the young. Many of these paintings have survived in the caves of southern France and northern Spain. They show contemporary animals – bisons, boars, aurochs, stags, and ibexes. They date from about 35 000 to 14 000 years ago. Other paintings and figurines have been discovered in Austria, Russia, South Africa, and Australia.

3   The Agricultural and Urban Revolution

Around 10 000 BC the last Ice Age drew to an end. Ice sheets which had covered much of Europe, Asia, and North America melted. The water previously locked up in them poured into the oceans and raised their level by some 430 feet (130 m), severing land-bridges that had connected the British Isles and Europe, Siberia and North America, Indonesia and Malaya. The rainfall increased and deserts receded.

Conditions for human existence became more favorable. The area in which these revolutions first took place is called the Middle East, encompassing Syria and Israel, Egypt, Iraq, and parts of southeastern Turkey.

Man had lived so far by hunting and by the gathering of plants, roaming the country to find new hunting grounds. The great breakthrough which occurred now in the Middle East was three-pronged.

Some of the hunter-gatherers had already harvested wild cereals, now they started to grow them themselves. Wheat appears to have come first, followed by barley, lentils and beans. By selecting the best strains the small wild plants were developed into bigger, domesticated ones. The earliest such development seems to have taken place in or around present-day Israel, but spread out soon to neighboring areas.

The second field of development was that of animal domestication. Dogs may have been the first ones, descending from tame wolves, who were trained first to help to hunt and later to drive and guard herds. Next came sheep, goats, cattle and pigs. Man thus obtained "living larders" by using their milk and meat and later also learned to use their wool.

There was no point in roaming any longer, fields had to be tended, herds and flocks had to be attended to. Man started to settle down, at first in small communities, later in bigger ones. The oldest such town found so far by archeologists is biblical Jericho, founded 9000 BC. It was surrounded by a 3 m thick stone wall, strengthened by a 9 m high circular stone tower. Jericho's basis was agricultural – cultivating wheat and barley, and raising herds of sheep and goats. A local shrine has been uncovered. By 7000 BC plastered skulls were used as cult objects.

This "Urban Revolution" spread out, first along the Jordan rift and along the eastern shore of the Mediterranean and later, around 7000 BC, also to Mesopotamia and Anatolia. Smallish urban sites have been discovered in all of these areas. The largest such site found so far is Çatal Hüjük, founded around 7000 BC, in Anatolia, covering 13 hectares. The settlement was built closely packed together and raised above the ground, so that access could be gained only with the help of ladders. Its wealth depended on the black obsidian mined in the nearby mountains. In a local shrine human skulls were lined up on benches, beneath reliefs of bulls' and rams' heads. In some of the houses figurines of goddesses were found, shown pregnant or giving birth, suggesting a fertility cult.

This period is called the Neolithic period (New Stone Age) by prehistorians and hence derives also the use of an equivalent term: the "Neolithic Revolution." Its achievements – domestication of animals, introduction of agriculture, urbanization – slowly spread out from the Middle East in all directions, to the Balkans and Europe, to Baluchistan and Eastern Asia, and to Africa. Their Neolithic periods are accordingly somewhat later than that of the Middle East. In America, similar inventions were made independently some millennia later.

These important achievements led to denser settlements as given areas of fertile land fed far more food producers than hunter-gatherers. It has been estimated that the total number of humans inhabiting the Earth may have reached some 10 million souls in the Neolithic period.

Further new inventions followed, such as that of textile weaving (initially using hemp) and of pottery making. Pottery replaced vessels made of stone, or baskets. The different styles and materials of pottery sherds serve nowadays as indispensable tools for the modern archeologist in identifying cultures and dating the layers of the sites which are being excavated.

In the seventh millennium BC casting of such metals as gold and copper was discovered, initially mainly for the preparation of ornaments. In the fourth millennium BC bronze was first cast – an alloy of cooper and tin – and used for tools and weapons. As deposits of tin were rare, long-distance trade routes had to be developed.

Part II

The Ancient Middle East

Many books which deal with ancient history in Egypt, Israel, Syria, Iraq, and parts of Turkey, call the area the "Near East." But the same area is called the "Middle East" when dealing with modern history. In order to be consistent throughout, we shall call it by its present name.

Prehistorians use many names both for complete periods (Mesolithic, Neolithic, Chalcolithic) and others for specific cultures (such as Yabrudian, Halafian, Natufian, Kebaran, Nebekian, Zarzian, Ghassulian, etc.). For non-specialists it is confusing to remember that Natufian is, in fact, late Mesolithic. As prehistory, like most sciences, is subject to its own changing fashions, one finds that after many years an old friend such as the Mesolithic period (Middle Stone Age) has fallen out of favour and is now called by some "Proto Neolithic" and by the majority "Epipaleolithic." So one has to shift the Natufians to either of these. But there is also often some disagreement as to whether a site or some development belongs to the Kebaran culture or the Nebekian, which is rather similar. Scientific papers abound with heated discussions on these and similar subjects. We have tried here, however, to use this nomenclature as little as possible, as the basic facts behind these shifting names are often much simpler than one is led to believe.

4 Sumer and Akkad

Mesopotamia early took the lead. Its northern area, along the River Tigris, had first been settled during the seventh millennium BC. Various cultures are identified in the next 2000 years, spreading out further, both westward and southward. The 'Ubeid culture (5500–4000 BC) is remarkable for the settlement of arid southern Mesopotamia, utilizing the spring floods of the River Euphrates to increase crop yield. New cities sprang up here with names later well known in history, such as Ur, Eridu, and Nippur. Eridu had already as many as 4000 inhabitants and its area spread over some ten hectares. Agriculture was intensified by the use of irrigation systems and of the plow. A complicated system of radial canals was constructed and maintained. The wheel was invented, and boats were being built and sailed.

The inhabitants of southern Mesopotamia called themselves Sumerians. Their language was unrelated to later Semitic or Indo-European languages. Their contribution to the advance of civilization is manyfold, but none of its strands can rival that of the creation of the first real states and of the invention of writing, both of which began late in the fourth millennium BC.

The first script was pictographic, on clay tablets, developing later into wedge-shaped marks called the cuneiform script. Some of the signs were used for words and others for syllables. The earliest use of writing was for accounts; but by 2500 BC it was used already for literary creations. The story of the Flood is well known in a later version from the Bible. The "Tales of Gilgamesh" can be read with some enjoyment even today. A very few love songs have survived, and also some animal fables, quite a few hymns and some lamentations.

Writing also enables us to study some of the other facets of Sumerian civilization. Some of their laws were changed and reused, until they reappear among the later laws of Hammurabi and among those of the Old Testament. The use of legal precedent began in Sumerian law.

The Sumerians had moral principles, but regarded them as derived solely from the will of the gods. As a god usually mirrors the character of the believers, let it be said that their gods were a much more decorous lot than those of Homer's *Iliad*. Their temples usually dominated their towns – physically as well as spiritually. The Ziggurat of Ur, for instance, was a three-storied building, 15 m in height, constructed of mud bricks in the form of pyramidal ascending terraces. It stood in a sacred precinct containing various temples and the royal palace.

Hundreds of practice tablets by pupils have survived from the late Sumerian period, indicating a developed school system. Most of the pupils came from the upper classes and all were boys – no girls seem to have been admitted. Discipline was strict.

Physicians were a recognized class and some of their remedies have been recorded. Most remedies derived from plants such as myrtle or thyme. Willow, figs, and dates were also used, and were usually prepared with the addition of some saltpeter and some sodium chloride. The physicians prepared healing salves and therapeutic draughts.

The Sumerians invented the potter's wheel. In warfare they used solid-wheeled chariots drawn by asses. The king was the commander-in-chief in war, and an absolute monarch in peace-time. His functions were also sacral – he represented his city before the gods. But there were checks on his power, both by law and common usage and by the considerable economic power of the temples. Private property was inalienable and even the king had to pay for any land he might desire.

Some Sumerian art in the form of sculptures and reliefs has survived. It is less impressive than contemporary Egyptian art, and shows the Sumerians as rather squat, round-headed individuals who do not correspond to our ideals of beauty. But these thick set, meaty men and women, with their big, staring eyes, occupy a unique niche in the annals of mankind: Both history and literature begin at Sumer. From here many of the initial achievements of civilization radiated outward in space and onward in time.

In one area Sumerian achievements were not significant: that of empire building. The rulers of the city of Lagash tried with some success, between 2500 and 2400, to spread their rule over all of Sumer and so did those of Ur, later in the third millennium BC; but otherwise this was a civilization of independent city states. Nor did the Sumerians try to expand northward. Their civilization and script spread in the early third millennium BC to the Semitic people who had settled north Mesopotamia, who are usually called Akkadians.

One of their rulers, Sargon I of Agade, founded in the middle of the 24th century BC the first empire recorded by history. Its spread – from the Persian Gulf to the Mediterranean – was astonishing, given the slow means of overland transport of that age. It included all of Sumer, neighboring Elam, and most of Syria. His grandson regarded himself already as divine and styled himself "King of the four regions," meaning "Lord of the Earth." But by 2250 BC the Akkadian empire had been swept away by nomads from the east.

Early in the second millennium BC the town of Babylon became an important center. Its king, Hammurabi, imposed his rule on all of Mesopotamia in the 1700s. An interesting change took place. Although the rulers of Babylon used the cuneiform script and their culture was deeply permeated by the Sumerian civilization, it was the Akkadian language which spread all over the Middle East, replacing Sumerian even in Sumer. For more than a thousand years it became the lingua franca of all of the Middle East. Even the Egyptians used it for their diplomatic correspondence, as shown by the el-Amarna letters.

Hammurabi is remembered for his code of laws, which survive to this day – albeit that most of the Sumerian laws on which it was based have disappeared. The Old Testament principle of "an eye for an eye, a tooth for a tooth" was already firmly established. From these laws quite a lot can be learned about the Babylonian economy. Barley served as local money, but silver was used already to pay for imports and for commercial calculations. Interest on loans amounted to as much as one-third of the sum loaned. There existed very clear social distinctions. Members of the upper classes had privileges not accorded to the lower classes. But even slaves could own property and marry a free woman. Women were not the equals of men. They received only half the food allowance of men and could be drowned if caught in adultery. However, women were allowed to own property and lend money. Men were allowed concubines.

Babylonian domination lasted for only 125 years after Hammurabi's death. Barbarians from the mountains to the east then conquered Babylon, and Mesopotamia dropped for several centuries out of the limelight of history.

There is, however, another "first" to Mesopotamian civilization: the first ecological disaster. After two thousand years of intensive irrigation, the resulting salinization of the soil may have been a contributing factor to the collapse of civilized life there.

5   Early Egypt

Among the harsh deserts of northeastern Africa it was only the River Nile which made the development of an advanced civilization along its banks possible. In the late sixth millennium BC farming was introduced from nearby Palestine. The unique advantages of the Nile made a dramatic increase of the population possible. In the fourth millennium villages increased in size, until the first walled towns appeared around 3300 BC in southern Egypt. Around 3100 a single kingdom, encompassing all of Egypt, was established.

Some historians and archeologists believe that these developments should be regarded as a mainly local achievement. Others believe that it was the impact of influences emanating from Sumer which caused the sudden flowering of civilization in the Nile valley. There is indeed some evidence of Mesopotamian influence in the formative phase of Egyptian civilization. It might also seem unlikely that the two earliest civilizations of the Middle East arose by chance at nearly the same time, without influencing each other. What is true is that the Egyptian civilization became very soon strikingly different from that of Sumer.

Ancient Egyptian history is basically the story of three lengthy periods of flourishing civilization, divided by shorter intermediate periods of decline and dissolution. The Old Kingdom lasted for some 850 years (3100–2250 BC) and was the most impressive era in Egyptian history. Most of the time the country was a strong, unified monarchy, engaged only rarely in foreign wars of

· conquest, being apparently content with what it had. Its capital was Memphis, near present-day Cairo. The utilizing of the waters of the Nile for agricultural purposes throughout the country necessitated an efficient administration and a strong, central authority. It is therefore not surprising that the pharaohs were soon regarded as divine.

A detailed list of kings has come down from Hellenistic times, which conveniently groups these kings in dynasties. Six of them are allotted to the Old Kingdom. The central position of the king in Egyptian life is shown by the enormous effort invested in building his tomb. The fact of death was seemingly denied and great care was taken to equip him properly for his existence in afterlife. Around 2650 BC the Third Dynasty started to build stepped pyramids for the pharaoh's last resting place, but these pyramids only reached their full development under the Fourth Dynasty kings Khufu (*c.* 2540 BC) and Khafre. Khufu's pyramid is 147 m high and consists of 2.3 million blocks of 2.5 tonnes each (on the average). It remains one of the largest buildings ever erected. The pyramids have been regarded as one of the wonders of the world ever since.

Egyptian art was perhaps even more impressive. It was at its best right from its inception early in the third millennium. The statuary is striking and lifelike and appeals to modern taste, in spite of a time gap of nearly 5000 years. It shows, for instance, pharaohs and their families marching towards the beholder, full of self-assurance, in spite of their scant apparel. The scene depicts squatting scribes alertly awaiting dictation, erect officials, and hard-working women.

Initially Egypt was a nearly classless society. There existed no real aristocracy. The sons of simple farmers could, and occasionally did, ascend the ladder of an administrative career. But in due time a class of professional officials crystalized, with sons following fathers into careers of governmental service and of power. There seem to have existed no private merchants, and all large-scale mercantile undertakings were organized on the king's behalf by his administration. The accumulation of great wealth was difficult, as property had to be divided equally between sons. Nevertheless, a class of great landowners seems to have started to develop by the end of the Old Kingdom. Real slavery was unknown, but free farmers were sometimes forced to become serfs.

Egyptian religion has usually a regional basis: Atum-Re was venerated in Heliopolis; Ptah in the capital Memphis; Osiris and Isis in the Nile delta; Anubis, with his dog head, in Assiut. Only Horus, the falcon, was venerated in many places. There was a strong tradition of life after death, in a nether-world presided over by Osiris. Hence the widespread custom of the mummification of the dead.

Much of what is known of Egyptian religious customs stems from surviving inscriptions in the small pyramids of the VIth Dynasty. Hieroglyphic writing is quite different from Mesopotamian cuneiform. Although it was written on papyrus (hence our "paper") and not imprinted laboriously on clay tablets, it reached its phonetic syllabic stage only much later. Bronze, too, came into widespread use only a thousand years later than in Mesopotamia.

The conservative adherence to old habits and customs became even more typical of Egypt as her civilization grew older. At the close of the VIth Dynasty too much government land had passed into private hands, seriously curtailing the income of the state; central power declined, the reigns of pharaohs became short, and local governors became semi-independent. A relatively short intermediary period of dissolution and decline followed.

Prosperity and strong government were restored by the Middle Kingdom (Dynasties XI–XII, 2130–1786 BC). Its dominant characteristic was that of continuity. Changes in religion, in art, and in administration were minimal. The social fabric became more hierarchical. Literature now had its golden age. Such tales as the later "Thousand and One Nights" originated then. Science, too, was developed, as shown by surviving papyri on mathematics.

Foreign policy became more aggressive. Egyptian expeditions to Nubia and the Land of Canaan had, however, commenced already under the VIth Dynasty. They were continued and intensified.

There is no darker age in Egyptian history than its second intermediary period of decline and chaos, after the Middle Kingdom came to its end. It lasted from 1786 to 1590 BC. In its later stage

Egypt was dominated by the Semitic Hyksos. In Part IV we shall describe the New Empire which arose after the Hyksos had been driven out.

6   Syria, Canaan, and Alphabetical Writing

Between Mesopotamia and Egypt further city states developed in the third and second millennia BC, in regions that belong now to Syria, Lebanon, and Israel. The earliest to be discovered so far was Ebla, near the river Orontes in northwestern Syria. Ebla achieved its greatest prosperity around 2400 BC. The city's area of 50 hectares was enclosed by a powerful rampart, 50 m wide at the base. Its Italian excavators had the rare luck to find an archive of some 16 000 clay tablets, inscribed in cuneiform script but written in a West Semitic language closely related to later Hebrew. Ebla ruled a state reaching from the Orontes to the Euphrates and as far north as the Taurus range. Some of the tablets are the correspondence between its king and his governors, but most relate to administrative matters and to the collection of taxes and tolls. The main export appears to have been cloth. The presence there of obsidian from Anatolia, alabaster vessels from Egypt, sea shells from the Persian Gulf, and lapis lazuli from Afghanistan indicate its wide trade connections. Tribute was paid in gold and silver. Amongst its gods was already the West Semitic Shalem – the god of the setting sun – after whom Jerusalem was later named.

Another treasure trove of documents (some 17 500 clay tablets) was discovered in Mari, on the upper Euphrates. They date from the 18th century BC. Mari covered all of 100 hectares in its prime, and was larger than any contemporary town in Mesopotamia. Its beginnings go back to the late third millennium BC. Its palace covered 2.5 hectares and contained more than 300 rooms. A nearby temple was dedicated to the god Dagan, who was venerated in Old Testament times. Mari's prosperity derived partly from its control of the river traffic on the Euphrates, but also from tribute from subject princes. In the end Mari was destroyed by Babylon.

Further to the north another archive has been found in Kültepe, in Anatolia, where Assyrian traders maintained a colony from around 1950 to 1750 BC. Its documents are concerned with matters of trade between early Assyria and Anatolia. Gold and silver was obtained in Anatolia and paid for by tin and textiles.

To the south were further city states, such as Qatana near Damascus and Hatzor in the north of present-day Israel. Each of them had a size of about 70 hectares. As no archives have been found there, less is known about them. Both belonged to that region settled by Western Semites, which can be called the Land of Canaan. Its great importance is that alphabetic writing was developed there during the second millennium BC.

Cuneiform and hieroglyphic writing were pictographic and ideographic – thousands of symbols were needed. The development of modern civilization is unthinkable with such a system, hence the enormous importance of giving exclusive phonetic values to each symbol, thus reducing the alphabet from many thousands of symbols to less than thirty, which can be learned easily. Several attempts were made. The first one, in 18th century Gebal (Byblos) in present-day Lebanon, was based on the hieroglyphic system. The next step was the 16th century Proto-Sinaitic system, in Canaanite language, reducing the system to 27 symbols, which still show their pictographic roots ("Aleph" is the frontal head of an ox, "Beth" a house, "Daleth" a fish).

In Ugarit, on the Syrian coast, a completely different system was tried in the 14th and 13th centuries, based on cuneiform symbols. This somewhat cumbersome system was later superseded by the Proto-Canaanitic system, in linear script. Some samples of it have been found in Lahish (13th century) and Bet Shemesh (12th century) in present-day Israel. There are 22 letters, all consonants. This Canaanite alphabet was brought around 1100 BC by Phoenician traders to Greece, and was called the "Phoenician" alphabet. It was written from right to left and still is, in Hebrew. At some point the Greeks started to write the alphabetic form from left to right and also added the vowels. The very word "Alphabet" is, however, Canaanite (or Hebraic).

Part III

The Diffusion of Civilization

Some of the great achievements of the Agricultural and Urban Revolutions in the Middle East, and of the later invention of writing and the working of metals, spread slowly outward throughout Asia and Europe.

From 4500 BC onwards there was a gradual transition to agriculture throughout western Europe. Forests were cleared in order to make room for farmers, population levels rose, usually at first in the fertile river valleys. By 2800 BC the wheel was being used in Denmark and the Netherlands; by 2500 the use of the horse had spread to Ireland. By the late third millennium BC bronze was being used for the casting of tools and weapons.

Agriculture came to Africa north of the Equator, through Egypt, from 5000 BC onwards. As the Sahara dried out, farmers were forced south. But south of the Equator hunting and food gathering were apparently too easy to be exchanged for more laborious agriculture. Also, the aboriginies of Australia never developed agriculture.

In the steppes of southern Russia and southern Siberia, animal domestication appeared after 4500 BC. Agriculture was secondary. Bronze was being used between the Urals and Lake Baikal from 1500 onward. Initially influences came from the west, meaning ultimately the Middle East, but after 1200 BC there were increasingly signs in its eastern parts of Chinese influence. By the first millennium Scythians and other tribes had developed full pastoral nomadism in the steppes.

These were beginnings, but these activities did not lead to the creation of civilizations. These did not start up separately in such diverse centers as the Middle East, Europe, India, and China. The development was one of diffusion from one center – the Middle East. From there, by trade and conquest, influences moved outward. First they seem to have reached western India (the Indus civilization of the third millennium BC), later Crete (the Minoan civilization from about 2000 BC onward), and later still, China (during the second millennium BC).

By the middle of the first millennium BC the peripheral civilizations seem to have caught up (as we shall show in later chapters), and seem to have reached a similar stage of development to those of the Middle East.

7   The Indus Civilization and the Coming of the Aryans

The first expansion of civilization beyond the Middle East was to the Indian subcontinent. From about 2500 BC to 2000 BC there flourished in the Indus valley an interesting and original civilization, with strong ties to Mesopotamia. Its cities have been uncovered mainly in present-day Pakistan. The two main centers uncovered so far were Mohenjo-daro in the south and Harappa in the north.

The big cities were well planned, with a citadel to the west and residential quarters to the east. Mohenjo-daro covered an area of 60 hectares and possessed an impressive bathing installation, perhaps for ritual purposes. In Harappa large granaries have been found north of the citadel, with adjoining workers' quarters, which indicate a relatively high standard of living. Wheat and barley were grown, also peas, sesame and cotton and perhaps also rice. Buffalos and fowl were the usual domestic animals. Tools were made of bronze.

Thousands of seals have been found, many with an inscription, but no writing on sherds has been uncovered. The pictures on the seals show some gods and various animals, such as tigers, elephants, rhinoceroses and buffalos. Maritime trade with Mesopotamia seems to have been lively. Archeologists have assumed that the Sumerians influenced the early Indus valley civilization. Overland trade was plied with Persia and Afghanistan. No signs of writing have been uncovered in the upper (later) layers of these sites and the local civilization seems to have declined and disintegrated around 2000 BC.

India was invaded from the northwest after 1500 BC. The newcomers formed the eastern branch of the great Indo-European movement, which left a common cultural heritage from Greece, through Asia Minor and Iran to India. They called themselves "Aryans." They arrived via Central Asia and entered India from the northwest. They moved only slowly down the Indus valley and eastwards along the Ganges. They were cattle-owning half nomads.

For a long time agriculture and not city life was typical of the Vedic culture, as their civilization is called. Its language was Sanskrit, used by the educated upper classes, in which the Vedic literature is composed. Initially this was an oral tradition – like the *Iliad* in Greece; its creations were written down only much later. Most of what we know of Aryan culture derives from the *Rig-Veda*, a collection of hymns transmitted orally by the Brahmans, the priestly caste. Other collections of hymns also survived. The great epic poems of Sanskrit, the *Rāmāyana* and *Mahābhārata*, came much later, from the late first millennium BC and the early first millennium AD.

The Aryan settlers tried not to mix with the dark-skinned older inhabitants of India. Although they did not succeed, they thereby initiated the caste system, which for three millennia has survived all the vicissitudes of Indian history.

The roots of present-day Hinduism, too, go back to the Vedic culture. Some of the original deities mentioned in the *Rig-Veda* were Indra, Mitra, and Varuna. Their names had also been mentioned in the inscriptions of the Middle Eastern Mitani Empire, showing the common roots of the early Indo-European cultures.

In the Mahābhārata such later deities as Krishna and Vishnu are already mentioned. The Aryan settlers made another important contribution – in the clearing of the land, especially along the Ganges valley, for large-scale agriculture.

The fully historical period in India begins around 600 BC, with the reintroduction of writing. Northern India was divided at that time into several separate states, none of which was of great size or importance. Thus Alexander the Great, on reaching India in 327 BC, did not have to face any unified resistance.

After his death there arose a strong state, the Maurya Empire (321–185 BC), which subjected to its rule a greater part of India than any other state, prior to the arrival of Islam and the British. Its administration was centralized and efficient.

8   Minoans and Mycenaeans

The first European civilizations developed in Crete, on the islands of the Aegean Sea and along the shores of southern Greece. Influences from the Middle East and especially from Egypt can be identified on Crete in the second half of the third millennium BC. From about 2000 BC onwards one can speak of the crystalization of a local higher civilization, for which are typical the erection of large-scale palaces (the most famous one at Knossos), the use of bronze tools, and the development of several differing systems of writing. One of them, called Linear A, is supposed to be written in a language other than Greek. This civilization has been named Minoan, after the legendary Minos, King of Crete before the Trojan war.

The buildings which have been excavated, and even more the many-colored frescoes found on Crete and Thera, give us a much livelier impression of this civilization than we have of many earlier ones. The pictures convey a sense of airy lightness, of good taste, and of elegance. There is no intrusive influence, so common elsewhere, of the martial arts. Animals are depicted, and so are the sport of bull baiting, plants, buildings, beautifully dressed women, ships, and fishermen. Seaborne trade seems to have been the backbone of the economy of the Minoan civilization and naval strength made the fortification of the palaces unnecessary. The trade specialized apparently in Middle Eastern, and especially Egyptian, artifacts, which were re-exported to Asia Minor and southern Europe. The Minoans themselves were skilled potters, carvers of gemstones and ivory, and metal workers. They worshipped a Great Earth Mother and other deities as well.

Minoan influence was brought to bear on the shores of Greece and some of the islands of the Aegean and there, too, were constructed Minoan cities, such as Akrotiri on Thera.

After some time there took place a change in mainland Greece and a different, harsher civilization developed there, called Mycenaean, after the city of Mycenae in the northeastern Peloponnese (1550–1150 BC). Its great cities were surrounded by cyclopic walls. The golden masks of Mycenaean rulers show rough, bearded faces. Some of their aristocrats used bronze cuirasses, figure-eight shields, and sometimes, boar's tusk helmets. Their reliefs depict lions and scenes of hunting and battles. They used war chariots, derived from the Middle East, and constructed extensive roads to facilitate their movement.

Around 1450 BC a catastrophe seems to have struck down Minoan civilization. The volcano on the island of Thera, north of Crete, erupted with enormous force. Most of the island disappeared, leaving behind only the rim of the volcano. Volcanic ash fell everywhere from Crete to Anatolia and Greece, and an enormous tidal wave swamped northern Crete and its palaces. Most of the ships which constituted Crete's naval power must have been smashed, leaving the way open to invasion. Soon after, Crete seems to have been invaded by the Mycenaeans and what had been left by the sea was captured and burned down.

In the aftermath Crete became a province of Mycenaean civilization. Knossos was rebuilt, but not the other palace-towns. Linear B writing supplanted Linear A. When deciphered, it turned out to be in early Greek. This caused a revolution in the approach to

Greek history, as it showed that Greece had been settled by the Greeks already in prehistoric times. The Mycenaean civilization constitutes thus the first appearance of the Greeks on the stage of history.

The Mycenaean world included Crete, the Peloponnese, Attica, Boeotia, some of the Greek islands, such settlements on the western shores of Asia Minor as Miletos and Halikarnassos, and others on the shores of Cyprus. Its wide spread would indicate highly developed trade as the main foundation of the economy, but this is not borne out by the Linear B records, which seem to indicate a mainly agricultural society. Wheat and barley were the main crops; olives, figs and grapes were grown too, sheep and goats were raised and so were also some cows, oxen and horses. Wool and flax were spun and woven and, according to Egyptian records, even exported. Weapons and some tools were made of bronze.

There is no trace, in the Mycenaean records, of a strong central power similar to Knossos in Minoan times. Many separate cities, each strongly fortified, seem to have gone each its own way. Each had its ruler, aristocracy and lower classes. Detailed Linear B archives have been recovered from two of them – Knossos and Pylos – in the southeastern Peloponnes. They indicate a strong, centralized administration in each.

In spite of their strong fortifications, the Mycenaean city-states seem not to have been well enough prepared in the military sphere, as in the 13th and 12th centuries they were attacked, one after the other, and destroyed. The attack at Pylos clearly came from the sea, and it might be reasonable to assume that the Sea People (see Part X, chapter 35) were responsible for most or all of these attacks.

On Cyprus, Mycenaean civilization lingered on somewhat longer, but in Greece itself a long dark age commenced, during which the art of keeping records was forgotten, international commerce decayed, and the old centers of the Mycenaean civilization disappeared. Some Mycenaean memories have survived in the *Iliad* and *Odyssey*, but they are diluted and changed beyond recognition by the six centuries which elapsed before they were written down.

9   Beginnings in China

Early man may have reached western China as early as 1.7 million years ago, according to finds at Yuanmou. The oldest finds there of human bones are some 600 000 years old. Rich finds of early stone tools come from Zhoukoudian in northern China, spanning the period from 700 000 until 130 000.

Cultural influences from the West seem to have reached northern China first and hence, apparently, the development of civilization occurred first in the valley of the Yellow River. The inhabitants of the Yangtze valley, and of what is now regarded as southern China, were initially regarded as barbarians.

Around 3000 BC the Yangshao Pottery Neolithic Culture flowered south of Beijing. Agriculture was introduced about the same time. Both are thus some 6000–7000 years later than in the Middle East – ample time for influences to have reached the Yellow River valley.

Traditional Chinese history reports the existence of an early dynasty, named Xia, from 2205 to 1755 BC. While historians tend to regard early Chinese traditional history as mythical, they sometimes use Xia as a term for a prehistoric Neolithic culture, centered in Shanxi province, south of Beijing, in approximately the above period. It had as yet no metal implements.

The following Shang dynasty (traditionally 1766–1122 BC) has fared better and archeological evidence tends to confirm some of its features. China was partly urbanized, its capital was successively Zhengahou and Anyang, in Henan province, both of which have been excavated. Beautiful bronze artifacts have been uncovered, showing that metal was being used for the first time in China. Also silk working may have commenced then.

Even more important is the beginning of writing in the Shang period – nearly 2000 years later than among the Sumerians. At first it appeared on oracle bones, tortoise shells, and ritual bronze objects. Some 2000 characters have been recovered. Originally their pictorial origin was still evident, but later they became more abstract. No real phonetic system was developed and the Chinese script has thus become very complex. To mention some examples: two signs for "tree" mean "copse," or small wood;

three signs mean "forest." The signs for "woman" and "child" mean, together, "good." But three signs for "woman" together mean "treachery." Some 50 000 signs have evolved, but even an educated person uses only about a fifth of them.

With the next dynasty, Zhou, we are passing from prehistory to history, as far as China is concerned. Its traditional dates, 1122–255 BC, are, however, of little use. The dynasty might well have commenced only in the 11th century, and it ruled a unified state, if at all, only until the 9th or 8th century. China encompassed then mainly the Yellow River valley and did not reach yet anything like its later size. Nor was it a centralized empire, but, apparently more like a feudal confederacy. This, anyway, was the situation from the 8th century onwards, when our sources become more trustworthy. Traditional Chinese historiography calls the period of 771–484 BC the "Spring and Autumn Period," and 484–255 BC the "Period of the Warring States," and stresses the weakening and disruption of central authority. Typical for these times are the numerous wars, usually directed by the nobles and conducted mainly by horse-drawn war chariots. Weapons were made mainly of bronze, until the 3rd century BC. But in agriculture and various crafts iron tools were used from the 7th century BC onwards. Although iron had been used earlier in Asia Minor by some five centuries, the Chinese were the first to develop a high standard of iron smelting and casting. From the 4th century BC onward the war chariots disappeared, to be replaced by archers.

The various states of this period did not develop an identity of their own, as did the national states of the later Western Civilization. The ideal continued to be a united empire, comprising all of China. Chinese civilization actually expanded in these times of troubles. Walled cities multiplied. Hill tribes and non-Chinese settlements were conquered and subdued. Marshlands were reclaimed and rivers navigated. Outlying regions were settled and incorporated by the various states. Their population increased rapidly. Some of the border states expanded more than the others and became more powerful. None more so than the western state of Quin, which was to unite all of China, and form a centralized and strong, but short-lived, empire (221–206 BC), aided perhaps by the iron swords used by its soldiers.

Part IV

Early Empires

Why invade other countries? Why expand frontiers? Why create empires?

The original answer was that in an agricultural society this was the most direct and simple way to enrichment. Both booty and tribute stimulated the economy and brought about capital accumulation. As a result successful imperialism was regarded from the second millennium BC until the middle of the 20th century AD as the very touchstone of political success.

Only slowly did statesmen and nations discover that ever since the Industrial Revolution this axiom did not apply any longer. Peace has become a much more efficient way to the same goal.

Below we shall discuss some of the very earliest empires which took the road of war and expansion.

10   The Hittites

Early in the second millennium BC there appeared in Western Asia peoples speaking Indo-European languages. Originally nomadic and pastoral they penetrated into Asia Minor and established there the Hittite state, with its capital at Hattusas (modern Boghazkoy, 110 miles east of Ankara). By the middle of the 17th century BC they had achieved control of central Anatolia and were attacking cities in northern Syria. In 1595 BC they captured Babylon, though only temporarily.

However, in the 15th and early 14th centuries BC the Hurrian state of Mitani, also controlled by an Indo-European aristocracy, had the upper hand in northern Syria and Mesopotamia, effectively reducing Assyria to vassalage and bottling the Hittites up inside Anatolia. The greatest of the Hittite kings, Suppiluliumas, sacked the Mitanian capital, and captured northern Syria (*c.* 1370 BC). For nearly two hundred years the Hittites were now one of the great powers of the Middle East.

Their main adversary was usually Egypt, under the kings of the XVIIIth and XIXth Dynasties. One of the most famous battles of that time, that of Kades on the Orontes in 1286 BC, was between Rameses II and the Hittites, and in spite of the boastful language of the Egyptian inscription, Rameses seems to have had rather the worst of it. The Hittites continued to control most of Syria.

Hittite dialects were written both in cuneiform (on clay) and in an original hieroglyphic script. In spite of the fact that most of them have been deciphered, the resulting information has been less than startling. The Hittites appear to have excelled in warfare, but in little else. Their chariotry appears to have been formidable. The chariots were heavier than the Egyptian ones and were manned by three warriors instead of the two on the Egyptian side. The remains of Hittite fortifications, too, are impressive.

In spite of its martial prowess, the Hittite Empire seems to have fallen early in the 12th century BC, an easy prey to the great invasion of the Sea People (see Part X, chapter 35). The Hittites disappeared from Anatolia and their place was taken later by the Phrygians; but some Hittite splinter states existed for some time afterwards in northern Syria and most of the surviving Hittite sculpture belongs to this late period.

The farthest Hittite splinter state to the south seems to have been Jebusite Jerusalem. Its rulers were called Hittites in the Old Testament and some of its aristocracy bore Hittite and Hurrian names. Otherwise Hittite history was completely forgotten for 3000 years, until its remains were unearthed by the spades of modern archeologists.

11   Egypt – the New Kingdom

Approximately in the middle of the 16th century BC the Hyksos were driven out of the northern part of Egypt. During the next three hundred years the armed forces of the XVIIIth (1550–1314) and XIXth (1309–1194) Dynasties advanced into Syria, where they battled such rival expansionist empires as Mitani, the Hittites, and Assyria. Lengthy inscriptions on obelisks and temple walls report their victories in great detail.

Some of the rulers are of exceptional interest. Queen Hatshepsut (1490–1468) assumed all the attributes of kingship, which was apparently unprecedented, and ruled successfully and (a rarity in that period) peacefully. Her nephew and son in law, Tutmose III (1468–1438), served as her co-regent and became after her death the most successful and important warrior of the New Kingdom. In seventeen campaigns he founded or consolidated Egyptian rule throughout Palestine and Syria.

His great-grandson Akhenaten (1364–1347) was a religious innovator, who proclaimed an early kind of monotheism, based on the cult of Aten, the sun disk. His reforms carried over also into the social sphere and even more remarkably, into art. The mannerist figures of the pharaoh and his family and the lifelike, impressionist portrait sculptures of his period have not their like until modern times. A significant part of his archives – the famous el-Amarna letters – have been found in his capital, which was abandoned soon after his death. The letters give a vivid picture of the intrigues of the petty princes of Palestine and Syria during a period in which Egyptian leadership was less energetic than earlier and later.

The most important ruler of the XIXth Dynasty was Rameses II (1290–1224), the pharaoh of the Exodus. In spite of his long reign and his many campaigns, he was not able to match the record of Tutmose III. The story of his greatest battle, Kadesh (1286 BC), against the Hittites, hewn in stone, is even more detailed than the record of the battle of Megiddo, left by Tutmose III. But there is one important difference: he seems to have lost his battle.

Aside from the imperialistic foreign policy and from such exceptional reigns as the ones mentioned above, there seems to have been an astonishing continuity in the social, cultural, religious, and economic sphere to life in Egypt for two and a half millennia – from the beginning of its history to the Macedonian conquest, and even beyond. No other civilization, not even the Chinese, was equally long-lived, with so little change to its social and cultural make-up.

It is therefore worthwhile to mention some specific changes which did occur. The Hyksos introduced horses to Egypt and as a result the battle tactics of the New Kingdom were based on the use of the war chariot. The capital was at Thebes in southern Egypt (and at Memphis near present-day Cairo, in earlier and later times). Egypt was never as fully urbanized as Mesopotamia, or classical Greece. Dresses changed, from simple white garments to multi-colored ones, woven on more sophisticated looms. Even tapestries appear in New Kingdom times. The bureaucracy became more numerous, a large professional army was established, and a numerous priesthood developed.

But mostly, techniques which had been innovative in the times of the Old Kingdom, stagnated afterwards. In literature the New Kingdom copied mainly Middle Kingdom classics.

Under the XXth Dynasty (1184–1080) a marked decline set in. A last great feat of arms was the victory of Rameses III (1182–1151) over the Sea People, which saved Egypt from the fate of the Hittite Empire. His heirs, all named Rameses, ruled each only for a short period of time, and the great days of empire were over.

Egypt continued to exist for another 750 years, until the Macedonian conquest. Even before Alexander the Great, she was conquered for various periods by Ethiopians, Libyans, Assyrians, and Persians. Her ancient civilization was not, however, greatly affected, nor did it show any signs of rejuvenation or revived originality.

12   The Assyrian Empire

The Assyrians were Semites, who lived in northern Mesopotamia. They emerged originally as one of the great powers of the Middle

East from approximately 1350 BC onwards. Their central geographical position in the middle of the "Fertile Crescent" enabled
them to expand in all directions, but also made them vulnerable
to such great nomadic movements as that of the Sea People in
the early 12th century, or the immigration of the Aramaeans into
Syria and Mesopotamia in the 11th and 10th centuries.

By approximately 950 BC they had overcome these setbacks and
now embarked on a career of relentless conquest and expansion.
None of the other early empires were quite so single-minded,
tough, cruel and efficient in the pursuit of imperialism as the
Assyrians. Their rulers, as pictured in the many surviving stone
reliefs, are shown as massive men, with rod-straight backs, highly
developed muscles and finely-coiffed black beards. They are usually shown fighting lions or receiving delegations of subjected
people. They all look pretty much alike and also the written
sources do not hint at great differences between them. Nearly
all of them spent their time in organizing campaigns or leading
them. It is worthwhile to mention by name only two of them:
Tiglath-Pileser III (745–727), who conquered Syria, Babylonia
and eastern Anatolia; and Assarhadon (681–669), who conquered
Egypt and under whom Assyria reached her greatest size.

In order to give permanence to their conquests the Assyrians
pioneered a system of deportations, by which the elite of one country was transplanted to another: Syrians from the area of Hama
were transferred to western Persia and to Armenia and Arameans
from southern Babylonia were transplanted to the northeastern
border regions. "So were Israel carried away out of their own land
to Assyria unto this day. And the king of Assyria brought men
from Babylon, and from Cutah (in southern Mesopotamia) and
from Ava (in the mountains of Iran) and from Hamath and from
Sepharvaim (in Syria) and placed them in the cities of Samaria
instead of the children of Israel" (2 Kings 17:23, 24). By mixing
thus the transplanted people, the Assyrians tried to uproot the
subject people and to create a more or less homogeneous mass,
which would be more pliable and less likely to revolt.

This policy had one unexpected result: Instead of the previous
national languages, such as Akkadian in Babylonia or Hebrew
in the Land of Israel, Aramaic gradually became the common

language of all of the Middle East. Parts of the books of Ezra and Nehemiah, and most of the book of Daniel in the Old Testament, were already written in Aramaic. The common people continued to talk in Aramaic even under Hellenistic and Roman rule. This was the language used by Jesus and the Apostles. Only a long time after the Arab conquest was Aramaic replaced by Arabic.

The efficient Assyrian war machine must have been also very profitable at its peak, in the 8th and 7th centuries. The successive capitals – Ashur, Nimrud, Khorsbad, and Nineveh – show how much treasure and care were spent on palaces, temples, battlements, and decorations. The stone reliefs found there are often of great beauty, especially in their treatment of animals. Their subjects were usually Assyrian victories, and palace entrances were guarded by colossal winged bulls and lions. Reliefs and entrances impressed visitors with the power of Assyria.

Assyrian might declined rapidly in the second half of the 7th century and collapsed by 612 BC. Nineveh fell to the Medes and Babylonians. The Egyptians wanted their share, but were defeated in 605 by Nebuchadnezzar II (605–562), the Babylonian ruler who became the real heir of the Assyrians. He captured Jerusalem in 586, and exiled the Judean elite to Babylonia. But he did not have the same might as the Assyrians and could not resettle the city with other exiles. Nor did he, or his successors, succeed in conquering Egypt. After several weaker rulers, their capital, Babylon, was captured in 539 by the Persians. Much of the Assyrian structure of empire was taken over first by the Babylonians and later by the Persians.

13   The Persian Empire

Indo-European nomads seem to have settled large parts of Iran around 1000 BC, quite some time after the arrival of the Hittites in Asia Minor and of the Aryans in northern India. Although the country is very large indeed, it was far less densely settled than nearby Mesopotamia or India.

The first state to evolve was that of the Medes, in its northwest, late in the 7th century BC. These nomads participated in the final victory over Assyria, and later conducted an inconclusive war against Lydia in central Anatolia. Their neighbors to the south were the Persians, who were first mentioned around 700 BC. Some of their early cuneiform inscriptions have been found, showing that already in the early 7th century these tribes, who only recently had been semi-nomads, were led by men who apparently could read and write. They were ruled by the Achaemenian dynasty. One of its kings, Cyrus (559–530), defeated the Medes and set up the Persian Empire. It was by far the largest of the early empires. Cyrus united all of Iran, conquered the Babylonian Empire (which spread all over Mesopotamia, Syria, and Palestine), defeated King Croesus of Lydia and captured most of Asia Minor, subdued the Greek cities of Ionia, and, turning eastward, captured parts of Afghanistan and of Central Asia. His son Cambyses (530–522) captured Egypt. Darius (522–486) had western India and Thracia conquered, subdued a revolt of the Ionic cities, but failed in his attempt to conquer Greece.

Darius reorganized his enormous empire. It was divided into satrapies, each of which was subdivided into smaller provinces, such as Judea or Samaria. Many of the governors of these provinces belonged to the local aristocracies. An enlightened system of self-government was mostly used, instead of the heavy-handed system typical of Assyrian or Babylonian imperialism. Local customs and religions were actively encouraged – such as the erection of a new Temple in Jerusalem. The provinces were often allowed to coin their own money, on which appear the names of the local governors.

Darius created a network of roads, which survived Achaemenian times. A legal code, partly based on such earlier Mesopotamian laws as those of Hammurabi, was drawn up and publicly displayed. The language employed by all the Persian chancelleries, from Egypt to India, was Aramaic. From the middle of the 5th century onwards, it was written on parchment. Under its influence the oldest Indian alphabet, Kharoshti, was developed.

Darius built large palaces at both his capitals, Susa and Persepolis. The style of the decoration shows both Babylonian and Greek influences. There was, however, a grandeur about its griffins, archers, delegations and processions, which was all its own.

Although agriculture was very much the economic basis of the empire, trade expanded and carried everyday products, and not only the luxury goods of previous times. The introduction of coinage (a Lydian invention) facilitated agricultural trading no less than the enormous area of the empire and the quality of its roads. While previously only rulers or temples had handled larger monetary transactions, now genuine private banks were established. They invested in houses, fields, slaves, cattle, boats and canals, operated as pawnbrokers, floated loans and accepted deposits. Inevitably taxes followed in the footsteps of trade and banking. There were tithes on sales, port dues, and taxes on property and industrial production.

The Achaemenian Empire existed for over two centuries. But after Darius there is little that is original in its achievements. Weak rulers replaced Cyrus and Darius. When a stronger prince, Cyrus the Younger, arose, chance cut his career short. Xenophon's surviving account describes the "Anabasis" (withdrawal) of the Greek mercenaries Cyrus had hired.

In the 4th century Egypt, Cyprus, and other provinces revolted and regained their independence. Repeated wars were conducted along the coast of Palestine and Phoenicia. The last two kings, Artaxerxes III (359–338) and Darius III (336–331), were again active rulers and suppressed the rebellions, regained the lost provinces, and re-established the empire in its old extent. But Darius III had the bad luck to be attacked by Alexander the Great and lost his life and his empire.

Part V

The Age of New Beliefs and Thought – the First Millennium BC

Rarely quite different civilizations seem to reach at approximately the same time a similar stage in their development. This is what seems to have happened around the second and third quarters of the first millennium BC in such faraway places one from the other as Greece, Israel, Persia, India, and China. It is as if they had reached independently a similar stage in their development. There is no indication of any direct influence between the widely varied beliefs, philosophies and religions, which appeared there quite suddenly. Most of them have one thing in common: They have stood the test of time and are, after two and a half millennia, still of the greatest relevance (the one exception being Zoroastrianism).

Most of them owed their success to some fortunate political or military event, such as the wide acceptance of Buddhism in India, as a result of King Ashoka's conversion; or Zoroastrianism's success in consequence of its propagation by the Achaemenian rulers of Persia; or in China the success of the teachings of the Legists as a result of their acceptance by the Quin dynasty and the acceptance of Confucianism, by the Han dynasty; or the wide diffusion of Greek values as a result of the conquests of Alexander the Great. Even Judaism owes much to King David's political success.

14   Zoroastrianism

Approximately in the 7th century BC a new religion was launched in Persia. It was named after its founder Zoroaster, about whom very little is known. He seems to have lived in eastern Persia, or the upper Indus valley, and from there his teachings spread westwards into Persia proper.

He transformed the old Iranian religion, in which Ahuramazda, the "wise lord," reigned supreme, into a dualistic system in which Good and Evil battled each other. Ahuramazda was turned into the incarnation of the Good, while the malevolent spirit was named Ahriman. The Good is equalled with light, which diffuses not only the world, but also the souls of the righteous. Darkness equalled evil. There was belief in an afterlife, with a paradise to receive the pious, while the wicked were punished. Internment of dead bodies was forbidden and they had to be exposed on mountains or specially constructed towers. The Zoroastrian belief in an afterlife influenced later Hellenistic Judaism, and early Christianity and Islam.

Zoroastrianism became in the 5th century the religion of the united Achaemenian Persian Empire and was indeed one of its unifying elements. However, its importance waned with the conquest of Alexander the Great. When a national Iranian cult was re-established by the Sassanian dynasty (224–640 AD), it was essentially the pre-Zoroastrian Mazdian faith, which stressed fire worship.

In the 8th century some of the remaining Zoroastrians emigrated from Persia to India, where some of them survive till today. They are called Parsees and form a small but prosperous community in Bombay. Much of their rich "Pahlavi" literature – mostly on Zoroastrian religious and historical subjects – has survived.

15   The "Hundred Schools of Thought" in China

Periods of political disorder are often also creative periods in which new beliefs and thoughts arise. This is what happened in China in the "Period of the Warring States" (484–221 BC). The power of the Zhou rulers had declined already for several centuries; subsequently several practically independent states faced each other in often interminable wars. Against this background several philosophers and innovators tried to find a way out of the predicament of the present, and searched for a viable philosophy of life.

Of course there never were anywhere as many as the "Hundred schools of thought" traditionally mentioned and some were not very important, but a few do merit discussion. The "Naturalists," for instance, explained the universe in terms of complementary forces – Yin and Yang, male and female, day and night. This concept was later taken over by Confucianism.

Mo Tzu (468–376(?) BC) founded the "Utilitarian School" (or "Mohism"), which deplored waste and recommended economy and also love between the inhabitants of all kingdoms, in order to prevent the fratricidal wars of that time. His influence was limited, but some of his ideas were taken up again in the 19th century.

More important was "Legalism," which taught that whatever a ruler wants is right. Its teachings were, not surprisingly, popular with rulers, and especially with Quin Shi Huang Di (259–210 BC), who united all of China under the short-lived Quin dynasty (221–206 BC). In accordance with Legalism's teachings, the activities of the population were tightly controlled for the best of the state. Divisive feudalism was eliminated and replaced by a centralized imperial bureaucracy. All books, except for the Legalist canon, were burned in 213 – a unique, if extreme victory for any school of thought, but a heavy blow to historians of China ever since. This type of totalitarianism went out of fashion with the Han dynasty (206 BC–AD 221). Yet some of its legacy can be found also in the deeds of later emperors.

Taoism is a borderline case, half philosophy and half religion. It was founded by Lao-Tzu (6th century BC) and named after his chief work, *Tao te Ching*. "Tao" means "the way" but is also a metaphor for nature. The Taoist solution for the ills of the time was to become attuned to nature and renounce all worldly ambition. Yet it searched also for longevity or, indeed, for immortality. Taoism was influenced by Buddhism, but regarded it also as a competitor and had it twice (in AD 446 and 845) proscribed. In 1281 most Taoist texts were burned by the Mongols.

The most important innovator was Confucius (551–479 BC), who stressed the importance of human relations and of propriety in the relations between ruler and subject. His teachings were further developed by Mencius (371–289 BC), who espoused the principles of goodness and filial piety. Rulers were urged to practice benevolence.

The simple practicality of these precepts proved highly suitable for the Chinese mind and character and they have been adopted by rulers and subjects alike ever since the Han dynasty. In later times some elements of Buddhism and Taoism were sometimes added. But Confucianism has basically remained the main guidance for Chinese thinking on the mainland until the times of Mao Zedong and Communism, and it remains the main guidance for many Chinese abroad. Some of the ethos of hard work, which in recent years has been one of the causes for the great success of Japan, Southern Korea, and Taiwan in the economic field, can be traced back to Confucianism.

16   Buddhism

From the 7th century BC onward, cities in northern India multiplied and grew, trade expanded, and the use of a script became common. It is against this background that the sudden flourishing of new schools of philosophy and religion, which covered a wide range of human affairs, have to be understood. The Ajivikas, for instance, believed that even the most insignificant action of a human being is completely predetermined. The Charvakas were atheists and did not believe in any hereafter, "When the body dies both fool and wise alike are cut off and perish. They do not survive after death."

Of greater importance for the future was Jainism. Some of its ideas were in circulation already in the 7th century BC, but they were given their real formulation by Mahavira, about 500 BC. Everything has a soul, and its purification is the purpose of life.

Non-violence is central to his thinking – even the unintentional killing of an ant is a sin. His beliefs spread mostly among traders and moneylenders and has remained associated with urban culture. The Jains have remained throughout history mainly a small but prosperous community in India.

Brahmanism (the later Hinduism) underwent a thorough reformation around the 6th century BC. In the Upanishads (the last section of the Veda) personal salvation is stressed and the individual soul is emphasized. The soul undergoes an endless cycle of rebirths, from which release can be obtained by the practice of yoga, in order to attain eternal transcendence and bliss. But this could be achieved only by the Aryan elite, under Brahmanic priestly authority.

Indian history is mainly not the story of secular wars, empires, and administrations, but the story of religious beliefs and developments. Therefore Gautama Buddha, who lived and taught in the 6th century BC, is to a great extent one of her real heroes – more than any emperor. The Buddha released much of the new metaphysics from their Brahman shell and made them available to everyone, regardless of caste. He simplified them, used the popular language instead of Sanskrit, introduced a stronger rational element, and dissociated them from the esoteric Vedic lore.

The Buddha's teachings developed into a new religion with a very wide appeal. Under the Mauryan King Ashoka (*c.* 270–233 BC) Buddhism was used to unify his vast empire, which comprised most of India. Active proselytizing introduced Buddhism to Ceylon and Southeast Asia.

Similar to the schisms of the early Christian Church, Buddhism split in the 1st and 2nd centuries AD into several sects, the more important of which are the more orthodox "Lesser Vehicle" (now to be found mainly in Sri Lanka and Southeast Asia), and the more innovative "Greater Vehicle," which soon became dominant in India and later in Central Asia, Tibet, Nepal, Mongolia, reaching also China, Korea, Vietnam, and Japan. The Greater Vehicle developed the doctrine of the Nirvana, the end to the cycle of rebirths. Buddha himself was regarded as a God, one in a line of incarnations.

In spite of its huge success outside of India, Buddhism declined in its homeland and more or less disappeared, after the arrival of Islam, early in the second millennium AD. In recent years it is having a modest renaissance there, especially among the class of Untouchables.

From the 5th century onwards magical rites, associated with the fertility cult, came to the fore. This type of Tantric Buddhism is prevalent in Nepal, Tibet, and Mongolia. In China and Japan one of the most interesting aspects of Buddhism has been its peaceful co-existence and actual mingling with Confucianism and Shintoism.

17   Israel

Israel becomes a historically comprehensive reality after the Israelites settled in the Holy Land. Modern archeology leaves little doubt that Palestine was not captured in one sweep, as described in the Book of Joshua, but was gradually settled by Israelite half-nomads, who had crossed the Jordan, from the 13th to the 11th century, somewhat on the lines described in the Book of Judges. The first settlements were established in the center of the country, later called Samaria. From there the Israelites moved on, to the north (Galilee) and south (Judea). The numbers involved were very small indeed: some 55 000 souls by the later 11th century BC.

The early settlements developed in the densely wooded but sparsely inhabited mountains. The valleys contained Canaanite towns and farms which could not be captured by the weak Israelite tribes. They were threatened also in their mountains, when attacked in the 11th century BC by the Philistines.

Under pressure, the Israelites had to unite, and a monarchy was formed, first by King Saul (c. 1020–1004) from the tribe of Benjamin, and after his death in battle against the Philistines, by King David (1004–965), from the tribe of Judah. David is the pivotal figure in the history of Israel. He defeated the Philistines, captured all of the Land of Canaan and turned it into the Land of Israel, captured Jerusalem and made it not only his capital, but the Holy City of Judaism (and, as a result, in a later age, also of

Christianity, and one of the holy cities of Islam). He conquered the neighboring countries of Edom, Moab, Ammon and Aram, built up alliances with Tyre, Gshur and Hamat, and created a sizeable empire, from the River Euphrates to the Red Sea. The great events of his time caused some of his contemporaries to write down their history and also surviving traditions of previous times and thus some of the basic material was created out of which the Old Testament was later to evolve.

His son Solomon (965–928) built the original Temple in Jerusalem, but did not further expand his empire. Although there existed strong ties to neighboring countries, cities, and cults, the beginnings of a different and unique development in the religious sphere had been initiated.

Near the end of Solomon's reign the empire created by David collapsed and the small neighboring countries regained their independence. After his death the union of the twelve Israelite tribes did not survive, and two kingdoms were formed – Israel in the north, made up of ten tribes, and Judah in the south, with Jerusalem as its capital.

Nineteen kings ruled the former, from 928 to 722, when its capital Samaria was captured by the Assyrians. Twenty kings ruled in Judah, from 928 to 586, when Jerusalem was captured by the Neo-Babylonian King Nebuchadnezzar and the Temple was destroyed.

The southern kingdom, though less involved in international affairs, was nevertheless more stable, as it was dominated by one tribe and ruled throughout by the Davidic dynasty. A stronger middle class seems to have existed there, while in the northern kingdom the social differences between rich and poor seem to have been more pronounced. Several dynasties took over one from the other and the government was less stable. It is thus not surprising that Judah survived much longer and it was there that the more important developments took place.

Nevertheless, the northern kingdom has not completely disappeared. The present-day Samaritans are the direct descendants of the old tribes of Menasse and Efraim, though initially the capital of Samaria was repopulated by the Assyrians with settlers from southern Babylonia and Syria.

The period of the divided monarchy is not one of brilliant political or military achievements in either country, as the big powers – Egypt, Assyria, and later Babylonia – overshadowed completely events in the Holy Land. This period is of unique importance in the creation of the first truly monotheistic religion, and in the writing down of most of the material which later made up the Old Testament. The prophetic movement and the priests of the Temple of Jerusalem channeled Judaism into new directions, which were very different from those of the other Semitic religions of the Middle East. The most important moment was the writing down of the book of Deuteronomy during the reign of King Josiah (640–609) of Judah, which stressed the exclusivity of Judaism and forbade services at high places or at altars other than those of the Temple in Jerusalem. The God of Israel was regarded as a universal God, and not only as a local deity. The prophetic movement contributed new moral and ethical values, such as a clear sense of right and wrong.

As a result Judaism survived its first diaspora, in Babylon, and developed some of the special characteristics which enabled it to survive also the much longer diaspora which followed the second destruction of the Temple, in AD 70. During the Babylonian "captivity" most of the Pentateuch was edited, and was brought back to Jerusalem by Ezrah in 458 BC. The building of the Second Temple there had been completed earlier, in 515 BC, while the restoration of the city walls by Nehemiah seems to have been accomplished later, possibly in 444 BC.

Although the Jewish population of Judea under Persian rule (539–332) was small, it was there that Judaism was further refined, the later books of the Old Testament were written, and its further editing took place.

To summarize: though the political events of the time of King David started off the later development of Judaism toward becoming the first truly monotheistic religion, and led to the writing down of the bible, the resulting developments took many centuries and were not yet completed when Alexander the Great conquered Palestine.

The relevance of the early history of Israel is much enhanced by the fact that Judaism itself has survived and that followers of such

Judaistic religions as Christianity and Islam make up a majority of present-day nations. No other book in history has reached the importance and popularity of the Bible, or has been anywhere as influential.

18   Classical Greece

In the fairly long annals of humanity there is nothing to compare with the flowering of the human spirit in Classical Greece.

The rare remains and records of Mycenaean times indicate that a highly gifted race had occupied the shores of Greece and its isles. After the chain of catastrophies which terminated the Mycenaean civilization around 1200 BC there followed dark centuries about which we know very little. But from the 9th and 8th centuries onward new life flowered in the narrow vales of Greece. The limited space available for agriculture and the invitingly long shoreline caused settlers to cross the sea, both to the east, to the coast of Asia Minor, and to the west, to Sicily and southern Italy, and to look there for more spacious arable land. Archeological finds show that some of the Ionian cities, such as Miletus, were a direct continuation of the earlier Mycenaean settlements, and that others, such as Rhodes, were resettled after a short period of abandonment. But most were founded later, from the 9th to the 7th century BC. In the west most settlements were started between the 8th and 6th centuries.

In the 11th century the Phoenician alphabet was introduced into Greece and was soon complemented by turning its "dead" letters, like Aleph, into vowels, like Alpha.

The great development of Greece started in the overseas settlements. Homer (probably 8th century) was a native of Ionia. The *Iliad* and *Odyssey* developed over long periods and were transmitted orally. Today they are the most important and most popular works of Greek and world literature.

The first Greek philosophers and scientists, too, lived in Ionia, in the 6th and 5th centuries. Thales of Milet founded (apparently) the science of geometry, may have predicted successfully the solar eclipse of 595 BC, and believed that the universe was constructed mainly of water. His contemporary Anaximander is credited with the invention of the sundial, the drawing of a map of the world, and the first use of prose writing. His pupil Anaximenes believed air to have been the primary basis of the universe. Heraclitus of Ephesos assumed all things to be in a continual state of flux. Democritus held the universe to be composed of atoms. Some of their ideas have been a starting point of philosophy ever since.

Some of the most impressive Greek remains have been found in the west, in Paestum, in Italy, and in Agrigentum, Selinus, and Segesta on Sicily, all erected in the 6th and 5th centuries BC. The doric temples there have a serenity to be found only rarely again. Some of the coins struck in Sicily in the 5th century are perhaps the most beautiful ones ever to be minted.

Most of the Greek cities were originally ruled by princelings, styled "kings" in Sparta, where their function survived into Hellenistic times. In most other places they were displaced by oligarchies or by what later generations called "tyrants," such as Pesistratus in Athens (561–528/527). But slowly there developed also other institutions, in which first nuclei of democracy can be distinguished, such as the boulé (the council of citizens), or the gerusia (the senate of elders), or the archons (the heads and chief judges) of some of the early city states. The city ("polis") was the unit of social and political life in Greece.

Late in the 6th century several of the tyrants were driven out; thus in Athens, Naxos, and Samos, democratic institutions were given the chance to develop and flourish in the 5th and 4th centuries. We are best informed of what happened in Athens. Solon, in the first years of the 6th century BC, released the farmers from serfdom, reformed the constitution on an oligarchic basis, and instituted the right of appeal for individuals. In the late 6th century Cleisthenes overthrew the ruling oligarchy and founded the Athenian democracy. He divided Attica into parishes and tribes, to one of which each citizen had to belong. Each tribe, in rotation, sent each year 50 representatives to the boulé and they served for one-tenth of the year as its executive. Some oligarchic elements remained: the archons had to belong to the two wealthiest classes. Completely outside the charmed circle of citizenry remained women, foreigners, and slaves – which in total comprised a majority of the population. The number of inhabitants of Athens has been estimated, for the middle of the 5th century, at 110 000 souls, of which only about 35 000 were citizens.

Greece was lucky to enjoy in these formative years near-immunity from foreign intervention, but there were exceptions. The cities in Sicily had to defend themselves against the Carthaginian power, based on the eastern part of the island. Under the leadership of Syracuse the Carthaginians were defeated decisively at the battle of Himera (480), and Syracuse, in the east of Sicily, remained its dominant power until the intervention of Rome in the 3rd century BC.

The outcome in the east was less fortunate for the Greeks. The cities of Ionia were often under pressure from the kingdom of Lydia (700–550). Later in the 6th century they came under Persian rule. Around 500 BC they revolted, initially under the leadership of Miletus, but were defeated and Miletus was destroyed. The flowering of literature and philosophy in Ionia wilted, and from this point on, continental Greece played the main part in Greek culture and history.

The Persians decided to extend their rule to Greece, from where much of the support for rebellious Ionia had come, and made two main attempts to conquer it. In 490 a Persian naval expedition was defeated by the Athenians, commanded by Miltiades, at the battle of Marathon.

In 480 a much larger expedition advanced into Greece, overcame a Spartan unit at the defile of the Thermopylae and occupied Athens, destroying the buildings on the Acropolis. The Persians were, however, defeated at sea in the battle of Salamis and on land at Plataea and had to withdraw from Greece.

This brilliant success showed the Greeks that they could stand up even to the largest empire the world had yet seen. Their self-assurance, their belief in their institutions, and their creativeness were tremendously strengthened, and this was to be reflected in the future in most fields of human endeavor.

Nowhere was this more so than in Athens, which regarded itself as the main architect of victory. Themistocles had advocated the creation of a sizeable navy already before the second Persian invasion. The navy became instrumental in the creation of an Athenian empire, as the security of Greece against the Persians seemed initially to depend on it. At its height this empire encompassed most of the shores and islands of the Aegean and Marmora seas, and controlled to a great extent the commerce of Greece. Its navy operated as far away as Egypt.

The city of Athens became the center of the cultural development of Greece. Here Aeschylus, Sophocles, and Euripides wrote their dramas, Aristophanes his comedies, Herodotus and Thucydides their histories; here flourished the most important philosophers of antiquity – Socrates, Plato, and Aristotle; here worked the greatest sculptors, such as Phidias and Praxiteles; and there arose the most famous creations of architecture, such as the Parthenon. Many notable figures, such as Herodotus and Aristotle, were not citizens of Athens, but came to work or lecture there. The political leaders of the Athenian Empire were Aristides, Cimon, and Pericles. The latter gave his name to the greatest days of Athenian and Greek culture.

Success, however, breeds envy. Athenian trade had been developed at the expense of such old trading towns as Corinth and her political influence, at the expense of Sparta's traditional position of political and military pre-eminence in Greece. In the Peloponnesian War (431–404) these two cities and their allies combined against Athens and, after many vicissitudes (Athens, led by Alcibiades, tried for instance, unsuccessfully, to capture Syracuse in Sicily and lost there most of her army), defeated her decisively. She was shorn of her empire, her democracy collapsed for some time, and Sparta remained very much the leading power of Greece.

But not for very long. Her institutions did not fit her for an imperial role. At Leuctra (371) she was defeated decisively by Thebes, led by Epaminondas, and was permanently weakened by the freeing of her dependency of Messenia. In later years Thebes and a second Athenian confederacy struggled for the ascendancy of Greece, until both were overcome by Philip of Macedon (359–336).

Macedon was something of an outsider in Greece, but like other frontier states before and after (for instance Rome, Quin in China, or the Ottoman Turks), it succeeded where others had failed and unified virtually all of Greece, creating thus the springboard from which Alexander the Great launched his epochal expedition eastward.

The influence of Classical Greece on later ages has been unequalled. Democracy began in Greece. The art and architecture of the western world has been for centuries a dialogue with Greek values. In philosophy the Greeks did not have all the answers, but they did ask most of the relevant questions. The roots of modern science are deeply embedded in Greek soil. Greek literature is not only the starting point of much of Western literature, but is enjoyed by millions of readers and theatregoers for its own sake. In short, the legacy of Classical Greece is still of the greatest relevance.

Part VI

Hellenism and Rome

Looking at a map of the world one is surprised to see how tiny were the cradle lands of future human civilization and religion, Greece and Israel. Their message might never have got across if wider spaces had not been opened to their influence. This did happen, for Greek civilization was widely dispersed – first by the conquests of Alexander the Great, later by the cultural influence of the Hellenistic empires, and later still by Rome. The same Roman Empire also became the domain in which the Bible found wide acceptance – at first diffused by the Jewish diaspora and later, in a different guise and with a somewhat different message, by Christianity. Ultimately the Roman Empire itself became Christian.

19 Alexander the Great

Alexander the Great (336–323) illustrates the effect of the unexpected in history. Not everything can be explained by the pressure of economic trends, the influence of religions or ideas, or the cyclic growth and waning of empires. Sometimes – though admittedly rarely – a mere human actor, on the vast stage of history, suddenly pokes his sword into the spokes of history and upsets the applecart. None more so than Alexander.

Let us try to elaborate this point:

- It cannot be claimed that Persia was on the downswing, that its empire was dissolving, only waiting for a foreign conqueror. The last two Achaemid rulers happened to be particularly able, active, and successful.
- The Eastern Civilization, of which Persia was then the last link, had not exhausted itself. It has been claimed, amongst others by Arnold Toynbee, that a thousand years after Alexander had snuffed it out, it rose up again phoenix-like, in the guise of Islamic civilization.
- Nor can it be claimed that the outcome of the military contest was preordained, because of the superior ability of the Greek soldiers. Darius III employed more Greek mercenaries than the total number of Alexander's soldiers! The same conquest had been tried before by other Greeks – the Athenians, the Spartans, Xenophon's "Ten Thousand" – all of whom failed totally.

Alexander's phenomenal success can only be explained by his personal qualities as a commander, by his often frightening, unpredictable behavior, and by the strength of his Achilles complex, which drove him *on* to outdo the mythical hero of the *Iliad*. It can be claimed that no other general in history was equally effective and successful. To give some substance to this bald statement, let us compare him with the greatest commander of later Western history, Napoleon:

- Alexander won all his campaigns (while Napoleon, though successful in most of his 65 battles, lost half of his 14 campaigns) and also all of his battles and was also very good at siege warfare, which Napoleon was not.
- Alexander's powerbase of Macedonia was much narrower than Napoleon's of all of France, and yet his conquests were even more far-reaching.
- Napoleon preferred to leave the tactical handling of his battles to his generals. Alexander not only handled them himself, but personally led his men against the enemy, setting an example of personal valor, which Napoleon usually left to his marshals and generals.

- Napoleon was very good at applying principles of warfare which had been worked out by others. Alexander was himself a brilliant tactical innovator and, more than once, he acted not at his leisure, but on the spur of the moment, in the face of the enemy. To mention just four of the more outlandish problems which he solved with misleading ease:

(1) When campaigning in Thrace in 336/335 he and his men were caught in a deep gorge, when the Thracians rolled their wagons down the slopes on top of the Macedonians. Alexander immediately came up with a complicated drill of opening ranks in order to let the wagons through, as well as instructing his men to kneel down in groups, covered by their shields, so as to let them pass on top of them!

(2) During the siege of Tyre (332) Alexander decided that there was no solution other than to connect the island on which the mighty town stood, to the mainland. It took six months, but was entirely successful. The land-bridge is still there today.

(3) At Gaugamela (331) Alexander faced a force five times the size of his own. He came up with a scheme similar to that used by Napoleon at Austerlitz: The Persians must be induced to draw troops away from their center, and when this had been achieved, he smashed through the Persian left center, towards the person of Darius III, who promptly took flight. The enormous Persian army collapsed. Here timing was everything, just as at Austerlitz. But Alexander had not had Napoleon's opportunity of trying it all out previously at Castiglione (1796), nor did he command a force of near equal size to that of his adversary.

(4) At the battle of the Hydapses (326) Alexander improvised correct tactics to deal with elephants. They were encircled, their mahouts were picked off by archers, and once they were leaderless, they were attacked with javelins, scimitars, and axes. Napoleon never showed any similar ability at tactical improvisation.

- Alexander's strategic grasp was better. Napoleon questioned, in a discussion on St. Helena, the wisdom of Alexander's movement southward, along the Syrian coast, instead of striking inland immediately after the battle of Issus (333). What he did not understand was that Alexander was carrying out a unique maneuver: By capturing the Phoenician and Egyptian home ports of the Persian fleet, he demonstrated how a land power can defeat a sea power on land and completely eliminate its fleet. Napoleon never found a similar answer to his problem with England's sea power.

Are all these details relevant? We believe they are. Not only to show that Alexander was the greatest military commander recorded by history, but also to give some color to our claim that he, more than any other single person, influenced the flow of history.

Let us turn now to the highpoints of Alexander's career. His father, Philip II, had succeeded in imposing Macedonian control over most of Greece. The opposition to his progress was most eloquently voiced by the Athenian Demosthenes, whose speeches have survived. The climax came with the battle of Chaeronea (338), in which Alexander led the decisive charge of the right wing. After Philip's assassination, Alexander eliminated all claimants to the throne, defeated his enemies in Thrace, Illyria, and Greece, destroyed Thebes to make an example, and crossed over to Asia in 334. He defeated the first Persian army at the Granicus, King Darius III and his army at Issus (333), and then moved south through Syria and Palestine (sieges of Tyrus and Gaza) to Egypt. Having covered his back he moved into Mesopotamia, where he defeated Darius again, at Gaugamela (331). After this success he was in effect master of the Persian Empire.

He gradually changed his policy from pure conquest to the setting up of an empire in which the conquered should have many rights and be near-equal partners to the conquerors. This way he helped break down the barriers blocking the spread of Greek values. But he had to overcome the disapproval of his Macedonians and he achieved this, where necessary, by brute force. Even his closest associate, and most important general, Parmenion, was eventually put to death.

Alexander chose to campaign further afield and to subdue all the provinces of the empire in Central Asia and western India, and even expand its frontiers. He created thus an enormous, though short-lived, empire; he opened up these lands to the penetration of Greek ideas, institutions, language, commerce, and art. He linked up different civilizations, which previously had barely known of each other's existence. Later in this book we shall discover other meetings of civilizations but this is the first such link-up and perhaps the most dramatic one.

Although Alexander died in 323 in Babylon at only thirty-two years of age, his achievements – except for the unified empire – proved not to be ephemeral. He wiped the previous Middle Eastern civilization off the map, and instead opened the gate for the Hellenistic civilization, which was, in its various guises, to rule much of the then known world for a millennium.

Would this have happened anyway, in due time, even if there had been no Alexander? We do not think so.

20   The Hellenistic Civilization

During twenty years after Alexander's death continuous wars were fought between his Macedonian generals for possession of his empire. A few of them tried to keep it together in its entirety, but they were defeated in the end by those who tried to carve private kingdoms out of it for themselves. Three main dynasties were eventually established: the Ptolemies in Egypt and Palestine; the Antigonids in Macedonia; and the Seleucids in Asia Minor, Persia, Mesopotamia, and parts of Syria. The only other Hellenistic state worth mentioning was Pergamum in western Asia Minor (262–133 BC). Being the largest, the Seleucid empire was the least stable. India was lost before 303, the Parthians gradually conquered most of Persia during the third century, but on the other hand southern Syria and Palestine were finally captured, after several tries, by Antiochus III in 198. Nine years later he lost Asia Minor, except for Cilicia, and in the 2nd century most of the rest was lost by the Seleucids, except for parts of Syria.

The Romans, in the end, occupied the remainder in the early 1st century BC, as they had already taken over Macedonia in 168 and 148/147 BC, and were to occupy Egypt in 30 BC.

In addition there were innumerable smaller wars. Political turbulence was typical of the Hellenistic civilization. It is interesting how this manifests itself in the cultural sphere. In a very real sense one can still *feel* it just by looking at the twisted figures of giants and gods on the great altar to Zeus from Pergamum, now available for all to see in Berlin.

New ideas flowed back and forth in the Hellenistic world in many fields, amongst them also that of science. The heliocentric theory was propounded in astronomy 1800 years before Copernicus, by Aristarchus of Samos and Seleucus from Seleuceia on the Persian Gulf, but was not accepted at that time. Euclid wrote the definitive textbook of geometry in Egypt. Archimedes of Syracuse founded the science of hydrostatics. Hippodamus of Miletus introduced a system of town planning, with the help of a rectangular street layout.

New philosophical schools were founded by Epicurus and Zeno, which superseded the more staid schools of Plato and Aristotle. Especially, Zeno's Stoa became more than any other the philosophy of the Hellenistic civilization. Its centers were at Athens and Rhodes. In the Hellenistic world a man was no longer only a part of the body of citizens of a city, rather he was an individual, with an individual's need for success, career, and self-expression. The new philosophies did not aim so much at the discovery of truth, as at the happiness of the individual.

The free flow of ideas was facilitated by the common language of the educated classes throughout the Hellenistic world. This was the "Common Speech" of Greek, which had developed out of Attic, and served still as the language in which the New Testament was written. Thus the Greek-speaker was a citizen of the world within the limits of this civilization. He felt equally at home in Bactria, Egypt, and Sicily. In most Greek townships there were gymnasiums with libraries – and none larger than that at Alexandria, in Egypt, which was the seat of the most important Hellenistic school of poetry, called, accordingly, Alexandrian. Of its poets it might be worthwhile to mention Kallimachos, from

Cyrenaica, and his rival Apollonius of Rhodes, who was actually an Alexandinian. The best known writer of comedies, Menander, came, however, from Athens. Alexandria was also by far the biggest town (until imperial Rome arrived on the scene) and estimates of the number of its population go as high as one million souls. This was, of course, no longer a Greek city state, though it did mimic some of its forms, but the seat of an imperial government. Outside of Greece the population of such cities was neither wholly, nor principally Greek, but included a privileged Greek-speaking class. Most of the inhabitants were locals, who continued to speak their language (Aramaic in the case of most Middle Eastern cities), but lacked political rights.

Nevertheless, the non-Greek elements participated vigorously in the economic life. There was even a Phoenician standard of currency, which eventually pushed aside the Attic standard. Trade increased after Alexander released the great amounts of bullion he found in the Persian treasuries, and turned them into coins. The Hellenistic world, with its common language and usage, was ideally suited for the intensification of trade and production. Slaves supplied the cheap labor needed in a society lacking mechanical means of production. The wealthiest cities were those fed by transit trade – Alexandria, Antioch, Rhodes, Ephesus, Pergamum, and Delos. Alexandria, for instance, imported metals, wool, dyes, marble, wine, spices, and horses and exported wheat, papyrus, glass, linen, perfumes, and ivory. Exports exceeded imports – hence the great wealth of the Ptolemies. They also controlled the island of Cyprus, which exported copper. Corn came from Egypt, Syria, and the Crimea. The finest wines were brought from Syria and Ionia. Wool came from Cyrenaica and Aeolis, but was spun and woven mainly in Miletus. Pergamum specialized in gold-woven cloth, Aeolis in carpets, Cilicia in rough cloaks. But very little cotton was as yet imported from India and even less silk from China.

Purple dyes were produced in Tyre, ivory came from India and Africa, pearls were found in the Persian Gulf, balsam was produced in Jericho, cinnamon came via Arabia, and frankincense from Yemen. The center of the spice trade was in Alexandria and Rhodes.

In spite of the relative economic prosperity there flowed some-times a counter-current of local beliefs and non-Greek, or even anti-Greek, sentiment. This was represented by the Parthian con-querors of Persia, by the Hasmonean rulers of Judea, by Mithri-dates, King of Pontus, by the corsairs of Cilicia, by the nomadic tribes on the border of the Arabian desert, such as the Nabateans and Itureans. But these, too, were influenced in their later stages by Hellenistic ideas and customs. There also existed nationalistic, anti-Greek movements both in Egypt and in Mesopotamia. The Greek elements may ultimately have been absorbed and discarded by the local populations, as the Hellenistic states lost much of their initial elan and energy, but just in time they were saved in most places west of Persia by the intervention of Rome.

21   Rome

Rome's greatness was not one of creativity, like that of Greece, but one of superior organizational ability. Her fame rested on her impressive empire, the strength of her legions, the quality of her roads and aqueducts.

The oldest archeological remains uncovered at Rome belong to the 9th century BC. Several villages united sometime in the 7th century to form a little town. Until the end of the 6th century the area was apparently under strong Etruscan influence.

Who were the Etruscans? they may originally have been one of the Sea People, the Teresh, mentioned by Herodotus as Tyrrhenians. Later they came under the cultural influence of the Greek cities in southern Italy and their surviving later art can best be characterized as rather provincial Hellenistic. They were, however, strong enough to keep the Greeks away from Etruria. When their power waned, Rome threw off their yoke (509 BC), and became an oligarchic republic. Power was vested mainly in two consuls and the Senate.

During the 4th and early 3rd centuries Rome commenced her career as one of the great conquerors of history and succeeded in spreading her influence or outright dominion over most of Italy, defeating the Celtic hordes coming from the north, the Samnites to the southeast, the Etruscans to the north, and the Greek cities in the south of the peninsula. Rome faced two rivals from beyond the sea. First, King Pyrrhus of Epirus, in Greece, who failed in his expeditions to Italy (280–272 BC), and afterwards Carthage, which had originally been founded by the Phoenicians in what today is Tunis. Two "Punic" wars were fought between them, in 264–241 and in 218–202. The first was fought mainly for the island of Sicily and for naval superiority. Rome was ultimately successful in both areas. The second was more dramatic, with the Carthaginian general Hannibal, based in newly conquered southern Spain, traversing the alps with his elephants, invading Italy from the north and defeating Rome's armies repeatedly (his most famous victory was at Cannae in 216) in spite of the great superiority in manpower of the Romans. With his final defeat, back in Africa, at the battle of Zama (202), Rome was left as the single strongest Mediterranean power.

During the 2nd century BC, Rome defeated or browbeat all the Hellenistic kingdoms and occupied Greece, parts of Asia Minor, Spain, and parts of North Africa. The Mediterranean became increasingly a Roman lake.

The strong republican traditions of earlier times commanded less loyalty, as Rome became an empire. For a hundred years civil wars took place (133–30 BC). The social background was that many small farmers were ruined in Italy by the cheap wheat grown by slave labor in Sicily and elsewhere. The farmers lost their land and moved to Rome, where the needy multitudes grew in numbers. The aristocratic faction of Optimates were now faced by the opposing Populares. The latter were first headed by the Gracchi brothers (133–121 BC), later by Marius (104–86), and finally by Julius Caesar. Marius was defeated, however, by Sulla; and Caesar had to fight his erstwhile colleague in the first triumvirate, Pompey, before he achieved sole control of the empire.

The same generals achieved victories and conquests abroad. Marius captured Numidia, in North Africa, and defeated an inroad of German tribes; Sulla helped in Numidia and pacified Greece and Asia Minor; Pompey annihilated the corsairs of Cilicia and occupied most of the Middle East; and Julius

Caesar conquered Gallia and invaded southern England. The result was a much extended empire, but also rootless armies, loyal only to their leaders. After Caesar's murder in 44 BC a new round of fighting broke out. A second triumvirate was formed and abolished. Then, at last, Octavian (the later Augustus, Julius Caesar's nephew) managed in 31/30 BC to vanquish the last of his competitors, Mark Anthony, capture Egypt, and put an end to the civil war.

Augustus (30 BC–AD 14) tried to rule at first as inconspicuously as possible and to preserve a façade of republican legality, but in fact he was not only the first of the Roman emperors, but also the most important one and the one with the longest reign. The "Roman Peace" he introduced in all of his enormous empire made it a tremendously popular institution. Historians tend to dwell in great detail on all the cabals and murders of his court and those of his heirs. But this affected only a few hundred persons, while the 75–100 million inhabitants of the empire at its peak enjoyed peace and relative prosperity for some 250 years. Foreign wars took place far away. It is only worth recording that the Emperor Claudius (AD 41–54) conquered England, and Trajan (98–117) conquered what today is Romania and, temporarily, Mesopotamia. Afterwards Rome went over to the defensive along all her long borders.

When we speak nowadays of Rome, we usually think of the empire as it was in those 250 years of its glory and power. The deep peace in the interior brought with it lively trade and a high standard of living, but, perhaps surprisingly, nothing to compare with the outpouring of creativity of Greece in her prime. Roman civilization is, indeed, a direct continuation of Greek and Hellenistic civilization. Its authors and historians tried – unsuccessfully – to equal those of Greece; its sculptors and architects continued to work in the Greek tradition. Most of the Greek masterpieces of sculpture are known nowadays only from their Roman copies. Most of what we know of Hellenistic stoicism derives from Cicero's Latin philosophical works. The eastern half of the empire continued to use the Greek language.

What, then, were Rome's contributions to civilization? First of all – Roman law, which, as codified under Justinian in the

6th century AD, is the foundation of law in most of Europe. In architecture the Romans pioneered the functional use of arches for bridges, aqueducts, gateways, and vast open interiors. They constructed an enormous road network, from Scotland to Arabia, not to be equalled until the 20th century. Another important contribution was the Latin language, which for over a thousand years after western Rome had disappeared, served as Europe's international language, and the language both of the Church and of science; Latin is still taught today. Rome encompassed the idea of a universal empire. Thus the German Empire in the Middle Ages was called "Roman." Nowadays, when a United Europe is being created, this precedent is again of great relevance.

It is perhaps worthwhile to name some of Rome's thinkers, such as Cicero and Seneca, some of her poets, such as Virgil, Horace, and Ovid – all of them living in the time of Augustus; and its historians, such as Livius and Tacitus. But they cannot hold a candle to Plato, Homer, and Thucydides. Most original is perhaps Caesar's terse report of his Gallic wars.

In the middle of the 3rd century AD the long period of stability and peace came to an end and Rome passed from a state defending itself against marauders to one that had to struggle for its very survival. New groups of German tribes appeared in Europe, and were pushed toward the borders of the Empire by the Sarmatians from southern Russia. Some broke through, into the Balkans, others reached Italy and Spain. Gothic pirates plundered the islands and shores of the Aegean. In the East, the new Persian dynasty of the Sassanids proved after 224 AD much more formidable adversaries than the Parthians had ever been. A Roman emperor was taken prisoner by them (260). For several years a state of anarchy and crisis existed, emperors were discarded speedily, and much of the Roman Middle East was ruled by the princes of Palmyra (one of them was the famed Queen Zenobia). Three emperors of Illyrian origin re-established the Empire. Diocletian, the last and most important of them (284–305), reorganized it completely. But it was a different Rome that arose now. The old prosperity did not return. The currency was debased. Peasants were gradually forced into serfdom. Taxes were oppressively heavy. The emperors were army leaders, nominated by their soldiers. The government became a despotism founded on the army. The army camp became the power center of the Empire. The economy of the West had suffered more severely than that of the East, and the latter became dominant in the empire. The Greek language, Christian religion, and Eastern art characterized the later Empire. Its capital was now in Constantinople, founded by the first Christian emperor, Constantine the Great (306–337).

Western Rome became of lesser consequence and when attacked in the 5th century by nomadic Huns and by German tribes, such as the Goths, Franks, and Vandals, it collapsed (476). Eastern Rome survived, however, as the Christian Byzantine Empire, for another thousand years.

It was in Europe that the name of Rome kept its magic touch. During the darkness of the Middle Ages and beyond, the name of Rome stood for order and good government, for achievements to be emulated, for a golden age to be remembered with nostalgia.

22   Hellenistic Judaism and Early Christianity

Christianity was the final outcome of the meeting between Judaism and Greek civilization in its Hellenistic guise. But already much earlier this meeting had affected Judaism more than that with any other civilization in its 3000 years of existence. This happened on two different levels, one religious and doctrinal, and the other secular and political. On the first level Greek thought and especially their ethics proved to be very influential. Neo-Platonism had a great effect on Judaism. Such late books of the Old Testament as Ecclesiastes were written under Hellenistic influence. This is even more true of such later authors as Philon of Alexandria. The doctrine of the immortality of the soul and of resurrection entered Judaism probably under Greek influence, without however abandoning completely the this-wordly emphasis of the earlier biblical period.

In the 3rd century BC increasing numbers of Jews in the diaspora started to speak Greek. In Alexandria the Old Testament had to be translated into Greek (the Septuagint) in order to be understood.

Turning to the second level, in the early 2nd century BC many of the aristocratic priests of Jerusalem became hellenized. The Seleucid King Antiochus IV Epiphanes (175–164) did his utmost to force hellenization also on the other strata of Jewish society. If he had been successful it is likely that Judaism would have disappeared and then neither Christianity nor Islam would have appeared at all, or, at least, not in the way they did.

The Hasmonean revolution of Judas Maccabeus and his family prevented this eventuality. A Jewish state developed, initially in Judea and later in all of Palestine. Most of the Aramaic-speaking rural population of Galilee, Idumea, and Transjordan was converted to Judaism. Only the Samaritans in the central part of the country held out and stayed loyal to their own version of the religion of Israel. The ties of the Jews of the diaspora to their religion and their center in Jerusalem, with its Temple, were strengthened.

This second period of Jewish independence lasted for barely one hundred years. Pompey's campaign in 63 BC put an end to it. For another 60 years the country was ruled by the Idumean family of King Herod, but there was no longer any active proselytizing. It now came under direct Roman rule.

Several sects arose in Judaism. The Saducees believed in a centralized temple-cult, while the Pharisees started to develop the *Halachah*, or oral tradition, modifying the precepts of Pentateuchal law according to the needs of their time. Strong eschatological elements were stressed by the various groups of Essenes, among them those whose "Dead Sea Scrolls" have been recovered in modern times at Qumran. The belief in an early deliverance with the help of a messiah was particularly stressed in the times of increased pressure under direct Roman rule.

The Roman procurators (AD 6–66) were rapacious and inclined to help the Hellenistic cities in Palestine against the Jewish population. These difficult conditions reinforced the belief in eschatological teachings. Many messianic movements and leaders appeared early in the 1st century AD. Many of them were motivated by political, anti-Roman feelings and they were usually put to death by the Roman authorities.

John the Baptist seems to have stayed some time with the

Essenes of Qumran, and there certainly are strong Qumranian influences in early Christianity. The Galilean group to which Jesus belonged seems to have been concerned more with moral precepts and less with politics. Hence, perhaps, the ultimate success of Christianity. Surviving sources place all of Jesus' life in Galilee, except for his last week, when he went on the traditional Passover pilgrimage to Jerusalem. After trying to drive out the traders from the precincts of the Temple and predicting its future destruction, he was arrested in the nearby Garden of Gethsemane. After a preliminary trial he was delivered into the hands of the Romans, who had him crucified.

From among his disciples he had appointed twelve apostles, who provided, after his death, together with some members of his family, the leadership for the nascent Church. Before it had time to crystalize its doctrines, or to widen the number of its adherents, it was uprooted from Jerusalem and Judea by political events.

The tension between Jews and Romans, and the encroachments by the last procurators, brought about the Great Revolt of AD 66–70, which led to the capture of Jerusalem by Titus and the destruction of the Temple. As a result, Judaism changed. The old cult of sacrifices and of a central Temple disappeared. Rabbinical Judaism came to the fore. It regarded the *Halachah* as the main link to its roots. Its more important judicial decisions were collected early in the 3rd century in the Hebrew-written *Mishnah*, and some three centuries later in the Aramaic-written *Babylonian Talmud*.

The Jews of Palestine tried several times to regain their former political independence. Their greatest revolt (ten Roman legions were involved – a third of the total strength of the Roman army – as against the four used by Titus) was that of Bar Kokhba, in 132–5, which was suppressed by the Emperor Hadrian. Most Jews were exiled from Judea, but a sufficient number remained in Galilee for another great revolt in 614, in conjunction with a Persian attack on Eastern Rome, during the time of the Emperor Heraclius. This, however, was the last attempt by the Jews of the Holy Land to try and play a political role, for the next twelve centuries.

The great advances of Christianity were achieved away from strife-torn Palestine, among the Greek-speaking populations of the Eastern Mediterranean. The earliest missionary journeys there had been undertaken by the Apostle Paul. As more and more former pagans were converted, Christianity ceased to be a Jewish sect and became a religion in its own right, claiming to be "The True Israel."

It accepted the Old Testament in its Greek translation and originally also the Apocrypha, which had not been included in the Jewish canon. In the last quarter of the 1st century the Gospels were composed. By the middle of the 2nd century a first New Testament canon had been accepted by the Church. A standard organization evolved, headed in each place by an overseer ("bishop"), helped by presbyters (later priests) and administrative assistants, called deacons. With the spread of Christianity throughout the Empire, its members were persecuted from time to time. As the Roman Empire changed from the 3rd century onwards, and became more orientalized, Eastern creeds gained increasing popularity. None more so than Christianity.

Early in the 4th century the Emperor Constantine started to patronize Christianity. Under his heirs it became the dominant religion of the Roman Empire. Civil and criminal law were revised in the Church's interest. Large funds were allocated to the bishops. Patriarchs were nominated in the five main cities of Constantinople, Alexandria, Antioch, Rome, and somewhat later, Jerusalem. The office of the Patriarch of Rome evolved later to that of the Pope. Pagans, Jews, and Samaritans were persecuted. By the end of the 4th century most of the inhabitants of the empire were Christians.

Ecumenical councils were convened in order to discuss major questions of faith. The first one, at Nicea (325), was called primarily to define the nature of Jesus Christ and to transfer the day of rest from the Jewish Sabbath to the Christian Sunday.

Much of the early literature of the Church was written by the Church fathers, from the 2nd to the 7th century. Among the more important churchmen were Origen Adamantios ("the man of steel") (185–254), who initiated many of the Christian dogmata; Eusebius of Caesarea (c. 262–340), who composed the first "History of the Church"; Jerome (died in 420), who translated both the New Testament and Eusebius' *History* into Latin; Athanasius (293–373), who was the main defender of Orthodoxy against the Arian heresy; Augustine (354–430), a prolific writer and determined defender of Orthodoxy, from North Africa; and Ambrose of Milan (340–97), who composed a guide on ethics and was the main initiator of the use of hymns in church worship.

There soon occurred the first schisms. Followers of Arius, from early in the 4th century, believed that Jesus was not a god. Nestorians, from the early 5th century onward, believed in the duality of Jesus as both God and human. The Monophysites, later in that century, stressed the opposite, and believed that his two natures had been fused into one. The orthodox position was that the union was perfect, but the natures remained distinct. The Monophysite hair-splitting soon became a cloak for the political disenchantment of the local inhabitants of the Middle East with the Greek-speaking Byzantine authorities. When Islam arrived on the scene, the Semitic Monophysists of Syria quickly converted, while the ethnically different Monophysists of Armenia and Ethiopia continued to adhere to their creed. For political reasons, Emperor Heraclius reached a compromise with the Monophysists, which survives to this day as the Maronite Church of Lebanon. However, the Orthodox Church continued to be dominant both in the West and in Byzantium, to split only in the 11th century into the Catholic Church, headed by the Pope in Rome, and the Greek Orthodox Church, with its headquarters in Constantinople.

In medieval times it was usually the Church which kept alive some of the values of the Roman civilization in western Europe.

Part VII

Asian Empires of the First Millennium AD

Throughout most of the history of mankind it is the Middle East, and later Europe, where the most momentous developments have taken place: from the Agricultural Revolution to the Industrial Revolution; from the earliest attempts at urbanization and the initial use of metals and writing, to the development of modern mass transportation and the scientific breakthroughs of the 19th and 20th centuries; from the Egyptian and Roman empires to the British, French, and Russian empires; from Socrates to Einstein; from the Bible to *Das Kapital*. There were few exceptions to this rule, the most conspicuous of which was Asia in the period under consideration now. Under the Han dynasty, Chinese civilization drew even with contemporary Rome and the West. During the dark centuries of the early Middle Ages in Europe, China under the Tang and Song dynasties drew far ahead. Here stable rule prevailed, while barbarism was the rule in much of Europe. Even such civilizations as the Byzantine and Islamic were usually less stable and well administered. They were also less creative and more imitative. In the first millennium China forged ahead in such technological fields as the invention of paper and the resulting literacy, the invention of the compass, of porcelain and silk spinning and weaving, and the early use of printing, paper money, and gunpowder.

The developments in India, too, were momentous. At the very time that Christianity and Islam expanded all over the Middle East, Europe and North Africa, Buddhism expanded into Southeast Asia, Indonesia, Central Asia, China, and Japan. The world was thus split on the religious front into the West (controlled by Judaistic religions) and India and the Far East (dominated, though less rigidly, by Buddhism and Hinduism).

Under Sassanian influence Islam turned into a basically Eastern civilization, which cut the umbilical cord that initially connected it with Greek Civilization.

Never before or after did Eastern Asian and Indian civilizations play so dominant a part for so long a period of history. This is of special interest today, when such Eastern Asian countries as Japan, China, Korea, Taiwan, and others are moving once more to the center of the stage of history.

23   The Han, Tang, and Song Dynasties of China

In the long course of Chinese history there has been no more important revolution than that of 221 BC, which utterly destroyed the feudal system of early China and ushered in the classical age of empire. The revolution was carried out by the ruler of the westernmost of the feudal states, Quin, who after he had unified all of China, styled himself Shih Huang Di, "The First Emperor." He abolished the many codes of law previously used; enforced the use of the laws of Quin throughout the country; standardized the coinage, measures, and weights in order to control trade; burned all the books he could lay his hands on; unified the system of writing for use by the new bureaucracy; and started to erect the Great Wall of China, to keep out the northern nomads. When he died in 210 BC his body was guarded by a nearby army of thousands of life-size terracotta soldiers and horses, which have been uncovered by modern archeologists.

His real heirs were the emperors of the Han dynasty, who overthrew the regime of Quin's son, and ruled China for more than 400 years, from 206 BC to AD 221. Instead of the brute force of the Quin period, a system of social control through mutual responsibility was evolved, based on Confucian ideals. The old feudal units were further split up and reorganized, and the old aristocracy was resettled elsewhere. A strong bureaucracy was organized, which was in charge of the day-to-day administration of the empire. Stiff entrance examinations ensured the high quality of its members. Nowhere else was a similarly efficient system of administration, based on merit, used during the first millennium AD. China was far in advance in many fields, relative to such contemporaries as the later Roman empire, the Islamic Caliphate, or the early medieval states. And this in spite of the fact that the Iron Age, for instance, had commenced in China seven centuries later than in the Middle East. Thus technical, social, economic, and administrative developments had to be very rapid during the Han period. Paper was invented before AD 100, calligraphy developed into a fine art, and literacy spread widely. The breast-strap harness for draught horses was developed by the 2nd century BC – 800 years earlier than in the West. The horse collar was introduced by the 5th century AD, 400 years earlier than in Europe. Double-acting piston bellows in air pumps were in wide use by the 1st century AD. In Europe, similar equipment was developed only in the 16th century. During the Han period, bellows for metallurgical furnaces, and deep borehole drills, were first used, and the wheelbarrow was developed.

The Han Empire expanded in all directions. The Yangtze valley was firmly incorporated in the area of Chinese civilization, and all of southern China, to the sea, was incorporated in the empire. In the north the Han engaged in a long struggle with the monadic Hsiung Nu, and advanced their borders well beyond the Great Wall. To the west, parts of Xinjiang were incorporated, and a Chinese expedition reached the Caspian Sea. Even such areas as northern Korea and northern Vietnam became part of the Han Empire. But Tibet and most of present-day Outer Mongolia did not. Thus China became less isolated, and economic and some cultural contacts were established with Southeast Asia, northern India, Central Asia, Bactria, Persia, and the eastern parts of Rome.

The population of China is estimated to have reached 50 million in Han times – a good deal less than the 75–100 million estimated for the Roman Empire in its prime.

Cultural activity was intensive. The first dictionary was composed and important books of history were written, such as the *Shih Chi*; the literary scene showed change and innovation. Instead of the many centers of the feudal period, with their local traditions, a more uniform national culture now evolved.

No important architectural monuments have survived and only very few paintings. Visually we have thus to see Han China today mainly with the help of later copies of paintings, pottery tomb models, and surviving bas reliefs and statuary, in both stone and bronze. Some Western influences can be discerned, but more in technique than in content. Porcelain was developed in China, and so was silk weaving and lacquer work. Jade continued to be carved. Art became more secular than previously. Animals are often pictured – perhaps under the influence of northern nomads.

A period of troubles followed the collapse of the Han civilization. In the 3rd century AD "Three Kingdoms" are mentioned, in the 4th and early 5th centuries there were "Sixteen Kingdoms" in the north alone, with separate dynasties in the south.

Political chaos went hand in hand with an intensification of religious belief. Otherworldly directed Buddhism and Taoism became nearly equally important with the much more worldly Confucianism. Their monasteries proliferated. Numerous statues of Buddha were carved. Chinese pilgrims visited holy sites in India and thus strengthened the ties between these centers of civilization.

The usual cycle of Chinese history followed, with unity re-established by the short-lived Sui dynasty (589–618). It was followed by perhaps the most impressive of all the imperial dynasties of China, the Tang (618–906), whose borders were less far flung than those of the Han Empire, as they only reached the Great Wall in the north. Thus it is not the wars of the Tang which impress historians, but rather the quality of their civilization. China was never again so far in advance of the rest of the world.

A great movement of population caused the center of gravity of China to shift from the north to its center and south. Many small farmers lost their holdings to large landowners, to the monasteries, and to members of the imperial administration. Interior trade utilized the many waterways of China. Large canals connected the various river systems. Exterior trade was largely in the hands of Indian, Arab, and Persian shipowners.

The textile industry developed rapidly. Concentrations of hundreds of weaving looms are reported from the Hubei and Sichuan provinces. The mining of metal was intensified. Canal lock gates were used, allowing boats to ascend canals in stages. The first suspension bridge was built over the Yangtze river. The first mechanical clocks were assembled.

The administration of China was refined and made more sophisticated. There was a clear division between the functions of the imperial government in the capital and of the provincial authorities. Initially there were ten provinces, to be increased later to fifteen. The armed forces were organized so as to avoid the concentration of too much power in one hand.

Two universities served higher education, each of which had faculties of law, mathematics, administration, and calligraphy. A higher education was the stepping-stone for the examinations which were necessary to enter public service.

The Tang period is regarded as the golden age of Chinese literature and especially of lyrical poetry. It boasts of such names as Li Bai, Du Fu, and Bai Juyi. Many of their poems are composed as a series of images, evoking a mood. Also, short stories were already popular. The invention of printing, using carved wooden blocks, made a wide distribution of books possible for the first time.

The oldest surviving architectural structure in China (Mount Wu Tai in Shanxi province) is dated to AD 857. Earlier and more impressive buildings have survived in Japan, inspired by Tang architecture. The Tang period is regarded as the classical age of Chinese painting and especially landscape painting. Only a few originals have survived, but quite a few copies of the Song period still exist today. Because brushes and not quills were used for writing, painting and calligraphy developed hand in hand. Many of the masterpieces were created on fine silk, which permitted no erasures. Li Chao-tao's "Travellers in a Mountain Pass" creates, for instance, in metallic blues and greens, a panorama of cloud-shrouded peaks and gorges, against which is shown a group of small horsemen and camels. Colored Tang pottery figurines of women, men, horses, and camels are so numerous in museums and collections as to raise some doubts whether they are really all authentic.

Tang civilization did not reach a sudden, catastrophic end, but merged into Song civilization. The Song Empire (960–1127) was smaller, and did not include some of northern China, the previous western provinces, and northern Vietnam. Later the empire shrank even more and included only southern China (1127–1279), while the north was in the hands of various nomad tribes and states, the last, and most powerful of which were the Mongols, who later conquered southern China and put an end to the Song dynasty.

In spite of its narrower borders, Song China was more densely settled and is estimated to have reached 100 million inhabitants – many more than lived either in medieval Europe or in Byzantium or under the Arab Caliphate.

Using the compass, developed in China, Song ships penetrated into the Indian Ocean and maritime trade boomed. Paper money was introduced, which also helped to intensify economic activity. The merchant class grew in size, wealth, and importance. Gunpowder was invented, but its potential for warfare was not fully understood. Printing was further developed and in the 11th century movable type was invented, with characters cast in ceramic. The textile industry was refined by the use of large mechanical reeling frames for silk cocoons.

The wealth of the new merchant class provided patronage for artists, calligraphers, and painters. Early Song painters specialized in vast and towering landscapes of such magnitude that they dwarfed all signs of man in them. Later, painters stressed more the importance of the human figure in nature. Polychromed wood statues and gilded bronze figures show a flowing line of drapery. Many of the sculpted faces are fiercely expressive. Pottery and porcelain are many-colored and beautiful. Song ceramics are regarded as classical. In spite of the fact that Chinese art continued for many centuries on a high level, it never really surpassed its achievements in the Song period.

In literature, prose creations took pride of place from poetry. The language of poetry was too far removed from that actually spoken to find any longer a wide audience. The essay came into its full bloom. Historiography became less rigid. Chinese drama and the novel had their real start only later, under the Mongols.

To summarize, there is no more brilliant period in Chinese history than the 1500 years of Han, Tang, and Song rule, nor is there one in which Chinese civilization was farther ahead of the rest of the world.

24   Pre-Islamic India

While both Chinese and Egyptian history seems to consist of a cycle of strong dynasties, followed by breakdown and chaos, Indian history is much less easily defined and described. Its great moments are not necessarily those of strong imperial government. Religion seems to have left a stronger imprint on Indian history than either political development or imperial conquest. Philosophy, literature, and art are all permeated by religion. A history of Indian religious development seems to be more relevant than an enumeration of Indian dynasties and military victories. While this might not hold true for the second millennium AD, it seems to be valid for the first.

The rise of Brahmanism, Buddhism, and Jainism has been discussed in Part V. The present period was dominated by the struggle between Brahmanism and Buddhism for the control of India, and the changes wrought within each of them. Buddhism seemed initially, after Ashoka's reign, to have had the inside track. Its appeal was to the wide strata of the population, which were regarded as beyond the pale by Brahmanism. But while Buddhism was weakened by its split into the sects of the Great and the Small Vehicle, Brahmanism was envigored by the inclusion of many indigenous deities, beside the original Vedic gods, thus strengthening its ties to many sections of the population. As a result there evolved traditional Hinduism.

Indian art reflects the difference between the two creeds. On the one hand the many impressive statues of Buddha, initially influenced by Hellenistic art, and on the other hand the wild proliferation of figures in Hindu temple art. Elephants, warriors, naked Yakshis, floral scrolls, and minor deities are thrown pell-mell together and yet controlled by one aesthetic framework. The same rich visual symbolism is turned into literature, in the two enormous epic works, the *Mahābhārata* and the *Rāmāyana*. In some of their parts one can find fused together divergent strands of cultic theism, worldly social theory, and speculative philosophy. Even sex was regarded as a function of religious law, as explained in the *Kama Sutra*, a treatise on the technique of love-making. So also was mathematical astronomy, as expounded by the antagonists of the greatest of Indian astronomers, Aryabhata.

The era from AD 300 to 700 is usually regarded as the classical period of Indian culture. In the political field its earlier part was dominated by the Gupta dynasty (*c.* 320–500), under which Hinduism got the upper hand in India. Western ideas and sciences – such as medicine, astronomy, geometry, and logic – reached India via Sassanian Iran.

Buddhism's missionary activity in Central and Southeastern Asia enhanced its overall importance, but it did so at the expense of its standing in its homeland. In the ritual of worship and of religious practice it had to compromise with Hinduism to such an extent that it could sometimes be regarded as no more than one of Hinduism's sects. By the end of the first millennium Hinduism was very much the dominant religion and Buddhism was about to disappear completely from India.

25   Parthians and Sassanians in Iran

After the death of Alexander the Great, Iran passed during the wars of the Diadochi under the rule of the Seleucid dynasty. Hellenism did not affect very deeply the greater parts of its population. When Seleucid rule weakened, in the second half of the 3rd century BC, some Scythian tribes settled in the north of Iran, east of the Caspian Sea, in the province of Parthia, from which they took their name. Expanding to the south, they soon formed a wedge which cut off Hellenistic Bactria to the east, from the Hellenistic world in the west. Many of the inhabitants of Iran appeared quite willing to exchange the Greek yoke for some sort of national government. The attempt of the Seleucid ruler Antiochus III (223–187 BC) to recapture Iran proved in the end fruitless, when he himself was defeated by the Romans.

Mithridates I, the true founder of the Parthian Empire, annexed all of Persia and Mesopotamia and parts of Afghanistan between the years 160 and 140 BC.

Throughout most of their 400 years of rule in Iran the Parthians had to fight a two-front war – against further nomadic invasions from Central Asia and against Rome in the west. While Rome had defeated all its neighbors and occupied their territories, it never managed to overcome the Parthians. In the years of Rome's greatness the Parthians were regarded as the only power of equal standing. In 53 BC, one of the original triumvirs, Crassus, tried to emulate Julius Caesar's success in Gallia by an invasion of Persia, but was defeated and killed with most of his army in the battle of Carrhae. While the heavily armed Roman legion was highly effective in the countries bordering on the Mediterranean, it proved decidedly inferior to the light and mobile Parthian cavalry in the deserts of the East. The verdict of Carrhae was never reversed, in spite of further Roman attempts. Parthian undertakings against Syria were usually half-hearted and were not crowned by success either. The upper Euphrates and the Syrian Desert remained for nearly 700 years the border between Rome and Persia.

There were strong economic ties between Rome and Iran, as the latter was traversed by some of the main trade routes from Rome to India, Central Asia, and China. The Augustean peace brought about an unprecedented increase in the volume of trade. Much care was taken in Persia to maintain the roads on which this trade moved, as it was a very important source of revenue.

In spite of the wars against Seleucids and Romans, there developed a strong Hellenistic element in the culture of the Parthians. The Greek cities were left undisturbed, the Parthian coinage imitated Greek coins, the Greek language was widely used, and Greek names were often bestowed on Persians. Only toward the end of Parthian rule did a national Iranian consciousness appear to have been reborn.

In AD 224 the last Parthian ruler was decisively defeated by a new dynasty, the Sassanians, who had their roots in the province of ancient Persia. Their rule was regarded as the rebirth of the Achaemenian Empire. Persian national feelings strengthened the Sassanian armies in their many wars with Rome and Byzantium. Persia was regarded also beyond its borders as the center of the reborn Eastern Civilization, which had been subjugated by Alexander the Great.

The most important Sassanian king, Shapur I, defeated the Romans repeatedly, took the Emperor Valerian captive (AD 260), reconquered Mesopotamia and Armenia, turned the Kushan Empire of northern India and Central Asia into a dependency, and reorganized the Iranian Empire. Ctesiphon served as its capital.

Similar to Constantine the Great, Shapur I was looking around for a new creed to help cement the foundations of his empire; he found it in the Manichean faith. Its founder, Mani, had advocated an Iranian form of simple communism, with redistribution of property and other far-reaching social reforms. The Manicheans practiced baptism and communion, and their clergy was celibate. After Shapur's death the strongly entrenched Mazdian priesthood reacted violently and re-established their dominance.

Farmers lost their independence in Sassanian times and often were forced to become serfs, in a Persian version of feudalism. A similar development took place in Eastern Rome, preparing the way for the social stratification of the Middle Ages.

Sassanian Iran did not decline – it committed suicide. Under Chosroes II (590–628) it engaged in a murderous war with Byzantium, which led first to the occupation of most of Asia Minor and the Middle East by the Persians, and later to the conquest of Iran by the Emperor Heraclius. Both sides were finally so weakened that when the armies of Islam erupted in the 630s from the Arabian Desert they found but little resistance. Sassanian Persia collapsed completely, and became a province of the Arab Caliphate.

But Sassanian civilization still had much vigor left. The transfer of power, in 750, from Umayyads to Abbasids, meant in reality an acceptance by Islam of the Eastern values of Sassanian Iran, as against the Hellenistic–Roman values of their predecessors. In the 1250 years which have elapsed since then, Islam has continued to develop its Eastern, Sassanian, heritage.

Part VIII

The Early Middle Ages

The term "Middle Ages" has been coined in Europe and describes, neatly enough, the sharp decline of civilization in countries like Italy, France, Spain, and England after the fall of the Western Roman Empire and before the Renaissance and Reformation. One has to remember, however, that this term is inapplicable elsewhere. Byzantium, the Islamic countries, China in the times of the Tang and Song dynasties, and even the prehistoric civilizations of America, reached the pinnacle of their development at this very time.

Some scholars have not been very keen on the term Middle Ages even when applied to western Europe. The Austrian Dopsch held the notion that there existed an unbroken economic and cultural continuity from the later Roman Empire through the Merovingian era and into the Carolingian period. The Belgian Pirenne claimed that this continuity was disrupted not so much by the invasion of the German tribes in the 4th century AD, as by that of the Arab tribes in the 7th. Both views should be treated with caution, but show that the events of this period are open to widely differing interpretations.

26   Byzantium

Byzantium existed as a political unit for a thousand years, and as a civilization even longer. In one of the darkest ages of Europe it survived often as a lone beacon of light and culture. The roots of much of later Western art, science, and law are Byzantine.

While the Byzantine state had a distinct end, it is less clear when exactly was its beginning. As an empire it is simply a continuation of Rome. Some of the Eastern elements of its civilization were present already in the 3rd century reforms of Diocletian. On the other hand, even its last emperor, Constantine XI, regarded himself in the 15th century as a Roman emperor. Many historians speak of the 7th century as "late Roman Empire." We, however, shall take here the foundation of Constantinople, in 330 by Constantine the Great, as the beginning of Byzantine history, and the Orthodox Christian faith of its inhabitants as its clearest characteristic. The use of the Greek language was its other characteristic (though in both cases there were some exceptions – the Court, for instance, used Latin in its first two hundred years).

Its most constant feature was the autocratic reign of the emperor in Constantinople. At first he ruled a vast empire, stretching from the Balkans to the Persian frontier and from the Black Sea to the first cataract of the Nile. In spite of barbarian invasions from the north, Persian wars in the east, interior upheaval (for instance the paganism of the Emperor Julian "the apostate" (361–3), and the Arian, Monophysite, and Nestorian heresies), the Byzantine Empire survived successfully the 4th and 5th centuries, even though Western Rome declined and finally collapsed (476) and most of Europe was overrun by German barbarians.

In the 6th century, under the Emperor Justinian I (527–65), the Byzantine state even made a formidable attempt to re-establish the Roman Empire and turn the Mediterranean again into a Roman lake. Italy, northern Africa, and parts of Spain were recaptured and reintegrated in the empire. The Ostrogothic and Vandal kingdoms there were annihilated and the Visigothic state was weakened. Justinian reformed the administration, revised and codified the existing laws, tried unsuccessfully to reform the Church, beautified his main cities with sumptuous buildings (none more impressive than the Church of Saint Sophia in Constantinople), and embellished some of his churches with impressive mosaics. His court historian Procopius was the greatest Byzantine writer of history.

Justinian was trying to achieve too much. The resources of Byzantium were not up to it. Both its finances and the motivation of its ruling class were exhausted. Under his successors the Byzantine armies were defeated by the Persians and the nomadic Avars, the Langobards captured most of Italy (Rome becoming semi-independent under the Pope), southern Spain was lost back to the Visigoths and, even more fateful, many of the hosts of Slavs moving westward, to fill the empty spaces left by the Germans, turned south and poured across the empire's Danubian frontiers, torn open for them by the Avars. Within a few generations all of the Balkans, including continental Greece, were settled by those marauders. In the homeland of Sophocles and Plato, Greek was spoken no longer. By the end of the 6th century the empire was much weaker than it had ever been before Justinian. But worse was to follow.

Early in the 7th century Sassanian Persia and Byzantium battled each other to the death. The Persians overran all of the Middle East and almost captured Constantinople. It did not matter very much that in the end Emperor Heraclius (610–41) was victorious and conquered most of Persia. Both powers were so exhausted that the gate was opened to the newly Islamized Arab tribes, who overran all of the Middle East, Persia, and North Africa. The Byzantine Empire barely managed to hold out in Asia Minor and part of the Balkans, but hold out it did. It was, however, so badly mauled by Arabs from the east and Bulgarians from the west that two of its emperors were already preparing the evacuation of Constantinople. In no other period of its long history was it as hard pressed as in the 75 years between Heraclius' death and the ascension of Leo III, the Isaurian (717–40). The latter was a gifted soldier, who repulsed the great Arab siege of his capital (717/718) and recaptured Asia Minor. His son Constantine V (740–75) repulsed the Bulgarians and defeated the Arabs once more. The Isaurian emperors made the grave mistake of trying to impose Iconoclasm (forbidding image worship) on their population. Image worship was, however, so popular in Europe that not only did they lose their remaining control over great parts of

Italy, but the Papacy turned against them and found instead new allies in the new Frankish Empire. After a century the new edicts had to be rescinded.

From these wars, struggles, and turbulations emerged a new Byzantium. With its Latin connections broken on one hand and its previous Monophysite subjects in the Middle East lost to Islam on the other, there remained a purely Greek empire.

Its great days came under the Macedonian dynasty (867–1057). The empire now held its own against its neighbors, and in the 10th and early 11th centuries went over to a counter-offensive in the east and west. Trade revived and the law was recodified in an anti-iconoclast vein.

A renaissance of secular learning, and particularly of classical studies, commenced in the 9th century. The university of Constantinople was restored. The Slavs who had overrun Greece were assimilated to the Greek language and civilization, and the Orthodox faith. If modern Greece claims direct ties to Homer and the Olympic Games it is misrepresenting history. Actually its roots are in the medieval Byzantine renaissance. Byzantine missionaries moved beyond the empire's frontiers and converted Bulgarians, Serbs, Russians, and others to their Orthodox faith. Thus, after the fall of Constantinople, Pravoslav Moscow claimed to be the "Third Rome."

Some great historians took up their pen in this age, none more important than Leo Diaconus in the 10th century. More numerous are the biographers, or, more correctly, hagiographers. The most prolific branch of Byzantine prose was letters. Poetry was not a strong side of the Byzantines, nor was the writing of novels. Yet this was a highly literate and sophisticated society, in its upper reaches. Among its historians were some members of the imperial family – none more important than Anna Comnena, the queen of woman historians, and an indispensable source for the First Crusade.

In the 11th century there was a great Classicist revival and Classical Greek became again the main vehicle of writing. But nowadays our interest in Byzantine letters is but small. We are more in debt to Byzantium for transmitting to posterity most surviving texts of ancient Greece.

Art was perhaps the field in which the Byzantine genius reached its greatest achievements. While Byzantine monumental architecture, such as Justinian's Church of Saint Sophia (in Istanbul), has sturdy roots in antiquity, and its tradition of ivory carving is a direct continuation of Roman ivory work, Byzantium reached its greatest originality in its mosaics.

Here there is a true meeting of east and west, of realism and disembodied religious belief, of vivid colors against golden backgrounds. Many early mosaics have survived in Ravenna; some of the most beautiful late ones in the Chora Church in Istanbul. But outstanding mosaics are to be found all over southern Europe: from Palermo to Daphni, and from Venice to Chios. Large frescoes have mostly survived in provincial centers in the Balkans, none more impressive than in Mistra, near Sparta. Beautiful miniatures survive in MSS in Paris and Rome, and icons in Italy and at St. Catherine's monastery next to Mount Sinai. Later Russian icons are in a direct continuation of this art. Some of the most impressive mosques of Istanbul and Jerusalem, and Christian churches in Rome and London, are derived from Saint Sophia in Constantinople – though built sometimes a thousand years later. The roots of Italian Renaissance painting has to be looked for in Byzantine mosaics and frescoes.

The most successful emperor of the Macedonian dynasty was Basil II, "The Bulgarslayer" (976–1025). But in the second half of the 11th century a sudden decline set in. This first became evident in the economic position of the empire. Its stable gold-based coinage and Constantinople's unique geographical position astride the trade routes both from north to south and from west to east had supported for centuries the empire's central position in world trade. But Europe's rising importance tended to make Venice and the other Italian trading towns more convenient trade terminals than Constantinople. Their traders and sailors also started to gain the upper hand elsewhere in the Mediterranean. They were often better supported by their governments than were the Byzantines. For short-sighted fiscal reasons the emperors tended to give privileges to the Italians, which in the long term were detrimental to their own best interests. With the advent of the crusades the trade routes shifted and much of the sea-borne trade moved from

Acre, Tyre, or Tripoli, directly to Venice, Genoa, and Pisa. This trade was plied exclusively on Italian boats, which did not call on Constantinople. The old Byzantine monopoly in silk spinning was broken in 1147 by the Normans of Sicily.

Even more critical was the decline of the central power in Constantinople. Weak emperors and strife between Church, aristocracy, and administration caused a breakdown at the center, at the very time when the empire faced new foes from both east and west. Southern Italy and Sicily were captured by the Normans, who commenced attacking Greece across the Adriatic Sea. Even more critical was the rising power of the Seljuk Turks in the east. In 1071, in one of the most important battles ever lost by the Byzantines, the Seljuks crushed their army at Manzikert. As a result the Turks overran most of Asia Minor. The Greek civilization, which had been deeply rooted there for nearly one thousand five hundred years, was now eradicated, except in some coastal regions. Turkish herdsmen roamed the country, eventually settling down. The empire thus lost its main granary and its main recruiting ground. It never fully recovered from this blow.

Matters were patched up by the Comnenian dynasty (1081–1185), but Byzantium did not regain its previous power and importance. In 1204 Constantinople and large parts of Greece were captured by the Fourth Crusade. Europe's main eastern bastion had thus fallen to its own short-sightedness, as shown by the later conquests of the Ottoman Turks. Venice and some European princes divided the spoils. A "Latin Empire" set up in Constantinople proved short-lived. The Byzantines regrouped in some of their provincial centers. In 1261 Constantinople was recaptured by them, this time with the help of Genoa, which was granted as a result not only the town of Pera opposite Constantinople, but also most of the Black Sea trade.

Byzantium lingered on for two centuries, under the Palaelogan dynasty (1261–1453), an empire no longer, and a shadow of its previous self. While Pera prospered, Constantinople dwindled. Soon it was surrounded, in Europe as well as in Asia Minor, by Ottoman Turkish possessions. Culturally Byzantium was as active as ever in these years of decline, and some of its most lovely frescoes and mosaics date from this period. In order to obtain help from the West, some of the last Byzantine emperors tried to reach some compromise with the Catholic Church, from which the Greek Orthodox Church had been estranged and separated ever since the 11th century. But this effort was in vain – the two churches were too settled in their ways and practices; each had its own conception of Christian authority and organization. Byzantine civilization lived on, however, in the Greek Orthodox Church, when Constantinople itself fell to the Turks on May 29, 1453, after a siege of seven weeks. Of the other Byzantine centers, Thessaloniki had fallen in 1430, the Peloponnese was captured in 1460 and Trebizond, on the Black Sea, was lost in 1461.

A sense of continuing Byzantine tradition survived, however, in the Romanian principalities, in the churches and monasteries of Mount Athos, Jerusalem, Alexandria, and Constantinople and, more importantly, in Pravoslav Moscow.

27   The Dark Ages in Europe

The barbarian invasions of the 4th and 5th centuries passed over Europe like a giant earthquake. Early shocks had been the Marcomannic wars of the late 2nd century, and the onslaught of the Goths and Sarmatians on the Danube and of the Franks and the Allemans on the Rhine in the 3rd, which nearly brought Rome down. But the Empire recovered and survived for two more centuries in the west and for twelve in the east.

The main tremor came in the 4th century. It was caused by the appearance in eastern Europe of the Huns, previously for centuries the scourge of the Chinese civilization. In 375 they overwhelmed the Ostrogothic kingdom and most of the East German tribes were thrown against the lower Danubian Roman frontier defences. In 378, in one of the fateful battles of European history, the Alan and Ostrogothic horsemen annihilated the Roman infantry near Adrianople. The day of the Roman legions was past. Henceforth German contingents became the mainstay of the Roman armies.

The German tribes turned their main attention to the west. In 406 they broke through the defenses of the Rhine and swamped Gaul, the vital center of the Roman defensive system. Alaric, King of the Visigoths, sacked Rome itself (410). His successors set up a kingdom in southern Gaul and in Spain. The Vandals crossed the sea and conquered North Africa. The Ostrogoths settled in Italy, after the collapse of Western Rome. Other German tribes moved into Central Europe on the heals of the Goths, Alans, and Vandals. The Burgundians founded a kingdom from the Rhine to the Rhone, the Allemans settled in Alsace, the Franks occupied Belgium, northern Gaul, and parts of what today is northwestern Germany. Their king, Clovis (481–511), of the Merovingian dynasty, expanded his power over most of Gaul, converted to Catholic Christianity (while most of the other German kingdoms initially accepted Arianism) and thus inaugurated the alliance between the Frankish kingdom and the Church, which became the cornerstone of early medieval Europe.

Further, slighter, tremors followed. After the Ostrogoths had been annihilated by Justinian's armies, the Langobards moved in the 7th century into most of Italy. The Saxons and Angles crossed the sea and settled in southeastern Britain, while its west remained in Celtic hands. Slavs moved westward and occupied all of eastern Europe and the Balkans. Steppe-nomads, such as Avars and Bulgars, moved into the northern Balkans. In the 7th century Muslims had occupied all of North Africa and crossed in 711 into Spain, conquering most of the Iberian Peninsula and continuing into southern Gallia. In the battle of Tours (732) they were repulsed by the Carolingian Charles Martel and nascent Christian western Europe was saved.

The Germans, who penetrated into the Latin-speaking countries of the south and west, did not displace the local population, forming only an upper class. Many of the previous Roman institutions survived. In the Frankish kingdom, German and Latin language and customs existed side by side. The medieval feudal structure had its antecedents in the latifundia of later Rome. Missionaries sent by Rome were soon at work to convert German rulers and subjects to Christianity.

The growing Frankish state slowly transcended tribal identity. When the Merovingian house (416–751) produced weaker rulers, it was replaced by the Carolingians (741–928). The outstanding ruler of this house was Charlemagne (768–814), whose 53 ferocious campaigns united most of Western Christianity, from Barcelona to the Elbe, and from central Italy to the North Sea, into one huge empire. The Pope was closely dependent on him and crowned him Emperor in 800. The idea of universal empire was a legacy from Roman times. Although often quoted by latter-day advocates of a United Europe, this idea did not stand up well to the realities of the 9th century and split apart, under Charlemagne's grandsons, into three parts, later reduced to two – France and Germany. Thus the most important division of later European history was achieved already in Carolingian times.

Scholars speak of a "Carolingian Renaissance," but the level of learning was actually low. Charlemagne could barely scrawl his signature, but nevertheless surrounded himself with men of learning, none of whom was a Frank. Much of Carolingian thought only echoed earlier Roman writings. The earliest medieval philosophical system was put forward by John Scotus Erigen, in the 9th century, but exercised no direct influence. Carolingian art and architecture were alternatively provincial Byzantine or self-consciously classical.

Perhaps more interesting are the first national cultural stirrings, which took place in Gaelic-speaking Ireland. They were based on the local monasteries, where Latin was cultivated, libraries were installed, and a local literary tradition grew up. Some of their churches and monasteries have survived and so have beautifully illuminated manuscripts, such as the 8th century *Book of Kells*.

Matters were not improved in the 9th and 10th centuries by the last tremors of the great barbarian earthquake. The Scandinavian Vikings unleashed their attacks on western Europe, putting an end to the early Irish civilization, and the Magyars attacked central Europe from the east. The Vikings settled among other places in Normandy and in Yorkshire. In the latter a Danish element has survived till today in the local dialect. Under Alfred the Great (871–901), King of Wessex, and his descendants, the Vikings were repulsed. By the middle of the 10th century these kings had united England as far north as the Clyde.

These last invasions ended in the creation of relatively stable states in a wide arc stretching from France and England, through

Scandinavia, to Hungary and Kiev in Russia. The Dark Ages of Europe were reaching their end.

28   The Rise of Islam

In Yemen an Arab urban civilization flourished as long ago as the late second millennium BC. Around the edges of the Arabian desert half-nomad herdsmen had existed from early times onwards, but it was only around the 12th century BC that the camel was domesticated, introducing the real nomad lifestyle. From this point on, the desert was opened up by the Arabs.

Some 1500 years later Jewish and Christian settlements were set up in Arabia, introducing its pagan inhabitants to Aramaic and Hellenistic culture and to monotheism, and preparing the ground for Islam. Muhammad (570/580–632) was born in the merchant republic of Mecca, but had to flee in 622 to Medina (the *hijra* – migration – serves as starting point of the Islamic calendar). From here commenced his conversion and organization of the Arab Peninsula (Mecca itself was recaptured in 630).

Islam's great chance came as a result of the suicidal struggle between Sassanid Persia and Christian Byzantium. Both powers were so weakened after twenty years of all-out war that they could not put up much resistance when the newly-united Arab forces erupted from their peninsula under the generals of the early caliphs. In the 630s Palestine, Syria, Egypt, Iraq, and Persia were conquered, to be followed later by North Africa, Spain, and western India. The slow process of the Islamization of the local population began. The Monophysites of some of these regions did not put up too much of a struggle, as they preferred fellow-Semites to their previous Greek overlords. Islamization took several centuries to complete, the reason being that under the Umayyad dynasty (661–750) the conquerors regarded themselves as Arabs first. They tended to keep their religion to themselves and preferred that the people pay taxes instead of converting to Islam. Their capital was in Damascus and they were influenced to a considerable degree by the Roman and Hellenistic civilization of the territories they had acquired. Saint John of Damascus, the important Christian polemicist, served as chief financial advisor to the caliph in the early 8th century. In Arabia, erotic poetry, influenced by Greek examples, was in vogue. Erotic frescoes – usually shunned by Islam – appear in the Umayyad hunting lodge of Kussejr Æmra, in what today is Jordan. One of the noblest examples of Islamic architecture to have survived, the late 7th century Dome of the Rock in Jerusalem, is strongly influenced by Byzantine art. Further examples abound.

But there were also other aspects to Islam. Already in the struggle for dominance which preceded the advent of the Umayyads, the fourth caliph, Ali, Muhammad's son-in-law, represented other, eastern, elements. After his death his followers formed the Shi'ite faction, which nowadays is dominant in fundamentalist Persia. Similar eastern elements gathered strength, until in 750 they overthrew the Umayyads and replaced them with the Abbasid dynasty. Only one of the Umayyad princes managed to escape; he set up an independent caliphate in Spain.

The Abbasids did not rule from westernized Damascus, but from Baghdad; and their cultural inspiration came from Sassanid Persia. They turned Islam into the severe, eastern creed it has been ever since. Their rule signifies also the coming full circle of eastern influences all over the Middle East. It had been Alexander the Great who had replaced the old established eastern civilization by Hellenistic culture. Now, a millennium later, eastern cultural influences were victorious. The Greek language was replaced everywhere, eastern customs replaced western ones, and many cities returned to their ancient names (for instance Acre in Palestine, after having been "Ptolemais" for 900 years, or Beisan, after having been "Scythopolis"). All signs of western art were eradicated. Non-figurative decorations, often including pious inscriptions, were preferred and local traditions developed. The pointed arch appears first in a cistern in Ramle, from the time of the caliph Harun al-Rashid (786–809), 350 years before it was adopted by Gothic architecture in the west. Poets, musicians, and artists were drawn to the court of this caliph, who is remembered as the *beau idéal* of Islamic kingship. This is the great period of Islamic civilization – of writers, philosophers, and scholars. Arabic served as their common language, though they themselves might come from Persia, Sicily, or Spain. Islam was no longer a religion only, but developed into a system of law, of administration, of society, thought, and art – in short into a fully grown civilization of its own. Although the sciences advanced, there was little of the innovative spirit of Ancient Greece or post-medieval western Europe. Islamic civilization looks particularly impressive when compared with contemporary Europe, but cannot be said to have been in advance of, say, Byzantine civilization under the Macedonian dynasty, and it certainly lagged behind the Chinese civilization of the Tang and Song periods.

The later Abbasids were not able to continue and hold together their enormous empire – from the Atlantic Ocean to India. Their troops were no longer Arabs, but mostly Turkish mercenaries, and their leaders showed from the early 9th century onwards a tendency to set up their own independent principalities in North Africa, Egypt, Syria, and Persia, leaving an ever-smaller area under the direct rule of the Abbasid caliphs. Of special interest is perhaps the Fatimid dynasty, originally established in 909 in Tunis. They were Shi'ites, and declared their rulers true caliphs (the only Shi'ite dynasty to do so). They first controlled all of North Africa, but lost most of it after they moved their capital to Egypt (where they founded the city of Cairo) and captured large parts of Palestine and Syria. They aspired to reach Baghdad and supplant the Sunnite (orthodox) Abbasids, but did not quite make it. They were the main adversaries of the crusaders when they first reached the Holy Land. Theirs was a brilliant court, and although not favorable to literature and science, they excelled in art, architecture, weaving, ceramics, and book-binding. Their ships ruled the eastern Mediterranean until the advent of the Italian trading cities in the later 11th century.

The Umayyad Caliphate of Córdoba, in Spain, was an important cultural center. After its fall in 1027 several petty states survived, until the last, Granada, was conquered by Spain in 1492. Its surviving palaces, gardens, and waterworks give a vivid idea of the opulence and the highly developed civilization which was to be found there. Altogether, Muslim rule in Spain or part of it continued for nearly 800 years.

29 The Beginning of Western Civilization

The early stirrings of Western Civilization in Europe are of special interest to us today, as no other civilization has had a similar impact on the history of mankind. Some historians claim that the Carolingian Period should be regarded as its beginning, but the 10th century seems to us more appropriate. Variety and not monolithic unity has been the mark of Western Civilization and by the 10th century Europe was already clearly divided along linguistic and political lines.

Germany was made up of several tribal duchies – Swabia, Bavaria, Franconia, Saxony – each with its own distinct dialect. They were all threatened by the hordes of Magyar horse archers, who brought devastation into their territories. In two great battles, at Unstrut in 933 and at the Lech in 955, the Hungarian invaders were decisively defeated by two Saxon rulers, Henry the Fowler (919–36) and Otto I the Great (936–73). As a result, the Magyar raids stopped and Germany was united under these highly popular Saxons. Otto I was crowned Emperor in 962 by the Pope and Germany was called for the next 840 years the "Holy Roman Empire of the German Nation." Its eastern border was initially the River Elbe, but gradually the empire expanded eastward, beyond that river, at the expense of the Slavs. Bohemia had to pay tribute and Austria was founded as a bulwark against the Magyars and Slavs. German knightly orders gained control of the Baltic littoral and Prussia. While the Saxon emperors (919–1024) were dominant throughout Europe, their successors, the Salian emperors (1024–1125), had to compete with the papacy.

France was similarly a collection of more or less independent fiefs. Here, too, the crown went ultimately to the descendants of rulers who had defended the country against foreign invaders, in this case the Normans. But here it took a century before the Capetingian dukes took the crown from their Carolingian predecessors. Fourteen Capetingian kings ruled France from 987 until

1328. Their seat, Paris, gradually became the capital of centrally governed France. Alsace-Lorraine and parts of Burgundy were German; Provence was independent, with a different language of its own (the langue d'oc); and much of the west of the country was under British rule. This came about initially by the conquest of England in 1066 by the Duke of Normandy, William the Conqueror (in England 1066–87). As a result England was ruled for two centuries by French-speaking kings and aristocrats, who introduced efficient, centralized government, thorough collection of taxes (based on the Domesday Survey), and trial by jury. Such French provinces as Normandy, Anjou, Guyenne, Auvergne, and Aquitaine were at various times under English rule.

In Scandinavia, unified states arose first in Denmark (initially around 800 and then again in the early 8th century) and later in Sweden (the south of which remained Danish), Norway, and Iceland. The populace converted to Christianity in the late 10th and 11th centuries.

Poland was founded late in the 10th century, mainly to combat the German settlers who were advancing eastward, into Slavonic territory.

The German Emperors claimed suzerainty over much of northern and central Italy, but could not always enforce it. Southern Italy and Sicily were taken over in the 11th century by Normans, who set up a strong, centralized state there. From time to time they supported the Pope in Rome against the Emperor or, alternatively, forced him to follow their political dictates.

The new Western civilization made its mark not only in the political field. The primeval forests of northern Europe were pushed back by advancing tillers of the soil. The major river valleys, from the Po to the Elbe, were drained and cleared. The population of many areas increased. Towns grew, none more so than the great mercantile centers of northern Italy and of Flanders. Trade and manufacture intensified.

Higher culture began to spread. A few universities were established in such centers as Bologna, Paris, and later, Oxford and Prague. At Bologna, law was studied, based on the rediscovered Roman law. In other places pupils flocked to cathedral schools, to learn, for instance, humanistic studies at Chartres, or Latin grammar at Orléans. Classical works were translated at Toledo, Palermo, and Constantinople. Theological subjects were the most popular.

European literature appeared in the 12th century. The Romance languages had by then freed themselves from their Latin roots. Chansons were composed for recitation to music, at feudal courts or at stages along the roads used by pilgrims. The subject matter was various: epic tales of adventure during the crusades; or fictional stories about Charlemagne's nephew Roland in Spain; or about Percival and the Holy Grail. In Spain other songs circulated – about the national hero, the Cid, and his fight with the Muslims. Another subject was courtly love, such as the story of Tristan and Isolde. The earliest Western vernacular in which poetry was written was Provençal:

> "In a leafy orchard, underneath a thorn,
> the lady clasps her lover in her arms
> until the watchman cries he's seen the dawn.
> Oh God! Oh God! How quickly dawn comes round!"

Similar themes were treated by troubadours in northern France, in Germany (where they were called "Minnesänger"), in northern Spain and later in Italy.

While pictorial art continued to be influenced by Byzantine models, western Europe developed its own architectural styles, especially in its sacred buildings. Classical and Carolingian architecture had been mostly horizontal, but the Romanesque churches from the 10th century onwards, and the Gothic structures from the 12th century onwards, pointed more and more insistently skywards. Looking today at restoration drawings of Cluny's abbey church, or at German Romanesque cathedrals, or Norwegian wooden stave-churches, or French Gothic cathedrals, one is aware that these structures heralded the arrival of a new civilization.

It is not by chance that sacral buildings are so typical of the new age. Christianity was undoubtedly the main motive force behind early Western Civilization. It was a pious age. Church reform was spearheaded after 910 by the Cluniac monastic movement. Other orders followed in the footsteps of the Benedictines of Cluny – in 1098 the Cistercians, in 1120 the Prenonstratensians, in 1209 the mendicant Franciscans, in 1215 the Dominicans. Churchmen invented the ideal of the Pax Dei, which often succeeded, where kings and rulers failed. From the middle of the 11th century the Cluniac movement was taken over by the papacy. In 1054 the old ties to Constantinople were cut. Gregory VII (1073–85) took on the German Emperor and humiliated him at Canossa. In 1095 Urban II summoned Christianity to the First Crusade. For two centuries popes and emperors were locked in a struggle for the supremacy of Europe. Emperors repeatedly removed popes by force, and popes repeatedly proscribed emperors and put them in ban. Public opinion leaned more and more to the side of the popes. In spite of the strong personalities of such Hohenstaufen emperors as Frederick I Barbarossa (1152–90) and Frederick II (1212–50), it was the Roman pontiffs such as Innocent III (1198–1216) and Innocent IV (1243–54) who were ultimately victorious.

The new and vigorous Europe pushed its frontiers outwards. By 1250 all of the Iberian Peninsula had been conquered, except for Granada. The Germans pushed beyond the Elbe, settled Austria, and even seized the Baltic littoral. The Normans captured southern Italy and Sicily from the Muslims and Byzantines. Such previous foreign invaders as Vikings and Magyars were settled, Christianized, and absorbed into the body of the new Western Civilization.

In conclusion, it is worthwhile listing some of the outstanding figures of the age:

- Peter Abelard (1079–1142) was a Breton philosopher and teacher, who first established Paris as a center of thought; he was the main founder of scholastic methods in philosophy. His best known work is, however, his exchange of letters with his pupil Héloïse. Their love affair ended with his castration and banishment into a monastery.
- Saint Bernard of Clairvaux (1091–1153) was a monk and a saint. He opposed Abelard's scholasticism and preached simple piety. His great political influence was used to found the Cistercian Order and launch the Second Crusade.
- Henry II, King of England (1154–89), was born in 1133. By marrying Eleanor of Aquitaine he gained her large duchy in

southwestern France and set up a vast west-European empire. He re-established, after some weak reigns, the central power of the monarchy, humbled the aristocracy, founded English rule in Ireland, and opposed attempts at intervention by the papacy (as a result of which Thomas Beckett, the Archbishop of Canterbury, was murdered). Henry's popularity was badly hurt and he died trying to supress a revolt by his sons.

- Philip II, August, King of France (1180–1223), was born in 1165. He was the most successful ruler of the Capetingian dynasty and succeeded in strengthening the royal power at the expense of the aristocracy. His 1191 participation in the Third Crusade was short and lackluster. More effective was his long war (1186–1214) against England (part of it while his fellow crusader Richard I [Coeur de Lion] was in Palestine), in which he recaptured Normandy, Brittany, Anjou, and Poitou. By early in the 13th century he was the most powerful ruler in Europe.

- Pope Innocent III (1198–1216) was born in 1161. Under him the papacy reached the pinnacle of its power. By a liberal use of the ban he frightened most of the secular rulers of his time into acknowledging his suzerainty. He widened the papal territories in central Italy by the addition of the Romagna, of Ancona, and of Spoleta. As a result of the Fourth Crusade even Constantinople acknowledged his overlordship.

- Emperor Frederick II (1212–50) was born in 1194. He was the adversary of the papacy in the last and decisive round of the struggle for supremacy. He was also King of Sicily, where he kept court, and of Jerusalem. He was proficient in Italian, German, Latin, Greek, and Arabic. During his crusade he obtained the cession of Jerusalem by diplomatic means, when under a church ban. He was a man of great cultural attainments, who wrote a book about falconry, but was apt to foment quarrels and bear a grudge. In spite of his accomplishments, he finally failed in most of his projects.

- Saint Thomas Aquinas (1125–74) was born in southern Italy and studied there. Later he became a Dominican monk and taught in Paris and Rome. He created a comprehensive philosophic-theological system, based mostly on Aristotle. His influence on later medieval theology was immense.

- Dante Alighieri (1265–1321) was the greatest Italian poet. He was active in the political life of Florence until he had to flee in 1301 and was sentenced to death in absentia. His greatest work is the *Divine Comedy*, which describes his visit to hell (where he claimed to have met several of his previous political opponents), purgatory, and heaven. The book is regarded as one of the most important works of literature in the history of Western Civilization.

30   The Crusades

The Spanish Reconquista and the struggle against the Muslims for Sicily and for supremacy in the Mediterranean had already given birth to a certain measure of crusading enthusiasm. When during the later 11th century the pilgrimage to the Holy Land and to the shrines of Jerusalem and Bethlehem became ever more difficult and dangerous because of the constant wars between Seljuks and Fatimids in Palestine, the scene was set for a grand expedition to the east. On 27 November 1095, Pope Urban II, at the Council of Clermont, summoned Christianity to a crusade, to recover the Holy Land. The response was overwhelming. Early parties, without proper leadership, were annihilated along the way, but a properly organized expedition made it to Constantinople and Asia Minor, captured Antioch and, after a difficult siege, took Jerusalem also (14 July 1099). The local Muslim and Jewish population was massacred.

Crusader states were set up in Edessa, Antioch, and Tripoli. In Palestine, a "Kingdom of Jerusalem" was created, ruled by members of the ducal family of Lower Lorraine.

Not everyone had come for exalted reasons. William, Archbishop of Tyre, said later: "Not all of them, indeed, were there on behalf of the Lord . . . Some were there so as not to desert their friends. Others were present lest they be thought idle, while others, still, were there out of frivolity or in order to escape their creditors, since they were loaded down with the obligations of many debts. All of them went for different reasons." Many younger sons of aristocratic families came out to obtain by sword or marriage a suitable fief. The Church kept the fires of crusading enthusiasm well stoked, both for obvious religious reasons and in order to secure its supremacy over the Greek Orthodox Church, to harness the machinery of feudalism to its chariot, and to strengthen its position in the struggle against the German Emperors.

In spite of all of these incentives the plain truth is that ultimately not sufficient settlers reached the Levant to turn it into a Frankish province. The main reason for this was that after the passage of the First Crusade, the overland route was closed again by the Seljuks of Asia Minor. The alternative sea route was too expensive and perilous for really large masses of western settlers to reach the shores of the Holy Land. As a result a relatively small Frankish minority had to rule over a large local majority, which was partly Muslim and partly composed of eastern Christians. These Christians had no part whatsoever in the running of the country and, as a result, felt little loyalty for it.

Against this background it is less than surprising that the crusading movement ultimately failed, than that it held out as long as it did. At first the Muslims were cowed by the obvious martial superiority of the Christians. The high point of Christian might was reached under King Baldwin II (1118–31) of Jerusalem. But his successors were less able or died too young, and a strong Muslim counter-movement commenced. This movement was headed at first by the atabeg of Mossul, Zengi (1127–46), who recaptured Edessa on Christmas Eve 1144. The Second Crusade launched against him (1148) proved ineffective. Later the sultan of Aleppo, Nur ed-Din (1146–74), spearheaded the drive against the Christians and, after him, Saladin (1174–93), who ruled both in Cairo and in Damascus and thus completely surrounded the crusader principalities. He annihilated the crusader army at the battle of the Horns of Hattin, in 1187, and after that easily captured all the towns and fortresses of the Kingdom of Jerusalem (except for the port of Tyre) and many of those of the other two Christian principalities. The Frankish presence in the Levant seemed doomed.

Crusading enthusiasm was, however, far from dead yet, and in the Third Crusade (1189–92), headed by King Richard I (Coeur de Lion) of England, the Christians re-established a much smaller kingdom along the coast of Palestine, with Acre as its capital. There, and in the two northern principalities, the crusaders held out for another hundred years, until the capture of Acre by the Mameluks in 1291.

Their "second kingdom" was a curious affair. Most of the time it was ruled in theory by representatives of absentee kings, but in practice by the local aristocracy, headed by the House of Ibelin. The great military orders were a law unto themselves, and so were the Italian trading towns – Venice, Genoa, and Pisa. Each of them had a quarter of its own in Acre and from time to time, in the off-season, when no ships could be expected from Europe, the Italians would battle each other in its alleys. The Venetians won out in the end and the Genoese had to withdraw to Tyre. As the Kingdom of Jerusalem, as it was called, depended on the Italians economically, nothing could be done to stop their outrages. Nor were the military orders much better. The Templars were the great bankers of the age, advancing loans near-indiscriminately to Christians and Muslims alike. The Hospitallers owned more real estate in western Europe than anybody else, which they had purchased with the huge alms they had collected for fighting the infidel. Most of the time each of the two orders followed, in Palestine, a different foreign policy from the other. One of the rare times they acted together was against Emperor Frederick II, during his crusade, but then a third one, the Teutonic Order, came to his assistance. Frederick was the only leader of a crusade who managed, after 1187, to obtain Jerusalem (1229), but found himself nearly alone, against the united wrath of the Frankish inhabitants of the kingdom, who disliked his absolutist rule, and in the end, the Emperor had to withdraw to Europe. Jerusalem was lost again in 1244.

One of the reasons the crusaders held out for as long as they did was the weakness and laxity of the Ayubite successors of Saladin; another reason was the importance of the transit trade through Acre and Tyre, from which the Muslims profited as well. But when in 1260 Muslim Palestine fell to the much stricter Mameluks (after they had defeated the Mongols at the same Spring or Harod where Gideon had fought the Midianites some 2350 years earlier) their fate was sealed.

The crusaders have always been regarded as great fighters and great builders of fortresses. But there was more to them than that. They not only inspired songs and poems written in Europe, but wrote themselves fables about animals and important works in the field of law, which later influenced feudal customs in Europe. William, Archbishop of Tyre, was one of the most important medieval historians. In their art they developed a distinct style of miniature and icon painting. They added to Gothic architecture the pointed arch, and developed in their fortresses round turrets, for improved defense, instead of the previous square ones.

After the fall of Acre there lingered on in Cyprus a last crusader principality, which was later (1489) taken over by Venice, and captured by the Ottoman Turks in 1571. Nor was the crusading spirit quite dead yet. In the 14th and 15th centuries there were many plans and a few attempts to renew the crusades, but none was effective. The Mameluks, however, took the precaution to destroy systematically all the ports of Palestine, and thus emptied great stretches of its coastal plain of its sedentary population. As it was not resettled later, they thus helped the earliest Jewish Zionist settlers to gain a foothold some 600 years later.

Part IX

Beginnings in America and Africa

East Africa is, of course, the cradle of mankind. But south of the Sahara, Africa's entrance into recorded history was relatively late.

America, on the other hand, was settled late by man. It is believed that this happened some time between 50 000 and 40 000 years ago, by groups coming from Siberia, which was repeatedly linked to Alaska. From there they moved gradually southward, first to North America and later to South America. Certain aspects of the American civilizations have raised speculations about later trans-Pacific influences, but nothing has, so far, been proven. Thus we find in this vast double continent several consecutive civilizations emerging apparently without any reference to what had gone before in the Old World.

Their very strangeness is, of course, the reason for their fascination for the historian. But in spite of their achievements, they did not get anywhere as far as the older civilizations of Asia and Europe. They never domesticated riding or draft animals, they had no wheeled vehicles, no plow, no firearms, no sea-going ships, no iron technology, and only in isolated cases any real system of writing. When attacked, in the early 16th century, by tiny groups of well-armed and ruthless Spaniards, their empires collapsed like houses of cards.

31 The Early Civilizations of Mexico

To a certain extent Mexico played in the New World the same role as the Middle East played in the Old World. From Mexico emanated many basic cultural influences. Around 5000 BC, or even earlier, there occurred in the Mexican highlands the local version of the Agricultural Revolution, with the initial cultivation of maize and other plants – such as beans, avocado, and squash. Cultivation spread south and other plants were added along the way – such as potatoes, tomatoes, red pepper, tobacco, and manioc.

The population began to grow in several of the centers where the best conditions existed. Similar to the development in the Middle East, some five thousand years earlier, there followed an Urban Revolution after the introduction of agriculture. But while several thousand years later writing had been widely introduced in the Middle East, this development remained stunted in Mesoamerica, though in the 6th century BC a rudimentary system of writing was developed by the Zapotec culture. The populace were not on the whole very literate and most of the other cultures remained mute and can generally be judged only by the artifacts they produced. To a certain extent their history is thus a history of art. In their latest stages these civilizations were described by the Europeans who had destroyed them and also by local annals. But much of what they reported does not apply to the earlier civilizations.

Perhaps the earliest of these mute civilizations is that of the Olmecs, 1300–200 BC, which evolved around the Gulf of Mexico, reached its height in the middle of the first millennium BC, and spread west to Central Mexico, and east to Yucatan and Salvador. One of the main Olmec shrines has been uncovered on a low island called La Venta. The great pyramid there is already typical for later Mexican and Mayan architecture, in its emphasis on external layout at the expense of the interior. The repeated reconstructions there have been explained as indicating the use of a sophisticated calendar, with cycles of 52 years.

What strikes modern viewers most is Olmec figure sculpture. Their loose-lipped, puffy baby faces look at us with distaste.

These features are evident in enormous stone heads, but also on tiny pottery figurines. Some are near abstract, others highly realistic. Later civilizations produced art that seems somewhat less impressive. Feathered serpents are typical of the large center of Teotihuacan, founded in the last centuries BC, to the southeast of the Valley of Mexico. It became one of the largest urban centers of precolumbian Mesoamerica, with some 200 000 inhabitants by AD 500, and continued to be the capital of an empire for a thousand years. There were hundreds of temples, many of them dedicated to gods known from later cultures – such as Quetzalcoatl, the feathered serpent, Tlaloc, the god of rain, and his consort Chalchihuitlicue. The largest structure was the enormous Pyramid of the Sun, but there was also an impressive Pyramid of the Moon, from which led an "Avenue of the Dead," with flat-topped pyramids to its sides.

Mexican civilization was apparently pacific and averse to the use of force. Its later period, in the mid-first millennium AD, is regarded as the classical era of precolumbian history. There is evidence of its influence in areas as far away as some of the centers of Mayan civilization.

The collapse of Mexican civilization in the 8th century AD left a void which was only gradually and partly filled by such later centers as Tula and Azcapotzalco. The first of these, some 40 miles northwest of Mexico City, was the capital of the Toltecs (10th to 13th centuries). Written records of late precolumbian times describe this period. The most prominent god was the feathered serpent, Quetzalcoatl. The surviving art of the period is typified by rather flat stone reliefs and lively pottery.

Further waves of nomads from the northwest, belonging to the Chichimec group of tribes, displaced the Toltecs. Several of these tribes were repeatedly fighting for supremacy, with the Aztecs emerging early in the 15th century as the dominant group. Here we are on sound historical ground, as they have been described in detail by the Spaniards, who arrived a century later, and in surviving annals in picture-script. Their capital was at Tenochtitlan, the present Mexico City (nowadays the most populous urban center on our planet). It must have been impressive even then – white buildings and green gardens, sited along canals, between blue lakes, ringed by lofty mountains. The Spanish historian Bernal Diaz reported the reaction of his comrades on first laying eyes on it: "It is like the enchantment they tell of in the legend of Amadis! Are not the things we see a dream?" The number of its inhabitants was large even then – some 300 000.

The Aztecs were a vigorous, war-like people. Their art pulsates with life, though much of it deals with death. They needed prisoners of war by the thousands, who had their hearts torn out as sacrifice to their war and sun god Huitzilopochtli. They believed that without these sacrifices the god would not be able in the morning to overcome the moon and stars of night, to pursue his journey through the sky. War was needed to supply these prisoners and was thus a central feature of Aztec religion. Also their economy was based on war, conquest, and payment of tribute. Their war-like qualities enabled them to dominate most of Mexico by the early 16th century. But because of their ferocious bloodthirst they were hated by the subjugated peoples, some of whom helped Cortés on his arrival to defeat their previous overlords and destroy their empire.

32   The Maya

The Maya occupied the country between Guatemala and Honduras to the south and Yucatan to the north. The roots of Mayan civilization go back to *c.* 2000 BC, when they started building their oldest cities. In the first millennium BC the Olmec culture of Mexico influenced them deeply. Some rudiments of writing were taken over from the Zapotecs and further developed, to make the Maya the only really literate civilization of precolumbian America. A basic calendar was taken over from the Olmecs, but was much developed and refined. The Maya showed great interest in astronomy and believed that the point at which the Milky Way appeared as a vertical band in the night sky represented the moment of creation. They calculated their calendar accordingly. Partly pictorial and partly phonetic inscriptions of great complexity recorded the dates and cycles they had calculated.

These inscriptions have been deciphered only in recent years. While it had previously been assumed that they dealt mainly with ceremonial religious centers, it has been subsequently recognized that in fact they are detailed historical records of some twenty Mayan city-states. These states were grouped in two loose alliances, centered on the cities of Tikal and Kalakmul. Tikal was the largest of the city-states, and had a population of some 40 000 inhabitants. Half a million inhabited its hinterland. A nearly permanent state of war seems to have existed between the two groups. Within each group, marriage alliances and payment of tribute held each of them together. The beginnings of these city-states can be dated to the 6th and 5th centuries BC, but their classical period was apparently between AD 100 and AD 800.

Mayan art is very distinctive: vast pyramids crowned with temples, intricately carved stone stelae, intertwined stylized bodies in low relief, and above all, the many-colored fresco paintings. Paintings which have survived at Bonampak show a great ceremony taking place. The paintings are full of life and expression – fierce fighting, dignified ceremony, the supplication of a prisoner about to be killed, the torturing of others, and the curious masks of performers representing nature gods.

The economy of such cities as Tikal was not only agricultural, but based also on the export of products such as jade and obsidian. The Maya imported metalwork from Mexico. A complex irrigation system sustained a population about 150 times the size of the present one in Yucatan; but some historians believe that at its center, in Petén, the economy of the Maya civilization was based on tropical slash-and-burn farming. When the population increased too much, it outstripped its diminishing food supply, with catastrophic results.

In 695 the old system of alliances came unstuck, when Tikal captured Kalakmul, and sacrificed its king. But Tikal did not succeed in taking over the city-states of its rival and chaos resulted. The canals silted up and the number of inhabitants declined steeply.

Most of the cities ceased to exist in the 9th century. Tikal is last mentioned in 879. It was apparently overrun by foreign warriors. By the year 1000 the population in the Copan valley seems to have declined by 90 percent.

In the late period some of the sites in Yucatan were reoccupied and surrounded by walls. Chichen Itza played a central role. It was occupied from the 8th to the 12th centuries and again from the 13th to the 16th. But the quality of the late stage of Mayan civilization is not comparable to its classical period. Strong ties to Mexico appear now, especially to Tula – perhaps an indication that Yucatan was dominated first by Toltecs and later by Aztecs. Its art shows a preoccupation with violence and death, such as reliefs showing jaguars and eagles devouring human hearts, or rows of skulls displayed on poles.

When the Spaniards reached this area, they met only the Mexicanized remains of this once great civilization. There was little resistance, as the Maya groups would not unite, and the Spaniards conquered one group after another. Some of the marks of previous glory – such as buildings, sculptures, and wall paintings – were luckily hidden by the re-emerging forests, and thus preserved for posterity.

But the Mayas did not disappear as an ethnic group. Their descendants are in recent years becoming conscious of their cultural heritage. They are using again their 260-day calendar, their comic books use old Maya stories, and they demand the use of Mayan languages in their schools. Some 190 000 of them were killed by the Guatemalan army in the 1980s, in an anti-insurgency drive, because of their nationalistic Mayan tendencies. These are also behind the recent Zapatistan revolt in southern Mexico. Thus, while the Aztecs and Incas have vanished from the stage of history, the Mayas have survived.

33 The Early Civilizations of Peru

Curiously, there is much earlier evidence for human settlements in Southern America (33 000 years ago, at sites in Chile and Brazil) than in North America. The local Agricultural Revolution, too, may have occurred as early as 8500 BC in Peru (squash, beans, and peppers). Maize appeared in the seventh millennium BC, but as the cultivated plants were practically identical with the wild ones, these dates might be too early. Llamas may have been domesticated already by 5400 BC.

Pre-ceramic cultures in Peru go back to *c.* 2500 BC along the narrow, arid coast. Pottery appeared in Colombia around 3000 BC and in Peru about a thousand years later. As a result of the low humidity, cotton fabrics have survived there with intricate patterns and so also have cotton fishing nets. During the 2nd millennium BC small states seem to have emerged in this coastal area, and also in the inland highlands. One state, the Chavin civilization, widened its influence around 900 BC, and spread during the first millennium BC over most of the Peruvian coastal area and the northern highlands as well. It continued to exist from 1200 to 200 BC, somewhat parallel to the Olmec civilization in Mesoamerica. Its statuary, artifacts, and pottery are, however, much less impressive than those of the Olmecs. Here, too, ceremonial centers arose, which survived for fifteen hundred years thereafter. The Chavin civilization declined and was replaced by different cultures in the various parts of the area.

The most impressive civilization in the Peruvian classical period was the Moché culture on the northern coast, about AD 0–600. Realistic colored Moché portrait vases are the most striking pieces of art produced anywhere in precolumbian America. Other beautiful pieces of pottery have survived – some showing buildings; others people with various diseases; weapons, warriors, prisoners, and some erotic scenes are also depicted. Gold and silver ornaments were produced. Copper was used for tools, weapons, and ornaments. Few impressive buildings have been found, nor important large statuary.

Another highly developed culture existed in the same period along the southern coast – the Nazca culture, which produced a distinct style of pottery and textiles.

Between *c.* AD 500–1000 two related cultures (and apparently also empires) existed side by side, the Huari culture in the north and the Tiahuanaco culture in the south. Both seem to have been influenced by the Chavin culture. The authoritarian system of the later Incas may have had its roots in the tight administration of these empires. The Huari civilization developed an urban culture and its sites replaced the previous ceremonial centers.

It was supplanted by the Chimu culture in the north, around AD 1300, which controlled much of the northern coastal area. Its capital at Chan Chan is an impressive site, composed of ten compounds, surrounded by walls, enclosing pyramids and other edifices. Its streets were long and straight, meeting at right angles. The Chimu placed greater stress on quantity than on originality. Their ceramic art is standardized, but their craftsmanship is impressive.

The south reverted after the decline of the Tiahuanaco culture to a rural way of life, but the final unification of Peru by the Incas started there, and not in the urbanized north. A small militaristic nucleus carried the Incas in the 15th century to widespread conquests, until they had created an empire stretching all the way from northern Ecuador to central Chile, covering a much larger area than that of the contemporary Aztec empire. Spanish sources reveal much knowledge about their state and its institutions.

The Inca empire was an autocratically governed welfare state. Each family was allotted just enough land to keep it comfortably fed, but without any disposable surplus. Additional land had to be worked by the farmers for the benefit of the state and the priesthood. In this way they contributed their share to keep a large class of nobles and priests comfortably provided for. The population was rigorously regimented and was left no initiative or independence. Each family had to construct its own tools and household equipment, and spun and wove its own clothing from wool supplied by the state. Each district had to supply a certain percentage of men for work in the mines, army service, and public works. The Inca emperor was regarded as divine – a descendant of the sun – and there were no limitations to his power. In order to keep his line pure he was expected to marry his sister. In spite of these incestuous marriages, the offspring provided vigorous and able rulers.

The success of the Inca armies was due to the efficient management of the logistics. Supplies were stored in government storehouses, spaced conveniently along the highroads that the troops had used for the movement of the army. Successful commanders were given lavish gifts. Soldiers were equipped with bolas (stones fastened to a cord, whirled around and thrown), slings, clubs, spears, and heavy wooden swords. But they were obviously no match for the firearms of the Spaniards.

34   Beginnings in Sub-Saharan Africa

Influences from Egypt began to be felt further south at an early stage, and by 3000 BC agriculture had been adopted in much of the Sudan, from the Atlantic Ocean to the Ethiopian plateau. Most of the cereals grown came from the Middle East, but in West Africa sorghum was added, and also a local variety of rice. No sign of a Bronze Age has been discovered so far.

The earliest known kingdom developed south of Egypt. Trading routes had crossed Nubia at least from pre-dynastic times onward. The first great Nubian kingdom existed from 2500 to 1500 BC, with its capital in Kerma. A remarkably high level of material culture was achieved. Beautiful sculptures, figurines, reliefs and jewelry were produced. A second, even more impressive Kingdom of Kush covered the period from 900 BC to AD 350. In the 8th century BC Egypt itself was conquered by these Nubians, who ruled there as the XXVth Dynasty, with their capital in Napata. They lost Egypt to the Assyrians in 676/666. A century later Kush pushed its frontiers southwards, beyond the desert and the cataracts to a line south of Khartoum. Its new capital was Meroe. It became a predominantly negro kingdom. There was plenty of iron ore near the new capital, which was worked intensively and formed the foundation of Kush's prosperity during the last centuries BC.

The iron-smelting technique was transmitted through Nubia to the Sudan. About the same time Southeast Asian food plants, such as the banana and the Asian yam, reached the Bantu-speaking black inhabitants of the belt of equatorial forests. Equipped with iron tools, these people spread slowly, until about AD 1500, throughout the southern half of Africa, planting the new food plants as they went. Similarly equipped negroes, speaking Sudanese languages, spread into western Africa. More backward earlier settlers were absorbed by the Bantu or driven back, as happened to the Bushmen, who were pushed into the most inhospitable and arid areas of southwestern Africa. Much of eastern Africa had been settled by Hamites, but they too were driven out by the Bantus. The Hottentots seem to have come into existence as the result of intercourse between these Hamites and the Bushmen.

The reason for Meroe's decline, from the 1st century AD onward, was the rise of a rival trading kingdom, with its capital at Axum. This rival kingdom was apparently the offshoot of a Semitic Sabean kingdom in present-day Yemen, and it itself signifies the beginning of an independent Ethiopia, which has been in existence ever since. Axum was the great ivory market of northeastern Africa and developed into a very wealthy city. In the 4th century its rulers accepted Christianity in its Monophysite guise. About the same time its armies attacked and destroyed Kush. Ethiopia's history is too involved to be treated here in any detail. Let it suffice to say that for most of its existence it has been involved in a struggle against encroaching Islam.

We shall turn now to the western Sudan. A trading center was first founded in Jenne-Jeno, on the upper River Niger, in 200 BC, reaching its peak late in the first millennium AD. It exported cereals and fish and imported iron ore. The trans-Saharan trade was intensified by the appearance of Muslim traders from the 8th century onward. Timbuktu, to its northeast, developed as a terminal for the trans-Saharan trade.

This trade was one of the reasons for the rise of kingdoms in western Sudan. The best known is Ghana, founded around AD 400, some five hundred miles to the northwest of its modern namesake. At the height of its power it spread from the northern curve of the River Niger to the upper reaches of the Senegal river. It imposed levies on the expanding trans-Saharan trade, and grew rich and powerful. It became well known to the Muslim world by its export of gold to North Africa.

While Ghana continued to be pagan, all around it Islam had been advancing southward. The desert nomads were converted within the next centuries and also the rulers of the states to the south of the Sahara found it profitable to accept Islam, in order to facilitate trade with North Africa. The fanatically Muslim Almoravids were launched in order to persuade by force the few who still held out. In 1076 they defeated Ghana and captured its capital. Subsequently all the main kingdoms on the southern fringe of the Sahara were Muslim. It is worth mentioning the kingdom of Kanem, east and north of Lake Chad, founded around 800, which accepted Islam in the 11th century. Its name changed to Bornu and it survived into the 19th century. Around 1300 the people of the town of Jenne-Jeno were converted to Islam, and in order to show that they had turned their back on paganism, they moved the city to a new site.

Mali became the successor of Ghana, further to the west, but was larger, reaching from the Atlantic coast in the west to the Niger–Benue confluence in the east. It included both Jenne and Timbuktu. It was also richer and better known in the Islamic world, especially after its ruler made the pilgrimage to Mecca, distributing largesse along the way.

The most interesting state to arise in the 11th to 12th centuries, in the forests of southern Nigeria, was Benin. Its trade was based mainly on slaves. It is renowned for its highly original brass statuary. And from the 15th century onward, there is evidence showing heads of chieftains, court ceremonials and, already, Portuguese soldiers.

Mali's existence was rather short – only from the mid-13th to the mid-14th century. It was succeeded by the even larger empire of Songhay, which united for the only time nearly all the western Sudan, west of Bornu. Its holy city, Timbuktu, was famed for its wealth and learning. By 1600, however, Songhay had been destroyed by the Moroccan army, which was equipped already with ample firearms. The Moroccan occupation was only short-lived, but the havoc it caused remained. The number of trans-Saharan caravans decreased and the wealth and civilization of the western Sudan declined rapidly.

In the ports of East Africa Swahili-speaking Islamic rulers controlled the rich maritime trade, but did not found large or lasting principalities.

The most important later contribution of the Africans is a passive one: as victims of the trans-Atlantic slave trade. Arab bands raided local villages, carrying off suitable men, women, and children and often slaughtering many of the others. At first the slaves were sold to Portuguese traders, but from the 17th century onward mainly to British, Dutch, and French slavers. The heyday of this trade in human beings was in the 17th and 18th centuries, but it was not entirely stopped until the second half of the 19th century. Those who survived the sea voyage ended up on the European plantations and in the mines of America. Some ten million slaves reached the New World, but many more died in Africa and during the sea voyage. Sub-Saharan Africa was ravaged for centuries by this scourge and some of its after effects linger still.

Part X

Civilizations Link Up

It is somewhat misleading to talk about "civilizations" as if they were watertight compartments, the one not intermingling with the others. There have always been contacts between civilizations, and influences passed from one to the other. In some cases these influences grew into mass-movements, both of people and of ideas and techniques. Some influences occurred so early in history that we do not know enough about them to describe them in detail. We shall discuss here the more important ones of those that are sufficiently well documented to merit detailed treatment. We shall in this case be less bound by chronology than elsewhere in this work, and that because of both similarities and dissimilarities between these cases, which we want to stress even though they are divided by lengthy periods of time. Furthermore we shall touch upon events occurring in different parts of this planet, divided sometimes by great distances. In fact the overcoming of distance is the common denominator of all the cases discussed here.

35   The Sea Peoples

Although the Sea Peoples are mentioned both in the Bible and in Egyptian inscriptions of the 12th century BC, much is guesswork about this group of sea raiders. Thus we do not know yet to what degree they are connected to the movement of people in the Balkans from the 15th to the 13th centuries BC. When they appear on the horizon of history they are living along the southeastern shores of the Aegean and on some of its islands. The Bible places the origins of the Philistines on Crete.

The Sea People seem to have ranged the shores of the Mediterranean much as the Vikings did those of western Europe two thousand years later. Among them were the Shardana, part of a group that landed in Cyrenaica and attacked Egypt from the west during the reign of Merneptah (1236–1223). Later they are mentioned as mercenaries in Egyptian service.

The Sea People seem also to have reached the western Mediterranean. The island of Sardinia is thought to be named after the Shardana, Sicily after the Sheklesh or Sikeloi. The arrival of the latter caused the inhabitants of the coastal plains to leave their villages and fields and to escape to the interior of the island. Some of the Sea People apparently settled in the abandoned fertile area. Herodot claimed that the Etruscans came from Asia Minor. Possibly they should be identified with the Tyrsenoi, another of the Sea People ("Tyrrhenians" was the name of the Etruscans in Greek).

The most interesting question is to what degree were the Sea People involved in the collapse of the Mycenaean civilization? Were they actually a part of it (as indicated by the location of the Philistines on Crete). Did they break away, starting out on a new career as freebooters and corsairs? The cyclopic fortifications of the Mycenaean townships may well have been erected against them. At Pylos, in the southern Peloponnese, the surviving Linear B records indicate that the attack was not unexpected. The absence of human remains indicates that the inhabitants escaped in good time. Were the Sea People the main cause of this breakdown, or only its outcome? Their migrations might thus have been the result of the political, social, and economic collapse which occurred in Anatolia and the Aegean around 1200 BC and not its cause.

Until that time the Sea People had made their mark mainly as sea raiders, but now they embarked on a large-scale land expedition. They must have collected a really threatening land force, as the mighty Hittite Empire demanded of its outlying dependencies, such as the city of Ugarit on the northeastern shore of the Mediterranean, that they send all their levies immediately to join the main Hittite army. The archives of Ugarit and of the Hittite Empire itself fall silent at that moment. What probably happened was that the Hittite army was totally defeated, the Hittite Empire was destroyed, and when the land force of the Sea People reached the Syrian coast there were no forces left to stop or even delay them. They moved south – men, women, and children – with their oxen drawn waggons and were stopped only by the Egyptian Pharaoh Rameses III (1194–62). A great battle took place around 1189 in the western Nile Delta. From Rameses' reliefs at the Medinet Habu temple we get a very lively picture of the appearance of the Sea People, wearing Indian-style feather headdresses. Other reliefs there show the great sea battle, in which was destroyed the naval arm of the Sea People, which had captured on its way south the island of Cyprus.

Rameses resettled some of the defeated Sea People along the coast of Palestine – the Philistines in its south, the Tjeker further north, and some Shardana apparently at Acre. It has even been suggested that the Israelite tribe Dan was originally identical with the Denye of the Sea People.

Once settled, the Sea People did not prove very interesting or creative. The Etruscans in the west soon came under Greek cultural influence. The Philistines in the east accepted the religion and the material culture of the Canaanites. Their only real mark on history, the name of Palestine, was bestowed in the 2nd century AD, a long time after their disappearance, by the Romans, who wanted to obliterate the then current name of Judea, for political reasons, after the failure of the Jewish revolts.

36   The Phoenicians and their Voyages of Exploration

The Phoenicians cannot be differentiated from the general mass of western Semitic Canaanites until fairly late in the second millennium BC. There were coastal cities to their north and south, which have not been called Phoenician, such as Ugarit and Alalakh to the north and Jaffa and Ashkelon to the south. What makes the few cities along the rocky Lebanese coast, such as Tyre, Sidon, Beirut, Aradus, and Byblos stand out, is mainly their importance in the first half of the first millennium BC as trading cities and sea powers.

Tyre is first mentioned in Egyptian texts of the 18th and 17th centuries BC. Archeological remains, especially in Byblos, are much earlier. But the really relevant period of Phoenician history starts only from about 1000 BC. By the time the King of Tyre is mentioned in the Bible, in the 10th century, the Phoenicians were already making their mark as merchant adventurers, bold entrepreneurs who sailed not only the Mediterranean, but the Red Sea as well. In the 10th century, under King Hiram I (c. 970–935), Tyre surpassed all its rivals, particularly Sidon and Byblos, and became the dominant city on the Phoenician coast. Its main industries were weaving, the production of purple dye, dyeing, ivory carving, and perhaps already the production of glass. It also exported cedar wood from Mount Lebanon, which was used in the construction of the Temple of Solomon in Jerusalem.

The Tyreans founded trading posts on Cyprus and occupied the northern coastal plain of Palestine, down to Mount Carmel. Their traders reached Greece and the shores of the Aegean.

In the late 9th century Tyrean trade to the central and western Mediterranean had developed sufficiently to found the city of Carthage, next to present-day Tunis. Other colonies were established in western Libya, in southern Sardinia, on Malta and on the Balearic islands. In the 7th and 6th centuries additional strongpoints were established along the Moroccan coast, in southern Spain, and in western Sicily.

Of great interest are the Phoenician voyages of exploration, which surpass any similar undertaking until the European expeditions of two thousand years later. At the bidding of the Egyptian Pharaoh Necho (609–593) a Phoenician expedition circumnavigated all of Africa – a tremendous feat, when one remembers how small their boats were. One of their later explorers, the 5th century Carthaginian Hanno, sailed all around Western Africa, and part of his description has survived. Other Phoenicians may have reached the Azores, where some of their coins have been found, and the Canaries. The Carthaginian Himilco visited the Atlantic ports of the Iberian peninsula, on the look-out for tin; he might just possibly might have reached England.

Although much of the information collected by their explorers was subsequently lost, the leaders of Tyre, Sidon, and Carthage must have had a fairly accurate picture of much of Europe, Africa, and southwestern Asia. Their traders ranged from the Indian Ocean, through the Mediterranean to the Atlantic Ocean.

When in the 6th century first Babylonia and later Persia occupied much of western Asia and Egypt, the Phoenician cities became their vassals. Babylonia had, for instance, to lay siege to Tyre for thirteen years to achieve this end. As Persia never succeeded in developing a fleet of her own, she was dependent on the Phoenician fleet (as well as the fleets of Ionia and Egypt) for her own needs. Thus her relations with the Phoenicians were not all one-sided, and she had to take into account their wishes as well. Most of the cities along the coast of Palestine were placed under the control of either Tyre or Sidon, and both these cities enjoyed under the Persians one of their greatest periods of prosperity. After their conquest by Alexander the Great (in the course of which Tyre was captured after a six-month siege) their importance waned and the Greeks took over much of their commerce. The main Phoenician cities became in Hellenistic and Roman times provincial towns whose upper-class citizens were Greek-speaking.

In the west, Carthage enjoyed a meteoric career of her own. Her widespread commerce was the foundation of her great wealth. She controlled all the colonies settled originally by Tyre in North Africa and Sardinia. Her trade brought her into conflict with the Greeks of southern Italy and Sicily. Her threat to eastern Sicily brought about the first Punic War (264–241), during which she lost Sicily to Rome, but afterwards, as a compensation, she built up her empire in southern Spain. From her bases there, Hannibal, her greatest general, invaded Italy in the second Punic War (218–202). After his defeat at Zama in 202, the great days of Carthage were over. After a short third Punic War (149–146) the city was destroyed by the Romans.

Yet the Semitic traditions, implanted by the Phoenicians, did not disappear completely, and resurfaced in North Africa, Sicily, and Spain, when they were conquered by Arab Islamic invaders from the 7th century AD onward. North Africa has retained much of this heritage to this date.

37   The Graeco-Roman Reach into Central Asia

Alexander's campaign in northwestern India failed to bring about a mingling of Greek and Indian civilizations. This did happen, however, in the 2nd century BC in the far-away province of Bactria, between the Hindu Kush and the Oxus. The first Greek settlement dated back to the 5th century BC, when Greek exiles had been settled there by the Persians. Later some 20 000 of Alexander's soldiers, who were sick or wounded, were settled there (none too willingly – they revolted and demanded to be repatriated after Alexander's death, but to no avail). The trading facilities of the region resulted in the growth of thriving cities.

At the end of the 3rd century BC Bactria became independent of its erstwhile Seleucid rulers, and local Indo-Greek rulers established there a state of their own. They were typical Hellenistic rulers, forever engaged in wars of aggression with their neighbors, or among themselves. Their Greek roots are shown by the coins they struck, some of them of rare beauty. Euradites' gold stater of 170 BC is reputedly the largest gold coin in existence. Their Indian roots are attested to by King Menander (155–130 BC), the Milinda of Indian legend, who is supposed to have converted to Buddhism. His coins have been found from Kabul in the north to Delhi in the south. Other Greeks converted to Hinduism, as shown by an inscription on a pillar in Besnagar, in western India.

Bactrian silver and metal work, showing scenes from Greek mythology, was much admired and copied in Central Asia and even in the China of the Han dynasty. Some of its other subjects were the bronze statuette of a gryphon, in a style similar to classical Greek work, and a silver dish in Hellenistic workmanship, showing an Indian elephant.

The main Bactrian principality was overrun sometime late in the 2nd century BC by Central Asian nomads (who found their traditional way into the grazing grounds of northeastern China barred by the newly-erected Great Wall) and some of their smaller principalities in Kabul and northwestern India were engulfed in the 1st century BC. Some of these nomads belonged to the Asian part of the Huns, whose European cousins much later attacked the Roman Empire. Others were the Kushans, who set up, apparently in the 1st century, a sizeable kingdom in Central Asia and northwestern India. It was an important caravan center, trading with China in the east, and Rome in the west. The Kushans adapted to their own needs the alphabet used by the Greeks of Central Asia. Their most important king was Kanishka, whose capital was in Peshawar (in northern Pakistan). This city was then part of a province named Gandhara, after which is named the important Romano-Indian art of the Kushan period. The Kushans were Buddhists and under their rule this religious tradition was welded together with Graeco-Roman influences into an original and distinctive art form.

Its stupa buildings often use Ionian and Corinthian capitals, its statuary is garbed in dresses with Grecian folds, and the images of Buddha mirror the youthfulness of some of the statuary of Apollo, with the typical tuft of hair, which was originally Greek too. Further, there are portrait sculptures, reliefs showing family scenes, chariots, Bacchic scenes, sculptures of satyrs, putti and garlands, and an occasional Trojan horse.

This style strikes one often as almost entirely Western, with but few roots in earlier Indian civilization. The subject matter, however, is Indian.

Art historians have discussed at some length the question to what extent Gandhara art should be regarded as an offshoot of Graeco-Hellenistic or of Roman art. But in view of the dependence of Roman art itself on earlier Greek art, we do not believe this question to be of much relevance. It seems, however, that much of the actual influence did come via trade with the Greek-speaking Middle East under Roman domination, and especially with Alexandria in Egypt. From Alexandria came the technique of stucco sculpture, replacing the use of expensive white marble.

From Palmyra came, apparently, influences in the fields of textile manufacture and jewelry. The stucco technique spread northward and eastward, with the spread of Buddhist monasticism, to the borders of China and beyond.

There were strong commercial ties also between Rome and southern India, where many Roman coins have been found. Many Roman artifacts made of pottery, glass, and stone have been discovered, for instance, at the site of a southern Indian port, called by its English excavators Arikamedu, and its French ones Virampatnam. They date from the 1st and 2nd centuries AD.

To return to the north of the Indian subcontinent. The Kushan empire continued to flourish until 500 AD, approximately. But Gandhara art survived its demise, and was in evidence in Buddhist centers in Kashmir and Afghanistan in the 7th and 8th centuries AD.

Buddhist art carried elements of Western influence with it, as it moved further eastward. Wall-paintings from the Turfan Oasis of northeastern Turkestan show in the 8th to the 10th centuries a meeting of Chinese, Indian, Western, and Iranian elements. But when Islam came to rule great parts of Central Asia, the traces of Gandhara art disappeared.

The Chinese art of the Tang period absorbed some of the Hellenistic and Roman elements of Kushan art. Pottery statuettes of dancers and musicians, or of a woman rider on horseback playing polo, look like late Tanagra work. Pilgrim flasks modeled after Western prototypes have been found in Chinese graves. Stucco horses, camels, and the head of a laughing boy show traces of Roman realism. In the 7th century some of the heads in frescoes show Byzantine influence.

Buddhist sculpture in later centuries also shows Graeco-Roman traces in the way draperies are treated, both in China and Japan.

38   The Vikings

In the last quarter of the first millennium AD Scandinavia stood apart from the main centers of civilization. It had been touched neither by Rome, nor by Christianity, nor by Islam. Sweden was in the 8th century already an organized and unified state, but Denmark and Norway were not. They both seem to have been suffering from overpopulation (perhaps as a result of widespread polygamy) and they possessed long coast lines and well-trained sailors. Their longboats had a shallow draught and did not need deep harbors. Suddenly there occurred a great eruption of naval raiding and expansion, in which younger sons could look for wealth, adventure, and property beyond the seas. As a result, during four centuries, from the 8th to the late 11th century, their ships sailed east and west and southward, and their martial prowess was felt from the Holy Land to the shores of North America.

The Swedes moved first, into Latvia and Estonia, both as traders and as conquerors. The earliest raid in the west, by Norwegians and Danes, is reported in 787 from the coasts of England. From then on nearly every year the Vikings plundered the islands of Scotland. The monastery of Lindisfarne was sacked in 793, that of Jarrow in 794, that of Rechreyn (in Ireland) in 795, that of Iona in 806. Most of the raids went unreported, as the ability to write was usually limited to monasteries.

Denmark was unified early in the 9th century and started to attack Friesland and the German shores beyond. Up until 834 the Vikings raided only, but in that year they succeeded in planting a permanent settlement in Ireland. After 840 they made similar settlements in England and Scotland. In 841 they plundered London. After the death of the Emperor Louis the Pious in 840, Carolingian power on the Continent declined, and as a result all of western France was raided by the Vikings. They sailed up the River Seine and devastated Rouen; similarly sailing up the River Loire to plunder Nantes, and the River Garonne in order to lay siege to Toulouse. The defence in France, Germany, and England was irresolute to start with. The local farmers tried to defend their property, but the aristocracy was at first less resolute. Further south, the shores of Spain were attacked.

The very success of their attacks caused more Scandinavians to join in these raids, the size of their fleets increased, Swedes sometimes joined the Norwegians and the Danes. The raids turned into colonizing ventures. The forces were built up on the beaches in winter and marched inland when spring arrived.

The Norwegians started by settling the Shetland, Orkney, and Hebridean Islands. The native Pictish population was subdued. In the last quarter of the 9th century recently unified Norway established a strong earldom on the Orkneys. Other Norwegians settled in Ireland, founded Dublin, and chased away competing Danish Vikings. Another Viking base was established on the Isle of Man. Danes settled in Yorkshire and other parts of eastern England. Further south the Norwegian Rollo, at the head of an apparently prevalently Danish force, established early in the 10th century the dukedom of Normandy.

As local forces became more organized, the Vikings found it more and more difficult to advance any further. In 891 they were defeated by the Germans and in 878 by the English under Alfred the Great. During the late 9th and early 10th centuries he and his successors recaptured all their English possessions.

In Normandy the cultural development was different. The Normans accepted Christianity and the French language. Indeed, on their capture of England in 1066, they transplanted their French language and customs to Britain.

In the meantime Swedish traders used the water route via the River Volga and the Caspian Sea to link up with the caravan routes of the Caliphate of Baghdad. The great quantity of Arab coins found in Sweden shows that trade was lively until well into the 10th century. Other traders reached Constantinople. Their constant journeyings and far-flung political ambitions made them unrivalled carriers of ideas and objects belonging to other civilizations. For this reason the cosmopolitan civilization that started to flourish along the river route from Scandinavia to Byzantium owed a lot to these middlemen.

Around the middle of the 9th century the Swedes had created the Khaganate of Rus, in Novgorod, from which the name Russia derives, and later founded a more important principality in Kiev. They were followed later by Varangian mercenaries of mixed Swedish and Russian stock, who formed the imperial guard in Constantinople. They saw service in Crete, Asia Minor, Syria, Armenia, Bulgaria, Apulia, and Sicily.

The Arab traveler Ibn Fadlan describes in 922 some of the Swedes – "I saw the Rusfolk . . . Never had I seen people of more perfect physique. They are tall as date palms, and reddish in colour . . . No one is ever parted from his axe, sword and knife . . . They are the filthiest of God's creatures. They do not wash after discharging their natural functions, neither do they wash their hands after meals. They are lousy as donkeys."

The descriptions of the Vikings in the west were not any friendlier, the reason being perhaps that they were pagans, while their victims were Christians.

Some of the most important Viking expeditions took place far to the north. Already in the 9th century Norwegians reached and settled the Faroe islands and Iceland. The later Icelandic Landnambok gives the names of 400 settlers, who were mostly from western Norway, but some came from the Viking settlements on the Scottish islands and from Ireland. No Danes are mentioned and only a few Swedes. Soon several thousand settlers had arrived and from the 11th century onward they began to regard themselves as a separate Nordic nation. They adopted Christianity around 1000.

Greenland was first discovered by Norwegians around 900. It was first colonized by Erik the Red in the 980s. He gave it also its rather misleading name, hoping to attract settlers. Modern archeologists have recovered his settlement and even his hut. Around 992 his son Leif Eriksson discovered the coast of North America, which he called "Wineland." Viking remains have been discovered in L'Anse aux Meadows in Newfoundland. The élan of Viking exploration had, however, nearly run its course by the beginning of the 11th century, and this epochal discovery was not followed up in any way comparable to what the Spanish did 500 years later.

The Vikings did not develop much of an original material culture. Their carvings, jewelry, and runic stones look rather primitive when compared with contemporary Irish, Byzantine, or Islamic work. Thus it is perhaps not surprising that they did not manage to develop a fully-grown civilization of their own, and were swallowed up, so to speak, by the nascent Christian western European civilization in the 11th century.

One last chapter of their history has still to be told. Norman adventurers intervened in the 11th century in the fighting between Muslims, Byzantines, and Italians for southern Italy and Sicily and carved out for themselves a sizeable kingdom, bequeathed in the 13th century to the Hohenstaufen emperors of Germany. Two of their barons, Bohemond and Tancred, were in 1096–9 among the most active members of the First Crusade. Bohemond founded the Principality of Antioch, which retained for some time some Norman characteristics. Tankred became Prince of Galilee and tried unsuccessfully to be crowned king of Jerusalem.

Viking activity spanned thus the shores of much of the then known world, and they are the real discoverers of America.

39   The Mongols

Beyond the Great Wall of China spread the fluctuating world of nomad tribes. Their mobility made them formidable antagonists and from time to time they would conquer great parts of northern China. In the late 12th century they were united, partly willingly and partly by force, by their greatest leader ever, whom history remembers by his title of "Universal Ruler" – Genghis Khan (1167–1227). The name of his Mongol tribe was used from then onward for all of these tribes. He captured early in the 13th century the empires of north China, but did not attack the Song Empire in south China. Then he moved west and subdued the Khwaresmian Empire of Iran and Central Asia. He attacked northern India and sent raiding parties to Russia. His victories and conquests were based on his ability to make spectacular use of the mobility of his forces, on a highly developed intelligence service, and on a realistic evaluation of prospects as against risks. He had also the rare ability among nomads to organize his conquests into a viable empire, which survived the death of its founder.

His heirs continued to advance in all directions, conquered Russia and invaded Central Europe. In spite of spectacular victories in Hungary and Silesia (1241) they did not follow this line of advance, which might well have crushed the young Western

Civilization. Further south the Mongols conquered Iraq and Syria, but were defeated in 1260 at Ein Jalud by the Mameluks. Two further attempts to conquer Palestine (the last in 1300) failed too. Their greatest success was the capture of the Song Empire of southern China, in 1276, by Khubilai (1264–94) – the first time that all of China was in the hands of a non-Chinese.

Thus an enormous arch was formed – from the Pacific Ocean right into Europe and the Middle East – an empire of unprecedented size. It served as a bridge between all the advanced civilizations of the Old World, a completely unprecedented creation. Caravans and trade moved freely through this Eurasian empire, as attested to by Marco Polo, who traveled safely between 1271 and 1295 from Venice, via the Mongolian capital of Karakoram, to China and after a long stay there, back again. This was not an exceptional achievement – in 1340 Pegolotti's *Merchant Handbook* stated that the road from the Black Sea to China "is now perfectly safe, whether by day or by night."

But the empire was too huge to be governed centrally for any length of time. Khubilai moved his capital to Beijing (called then Khanbaligh) and ruled mainly as a Chinese emperor. His dynasty there was called Yüan (1276–1367). The other main parts became slowly independent, under other Mongol princes, such as the Central Asian Khanate, the Khanate of the Golden Horde in Russia, the Khanate of the White Horde in Kazakhstan, and the Persian Ilkhanate. The various courts co-operated in many ways, with that of Beijing being regarded as the senior one. Each was influenced by local customs, and after some time the Persian Ilkhanate accepted Islam, at Khubilai's court Buddhism flourished, and in some of the other parts of China lived Christian Nestorians. Catholic missionaries (mainly Franciscans) moved freely through the Mongol realm, but their success was very limited.

A great exchange of ideas and techniques took place. The Chinese were much impressed by the big horses brought from Europe. Gunpowder reached Europe from China. The transit trade was mainly in the hands of Central Asian Muslims. The economy was sophisticated enough to make the widespread use of paper money possible. French artisans were to be found in Karakoram, Arab revenue officers in China, Genoese consuls in

Tabris, Venetian merchants in Beijing, Mongol ambassadors in Northampton and Bordeaux. The Pax Mongolica was, for over a century, as real in a much larger empire as the Pax Romana had been.

In the later 14th century the Mongolian states declined. Their economic basis, the intercontinental caravan trade, could not compete with sea trade, which could carry heavier loads more cheaply, in spite of the longer route. The jewel in the crown, China, was recaptured over the period 1365–82 by a local dynasty, the Ming (1368–1644). The Persian Ilkhanate declined and split up.

A revival was attempted by Timur (1368–1405), whose original base was between Lake Aral and the Hindu Kush. He defeated the Golden Horde, conquered Persia and most of Central Asia, invaded Iraq, Syria, and Anatolia, decisively defeated the Ottoman Empire, capturing its Sultan, and invaded India and captured Delhi. His greatest campaign was to have been the conquest of China, but he died during its preparations.

Timur was a great warrior, but not a realistic statesman like Genghis Khan. Although he erected some beautiful buildings, his fame rests on his legendary cruelty. In many of the captured towns, many of the inhabitants were slaughtered, and their skulls were piled into enormous heaps. There was no common economic basis to his far-flung conquests, and his empire declined quickly after the death of his son in 1447. However, his court and that of his descendants was an important center of Islamic architecture and of Persian literature and miniature painting.

His later descendants ruled in Kabul, from where one of them, Babur, established early in the 16th century the Moghul Empire of India.

40   Expansion of Islam into India and Indonesia

In 711 the Arabs crossed the straits of Gibraltar in the far west and started the conquest of Spain. One year later they captured the province of Sind, their first foothold in India, and their farthest expansion yet eastward. It took 300 years before they continued to advance into India.

In the meantime Muslim travelers and geographers – such as Masudi, Ibn Haukal, el-Bekri and Ibn Battuta – ranged far and wide over all of the enormous spaces from Spain to India and beyond and described what they had seen and heard. The educated part of the population of the Muslim world had in the Middle Ages a far clearer picture of the world than their European contemporaries.

When the Muslims renewed their advance into India it was no longer by Arabs, but by Muslim Turks. One of them had set up the principality of Ghazni, in Afghanistan, and from there his son, Mahmud of Ghazni (998–1030), started his raids, in which he plundered the rich temple cities of northwestern India. Temples were the depositories of money, jewelry, and golden ornaments, and combined thus the lure of monetary gain with fulfilling the Islamic commandment of destroying pagan places of worship. Tens of thousands of local Indians were sold into slavery. Indian historians have always regarded Mahmud as the very prototype of a barbarian Muslim, bent on destroying all that was holy to the Indians. Yet there was another side to his character too. He developed the trade routes of Central Asia, beautified his capital and sent scholars like Alberuni to India, who wrote the important geographical work *Tahqiq-i-Hind*.

Although most of Mahmud's empire spread throughout Central Asia, he did control also, at the end of his reign, the upper Indus Valley and the Punjab to the very gates of Delhi. He left the northern Indian states badly shaken. They had not found any answer to his tactics, which were based mainly on a highly professional and mobile cavalry. His heirs lost most of his non-Indian possessions, but their court at Lahore became an important center for Islamic learning and Persian culture.

The next stage of the Muslim invasion of India came under another Turkish prince, Muhammad Guri (1173–1206). He and his brother controlled Afghanistan, and when he invaded India he used similar cavalry tactics in order to overcome the local Muslim and Rajput armies. In the second battle of Tarain (1192) he defeated the Indian levies and thereby gained control of the kingdom of Delhi, much of the Ganges valley, and part of Bengal.

Before he had time to organize his conquests he was assassinated and his direct heirs lost control of his Indian possessions. These passed under the control of his Turkish generals, who had commenced their careers as his slaves. Their realm was called the Delhi Sultanate. They are of the greatest importance in the history both of Islam and of India. They controlled all of northern India and were, by far, the rulers of its most powerful state in the 13th and 14th centuries. Thus they broke down the isolation of the subcontinent, which previously had only been dented by the Greek rulers of Bactria, 1200 years earlier. They sank deep roots in India, and while the later English rule has been completely swept away, the present states of Pakistan and Bangladesh attest to the survival of the Islamic inheritance.

As usual, the conquerors had no very high opinion of the conquered. Alberuni says about the power of reasoning of the Indians: "They are in a state of utter confusion, devoid of any logical order, and in the last instance always mixed up with silly notions of the crowd. I can only compare their mathematical and astronomical knowledge to a mixture of . . . pearls and of dung . . . Both kinds . . . are equal in their eyes."

No stable dynasty was established, but some of the Turkish generals who seized power were formidable commanders and twice, under Ala-ud-din (1296–1316) and Muhammad Tughlug (1325–51), most of the subcontinent was conquered or frightened into submission. These were, however, short-lived achievements. The strong, centralized system of government, introduced to India by the Sultans of Delhi, applied only to the northern part of the subcontinent, while in its south the old, local Hindu dynasties continued to rule, though often under Muslim suzerainty. When the central government weakened, in the second half of the 14th century, they regained their complete independence.

The decline of the sultanate was sped along by Delhi's capture by Timur (1398). During the 15th century India relapsed into several regional states – those in the north under Muslim rulers, those in the south under Hindus. Muslim cultural influence was, however, not diminished. Delhi, and some of the regional capitals, continued to be important centers of Islamic art and theology, and Persian literature and science. Many members of the Hindu upper classes adopted Persian dress and manners, and many members of the lower classes embraced Islam. Notwithstanding, the vast majority of the population, except in the northwest and north-east, continued to be Hindus. But Islam could not be absorbed and overcome like previous foreign influences and continued to exist side by side with Hinduism, each religion and civilization influencing the other.

In the 16th and 17th centuries Muslim influence reached its peak in India under the Moghul dynasty.

In the meantime Islam had already continued to spread out further eastward, into southeastern Asia and especially Indonesia. There it found several layers of previous cultural influences. The geographer Ptolemy had already in AD 150 indicated it roughly on his map. Chinese remains of the Han period have come to light, and parts of Vietnam were directly under Chinese control. But the main influences – religious, cultural, and economic – had been Indian. Buddhism had developed in all these areas a strong missionary activity, the impressive architectural remains of which can still be seen in Borobudur in Java (8th to 9th centuries) and in Angkor in Cambodia (12th century). Buddhist and Hindu states arose, from Burma to Java, and the Buddhist ones survived into the 19th and 20th centuries in most of the mainland, except the Malay Peninsula.

There, and in Indonesia, Islamic influences were mentioned from the late 13th century onward. Marco Polo relates in 1292 that many of the inhabitants of Perlak, in northern Sumatra, had been converted to Islam by the foreign merchants who visited there. Mostly they seem to have come from Gujarat on the west coast of India, and from only recently converted Bengal, on the northeast coast. The carrying trade of the Indian Ocean was at that time in Muslim hands, and Muslim traders exported the spices to Indonesia, which gained great popularity in Europe.

The Chinese, too, were interested in the sea-borne trade of this ocean, and they backed a prince when he established a trading post around 1400 in the port city of Malacca, which controlled then the transit trade, very much as nearby Singapore did later. In 1414 this prince embraced Islam, which had widespread repercussions. Other rulers of port cities and of coastal principalities, whose wealth derived from trade, followed his example. During the 15th century and after, a majority of the inhabitants of the Malay Peninsula and Indonesia converted to Islam, which even reached the far-off Philippines.

Islam thus linked previously independent civilizations, from the shores of the Atlantic Ocean, via the Mediterranean and the Indian Ocean, all the way to the shores of the Pacific Ocean, half-way round the earth.

The Muslims were, soon after, followed into Southeast Asia by European Christians, explorers, traders, and colonizers, from the 16th century onward. But while the later Dutch and English domination has left few vestiges, Islam continues to be the main religion of both Indonesia and Malaysia. About one-fourth of the present-day 800 million Muslims live in Indonesia.

41   The European Age of Discovery

Generations of historians have regarded the great European voyages of discovery overseas, of the 15th and 16th centuries, as a unique phenomenon in the history of man. There is of course much truth in this, yet less than has generally been assumed. We have tried to show in the previous chapters that the process of linking up the main civilizations of this world had been going on for quite some time, before the Europeans of the 15th century became involved: the Sea People had roamed 2500 years earlier all of the Mediterranean; the Phoenicians had circumnavigated Africa 2000 years earlier; Hellenistic and Roman influences had reached India and Central Asia 1500 years earlier; the Vikings had discovered America 500 years earlier; the Mongols had united under one rule most of central and northern Eurasia 250 years earlier; and the Muslims had expanded their rule, religion, and civilization not only into India, but right up to the edge of the Pacific during the last few centuries before Vasco da Gama.

Thus the European Age of Discovery was more in the nature of a continuation in the process of the linking up of civilizations than a completely unique event in history. This does not mean, however, that we should detract from its importance: it certainly was the culmination and high watermark of this process.

The spirit of the Renaissance freed Europeans of the 15th century from many of the shackles of religion and prejudice of the medieval period and enabled them to move ahead in many directions. One of the most consequential was that of geographical discovery.

The lead was taken by the countries of western Europe and especially those of the Iberian Peninsula. There contact with the Muslim civilization had been especially close: not only had nearly all of it been previously part of this civilization, but until 1492 there continued to exist the Muslim kingdom of Granada on Spanish soil.

In 1415 the Portuguese captured Ceuta, opposite Gibraltar, and from there started to make their way down the western coast of Africa, searching for trade and gold and attempting to convert pagans to Christianity. The initiator and organizer of this movement was Prince Henry the Navigator. Only gradually were these aims refined to the clear purpose of finding a path to India. The means were already at hand – larger and more sea-worthy ships, better compasses, anchors, sounding lines, charts, astrolabes, and quadrants. During the slow advance around West Africa these were further refined and captains, crews, shipbuilders, and sailmakers gained further experience.

In 1483 Diego Cão reached the mouth of the River Congo, in 1488 Bartolomeo Diaz the Cape of Good Hope, in 1490 Petro da Cavilhã reached India by the overland route, in 1498 Vasco da Gama reached it by the sea route, and in 1513 the first Portuguese ship had reached Canton in China. The Portuguese established bases in India, at the mouth of the Persian Gulf, and at the tip of the Malay Peninsula. Their aim was not conquest, but trade. They were prepared to fight ferociously for the control of the trade of the Indian Ocean, but not for the capture of large territories. This was dictated by common prudence, as the states of southern and eastern Asia were far too strong to be subdued by their limited forces. Their forte was sea power and not land power.

Spain was much more powerful than Portugal, and intended not to be left behind in the race for India and trade. On its behalf in 1492 Christopher Columbus sailed westward, assuming this to be a shortcut to eastern Asia and India. He made three further voyages (1413–1504) and never knew that actually he had discovered a new continent, which blocked the direct passage to the Far East. The Spanish exploration soon turned into conquest, with the help of firearms and horses, which were unknown to the inhabitants of America. Hernán Cortés subjected the Aztec Empire of Mexico in the period 1519–21 and Francisco Pizarro the Inca Empire of Peru between 1531 and 1538. All of the New World fell to the Spaniards, except for Brazil, which became Portuguese, in accordance with the Treaty of Tordesillas (1494).

The Spanish hoped to reach Asia from the west and to beat the Portuguese in the race for the spice trade. They sent Fernando Magellan out in 1520. He found a way round South America in the south, made the first crossing of the Pacific and was killed in the Philippines. One of his five ships managed to return to Spain and to complete the first circumnavigation of the Earth.

The Portuguese soon derived great profits from the spice trade round the Cape of Good Hope, and the Americas yielded silver and gold to the Spanish. Other nations tried to imitate them, such as the English, who sent John Cabot to North America in 1497, and the French, who in 1534 and 1541 sent Jaques Cartier there too. But there were no immediate results to their travels, except for a further broadening of the geographical horizon.

While some of the previous voyages of exploration – such as the Phoenician circumnavigation of Africa, or the Viking discovery of North America – had not had any long-range results, the outcome was different this time. The planet Earth was now known in its general outline, and this knowledge was never again forgotten. Some outlying places, such as Australia or Antarctica, were discovered in later outbursts of European exploration. But the contact between the various civilizations of the world had been established now on a secure basis and was never quite broken off again.

Part XI

The Later Empires of Asia

In spite of the increasing linking up of widely divergent civilizations there did evolve, outside of the area influenced by Europe, several great empires, which developed cultural strains of their own. First we shall discuss those of China and Japan and then we shall move on to three different empires, all of which belonged to a late stage of the Islamic civilization. In India also strong non-Islamic elements took an active and creative part. What interests us today is not only the external trappings of these empires, but the varied cultures they developed. They represent a last moment when the old Islamic civilization was still flourishing, followed by a long period of decline and stagnation. At the same time Europe forged ahead and in the following centuries influenced the Islamic world from a cultural, economic, and political point of view. In our own times the Islamic world is moving ahead once more, but has never quite forgiven the Western Civilization for its own period of backwardness.

42   From the Ming Dynasty to Mao Zedong

After a century of Mongol rule in southern China, and nearly 500 years of foreign dynasties in northern China, rebellions broke out throughout the country, the Mongol Yüan dynasty was hard-pressed and a previous Buddhist monk established for the last time a native Chinese imperial line, the Ming dynasty (1368–1644). Luckily perhaps for China none of the fifteen later Ming emperors proved to be a great warrior, and in the ensuing peaceful times an unprecedented number of books were printed and circulated, literacy spread widely, and so did vernacular literature. Novels were very popular, though not highly regarded.

Peace and economic security permitted a hedonistic way of life among the ruling and prosperous classes, which did not, however, prove conducive to great achievements in literature, philosophy, and art. Although more paintings and buildings have survived from this than from any previous period, they are not innovative, and continue on lines established under the Southern Song. But some of the Ming porcelain and ceramic ware is highly valued by collectors. Scholars preferred to turn to history, to study the literature and art of the past, and to produce beautifully illustrated books.

Chinese civilization began for the first time to lag behind that of Europe. When Marco Polo had visited China in the early period of Mongol rule, the civilization he described was far superior to that of medieval Europe. But by the end of the Ming period Europe had forged ahead and left China decisively behind. This trend became even more pronounced during the ensuing period of Manchu domination. The concluding years of the Ming dynasty were chaotic, and the Manchu tribes which had controlled northern China once before (1115–1235), moved once more southward early in the 17th century, and this time established their domination over all of China (1644–1911).

Outwardly this was an impressive period. China's frontiers were far flung, including Mongolia, Tibet, and Central Asian Xinjiang (Turkestan), none of which had been included in the Ming Empire. Even Burma, Vietnam, and Nepal recognized for some time China's suzerainty. In order to ensure their continued dominance over China, the Manchu tried not to be assimilated, marriage with Chinese was forbidden, and the Chinese were forbidden to settle in Manchuria.

The 18th century was the high-water mark of their reign. They were accepted now by most of the population as legitimate rulers, they identified with the Confucian tradition and sponsored huge scholarly projects, such as *The Complete Poems of the Tang Dynasty* or the *History of the Ming*. China's greatest novel, *The Dream of the Red Chamber* – a complex story about the decline and restoration of a wealthy family – was written at this time. Porcelain and lacquer wares were produced in great quantities and exported to Europe and Istanbul. If imitation is the greatest flattery, early in the 18th century Europe succeeded in producing its own porcelain.

The long period of peace made possible the cultivation of previously unused lands. New crops, imported from abroad, such as maize, the sweet potato, and the peanut (used for cooking oil), were utilized. The population multiplied, reaching some 300 million by 1800 – far beyond the numbers of inhabitants of Europe or India.

Many problems inherent in the Manchu regime started to be felt in the 19th century. The conservative Confucian outlook of the official hierarchy was not suitable to cope successfully with the many new problems brought about by the sudden close contact with the European powers. While the court was tucked away in Beijing, in the furthest northeastern corner of the empire, the chief center of trade was in Canton, in the equally inaccessible far south. Thus contact between them was poor and slow. European trade and power were felt in the south, but not understood properly in the north. Stagnation and corruption became endemic. The 19th century in China is characterized by misrule, internal rebellions, and disastrous foreign wars.

While there had been contacts with Russia ever since the 17th century, the real problem was posed early in the 19th century by Great Britain. England needed an export staple to pay for the large amounts of Chinese tea, silk, and porcelain it imported; and found it in the opium grown in India. The "Opium War" (1839–42) was fought by China for the suppression of this trade and by Great Britain for free trade and diplomatic access. The British were successful; China had to cede Hong Kong, to open five ports to foreign trade, and to recognize the diplomatic equality of the

Europeans. Not all these stipulations were fulfilled, and in the "Arrow War" (1857–60) the British and French fleets (joined by American and Russian envoys) captured Canton and their troops forced their way into Beijing. Their demands had to be met.

European influence became even more dangerous on a different level. Christian doctrines were included in the ideology of the Taiping movement, whose leader declared himself to be the younger brother of Jesus Christ. The movement spread widely and its troops captured much of central China, but failed to take Beijing (1850–64). It was finally crushed by a Western-trained Chinese force commanded by the British General "Chinese" Gordon (who was to gain even wider fame by being killed in Khartoum, by the forces of the Mahdi, in 1885). Casualties amounted to some 20 million. It is just possible that China missed there a chance of an easier way to European-inspired reforms than the one ultimately taken in the 20th century by the local Communists.

By the end of the century China's power was in full decline. In 1875 the Ryukyu islands, including Okinawa, had to be ceded to Japan; in 1885 Vietnam was ceded to France; in 1886 Burma to Great Britain; and in 1895 Taiwan and rights in Korea were ceded to Japan. The Boxer rebellion brought about in 1900 the siege of the members of the diplomatic corps in Beijing, by both rebels and imperial troops, until the capital was entered by European soldiers. The Chinese court had to withdraw from its own capital. Within a century once mighty China had declined to the status of a powerless colossus.

Attempts at reform from above failed in 1898, strengthening the revolutionary tendencies, mainly in the more advanced south. The Manchu dynasty was discredited and was finally overthrown in 1911. Most of China passed eventually into the hands of various local warlords. But around Canton the nucleus of a reform-minded republican China was established by Sun Yat-sen (1866–1925). He established there the Kuomintang party, which was led by his successor, Chiang Kai-shek (1887–1975), to victory in most of the country (1927–8). Its Communist-inspired left wing seceded, and set up after its Long March (1935) an independent region at Yenan, under Mao Zedong (1893–1976). Chiang Kai-shek headed China officially throughout World War II (which started with a

Japanese attack as early as in 1937), but his real strength eroded, and Mao and the Communists were able in 1949 to capture all of continental China. Chiang and his followers withdrew to the island of Taiwan. There, surprisingly, he and his successors, who had so spectacularly failed in China proper, were very successful, and small Taiwan was formed into one of the great industrial powers of the Pacific Rim. Also Chinese-run Singapore and Hong Kong were spectacularly successful.

Mao and his successor Deng Xiaoping (1902–97) gave China, with a population of over 1000 million inhabitants, strong leadership, but bewildered the world by their ideological zigzagging. The "Hundred Flowers" movement of 1957, the "Great Leap Forward" of 1958, the disastrous "Cultural Revolution" (1966–76), the opening up of the economy by Deng, and the Tiananmen Square massacre of 1989, each seemed to point the enormous country in a different, previously uncharted, direction. It says much for the capacity of the Chinese for sheer hard work and for organization at the grass-roots level that the country has not sunk again into chaos.

Towards the dawn of the new millennium China can show impressive economic achievements and enjoys new prestige as a world power, second in standing only to the United States.

43 Japan

Most of Japanese history has been played out against a background of Chinese influences. Chinese institutions had to be adapted to the quite different geopolitical conditions of the Japanese archipelago, with its safe maritime borders and limited space. The easy ability to adopt whatever foreign traits seemed desirable, while resisting whatever did not suit her circumstances, was to stand Japan in good stead when applied in the 19th and 20th centuries to Western influences.

Her traditions of an empire going back to 660 BC are quite baseless. In fact, at that stage the island people were still deep in their neolithic era. Only around AD 500 did Japan enter her historical period, and some fifty years later Buddhism reached her from Korea. Chinese civilization was adapted and even the Chinese language was used for several centuries in written communications. But the strong native feudal traditions made the adaptation of a system similar to the Chinese civil service impossible.

The Japanese emperors ruled at Nara (710–94), and later at nearby Kyoto (794–1185). The Nara period signifies the high-water mark of Chinese influence. When emperor Kammu transferred the capital in 794, he did so as a reaction against too great a surrender of Japanese cultural independence. The Nara period marks also the high watermark of Buddhist sculpture in Japan, mostly of bronze and dry lacquer. In the field of architecture the beautiful monastery of Hōryūji was started already in the 7th century and survives virtually intact to this day. Nothing of similar interest and age has survived on the Chinese mainland.

Kyoto's period as capital is called the Heian period. Painting overtook sculpture in importance. Around 1000 the greatest work of Japanese prose, and her first true novel, *The Tale of Genji*, was written by Murasaki Shikibu, one of the court ladies. The emperor's power declined soon after Kammu's reign, and members of the Fujiwara clan became the actual rulers in the 9th and 10th centuries, leaving the emperor a powerless figurehead. The aborigines of the islands were subjugated, but the military aristocrats carrying out this task replaced their predecessors. During the Kamakura period (1185–1333) they ruled the land, with the title of "Shogun" (general-in-chief). Their greatest triumph was the repulsion of two Mongol invasions (in 1274 and 1281), with some timely help from typhoons (the "Kamikaze" of World War II renown).

Zen Buddhism was introduced from China in 1200 and became popular during the period of social disruption, until 1573. Feudal lords ruled large, near independent territories. Their attendants were called "Samurai." Never before or after was Japan so marred by dissent and strife. The shoguns were nearly as powerless as the emperors. The near independent provinces were much of the time at war one with the other. Memories of these times have caused the later Japanese preference for a strong, united government.

Japan was reunited by three military commanders during the

period 1568 to 1616. The second, Toyotomi Hideyoshi, initiated a policy of foreign expansion by attacking Korea in 1592 and 1597; he seems also to have planned to attack Ming China, but this did not materialize. He left a heritage of foreign aggression, to be taken up again in the 20th century. He had numerous castles built and their decoration gave rise to a vigorous style of painting, mainly of landscapes. Wall panels and screens painted in thick colors against a ground of gold leaf attained great popularity.

Overseas commerce flourished, partly as a result of the arrival of the Portuguese (after 1542), and the Dutch and English (after 1600). The introduction of firearms aided the reunification of the country, but the rapid spread of Catholic Christianity caused new dissent. Hideyoshi turned against the new Christians and had them persecuted. In 1638 the Christians were defeated, after they had tried to revolt; most were expelled.

From 1640 to 1853 Japan was closed to all foreigners. Only a few Dutch merchants were allowed to trade in Nagasaki. The islands were administered during this period by the Tokugawa shoguns, whose line had been established early in the 17th century by Ieyasu, the third and last of the three military commanders. Their capital was at Edo, later renamed Tokyo. The system of government was feudal. The samurai formed an aristocracy which controlled most of the administration, the judiciary, and the learned professions. In the main cities, however, the merchant class grew in size and importance.

The deep peace and relative prosperity produced a cultural renaissance. Novels, puppet plays, and especially *haiku* poems (of 17 syllables) were widely popular. Woodblock prints were produced by many important artists and reached their peak with the landscapes of Hokusai (1760–1849) and Hiroshige (1797–1858). Eventually they were to influence Manet and the Impressionists.

The population of Japan was about 30 million early in the 19th century. Neo-Confucian academies diffused a high level of education, which spread widely, especially in the towns. Literacy became about as prevalent as in western Europe. Thus when Japan's long seclusion ended, as a result of the intervention of the US navy in 1853, she was better situated to compete with the West than any other non-European nation. It was felt that the

Tokugawa shogunate was not up to the task, and it was toppled by local uprisings in 1868. Instead, ultimate power was returned to the emperors, who had vegetated for close to a thousand years as mere figureheads in Kyoto.

Under the Meiji Emperor (1867–1912) there began the break-neck modernization of Japan. He transferred his seat to Edo, renamed Tokyo in 1868. The cherished feudal system was overthrown, the administration was centralized, and class qualifications for military or political office were abolished. Western models were copied unhesitatingly and efficiently. A general staff system was created for the newly modernized armed forces, modeled on that of Prussia. A large loan from Great Britain made the construction of a railway system and of telegraphic lines possible. Strategic industries were given priority, followed by export industries, in order to earn foreign currency. This was the heyday of Western imperialism, and Japan decided early not to be outdone in this field. As early as 1873 a scheme to invade Korea was considered. Korea was also the real issue in the Sino-Japanese war of 1894–5, in which Japan obtained Taiwan, and in the Russo-Japanese war of 1904–5, in which she acquired a protectorate over Korea (which was occupied outright in 1910). Japan also obtained Southern Sakhalin and concessions in Manchuria. The victory over giant Russia was a sensation, the first time that one of the great European powers had been defeated by an Asian nation in modern times. In World War I, Japan sided with the Allies and tried to obtain domination over China. Although she was not fully successful, she was rewarded with some of the German colonies in the Far East. Manchuria was occupied in 1931, China was attacked in 1937 and large parts of its area were captured. But not all of it. The war between both nations continued, to become part of World War II.

The political system was based on the rule of a small, self-perpetuating oligarchy in whose hands both the emperor and democratic institutions were but empty trappings. Even the militaristic extremists of the 1930s could not completely eradicate it. Basically this system has changed surprisingly little, in spite of the upheavals of World War II and the American occupation which followed it. It has had to adapt, however, outwardly. Japan practices democracy, but in reality the self-perpetuating oligarchy is still there, to be found in the upper reaches of the ruling Liberal Democratic party.

National priorities have changed. The disastrous outcome of World War II has ended, for the time being, all territorial overseas ambitions. The tremendous organizational abilities of the Japanese and their high work morale have been tethered to economic goals – again with spectacular success. Japan is now one of the three great economic centers of the world, on an equal footing with the much more populous United States and the European Union. Many industrial lines are dominated by Japan worldwide. Her banking system is the most powerful in the world, and she is producing more automobiles than the United States. But the 1990s have seen serious economic recession.

44   The Moghul Empire in India

After Timur's sack of Delhi in 1398 India was, for over a century, split up into numerous principalities, mostly Muslim in the north and west, and Hindu in the south and east. Ethnically the various princes were Afghans, Turcomans, Rajputs, Telugu, and early Maratha. The most important kingdom was Hindu Vijayanagar in the south, the capital of which matched Renaissance Rome in size and approached it in cultural activity. Most of the courts of the Muslim principalities in the north and center were influenced by Persian culture.

Babur, a descendant of Timur, but otherwise mainly of Turkish background, invaded India repeatedly, from 1517 onward, defeated the Afghan and Rajput armies which confronted him, captured Delhi, and established the Moghul Empire in northwestern India. He was a many-sided prince who laid out Persian gardens and wrote a highly readable book of memoirs.

His grandson Akbar (1556–1605) completed the conquest of northern and western India and organized the new empire. By giving the Rajputs employment in a senior capacity in both the army and the administration, the Hindu community came to accept the Moghul government as, in some sense, their own. This achievement was matched neither by the earlier Sultans of Delhi, nor by the later British rulers. Akbar created the imperial idea in India and forged an imperial service and a bureaucracy. He established a cult of the monarch, to present him as a semi-divine being, whom it was a sacrilege to oppose. The senior nobles were rotated in office so as to avoid the formation of hereditary feudal ties in the provinces.

Historians believe that the standard of living compared favorably with that of contemporary Europe. The main industry was cotton spinning and weaving. Spices were exported from the Malabar coast, indigo dyes from Gujarat. The trade balance with the Middle East and Europe appears to have been favorable. The number of inhabitants may have reached already a hundred million.

The government was conducted mostly in the Persian language, and indeed the Moghuls, in spite of their Turkish roots, spread mainly Persian culture in India. This is evident in the arts of the period, and especially in its paintings. Two styles evolved. One, Islamic and Persian in origin, was basically more naturalistic. The other, more traditionally Hindu, used a deliberate simplicity and flatness, with bright colors. The latter flourished also after the fall of the Moghul Empire at the Rajput courts of northern India.

Moghul architecture developed from an initially close reliance on Persian models, to an independent style of its own, represented in its full glory by the Taj Mahal in Agra (1630–48). In Moghul times evolved some of the modern Indian languages, such as Hindu, Benghali, and Marathi. The roots of the Sikh religion date from the 16th century.

Akbar's immediate heirs succeeded in supporting the delicate balance established by him. It was upset, however, by the last important Moghul ruler, Aurangzeb (1658–1707). He managed to extend his empire over nearly all of the Indian subcontinent (Vijayanagar in the south had been eliminated already in 1565). But this was no longer a balanced Muslim–Hindu edifice, and became totally Muslim instead. His was the Sunni Muslim creed, untouched by any Shia influence from Safawid Persia. Aurangzeb is nowadays highly regarded in Pakistan, while otherwise the Moghuls created the administrative basis both for British India and for present-day independent India.

After Aurangzeb's death the Moghul Empire declined. His Muslim extremism forged the equally extreme Hindu Maratha movement in response, which, for a short period, became the dominant actor on the Indian stage. Later in the 18th century the French, and especially the British, started to dominate the subcontinent.

45   The Safawid Empire in Persia

In the 850 years between the end of the Sassanian Empire, in the early 7th century, and the rise of the Safawids, late in the 15th, the existence of a national state embracing all of Iran was very much the exception and not the rule. Most of the time Persia was only part of huge Islamic or Mongol empires; in the late 9th and 10th centuries it was divided into many Islamic principalities. Only the Seljuk Empire of the 11th and early 12th centuries, and the Mongol principality of the Ilkhans of the later 13th and 14th centuries, were centered in Iran – but their ruling class was not Persian.

Seljuk Persia was an important center of a distinctive art – excelling in sacral and secular buildings, with large gateways, often decorated with colored tiles, in a flowery style of calligraphy (unlike the earlier square Kufic characters of Arabic writing), and in the earliest famous Persian carpets. Literature, too, flourished. Although the epic poems of Firdausi belong to an earlier period (10/11th century), Omar Khayam (11/12th century) was both a poet and a mathematician, who introduced an improved calendar. His four-line poems range from skepticism to mysticism. Sa'adi, in the 13th century, was the most important didactic poet of Persia and I cannot overcome the temptation to give an example of his work:

Straightforwardness becomes a man
  As snow becomes a mountain
Or as becomes the hush at dawn
  The music of a fountain.
No man has ever yet got lost
  Who in his heart would say:
'In God alone I put my trust –
  He maketh straight the way.'

In the 14th century, Hafis combined the study of the Koran with the writing of poems about the beauty of nature, and the pleasures of wine and homosexual love.

The inhabitants of Persia seem to have adhered only partly to the fundamentalist teachings of Shia Islam. A majority appear to have been Sunnites. From crusader history however, the Shia sect of Assassins (meaning "Hashish-takers") is well known; the sect was first formed in Persia, and was finally annihilated there by the Mongols. They used the murder of outstanding leaders as their main political tool. Their emissaries were promised eternal bliss in paradise, if, as was likely, they were caught and executed. This type of fanaticism has resurfaced in our own days in Khomeini's Iran and the Hezbollah movement in Lebanon, both, of course, again extreme Shia movements.

There are several sects in Shia Islam. The one which gained control of Persia under the Safawids was that of the Twelve Imams, with the last of them to be the expected Mahdi, or Messiah. In the 14th and 15th centuries this creed spread among the Turcomans of Iran and eastern Anatolia. The Safawids originally headed, from the early 14th century, a religious order in Azerbaijan. In the second half of the 15th century they organized their followers into a military force. When the coalition of Turcoman tribes, which controlled western Persia, collapsed at the end of the 15th century, the Safawids were ready and willing to fill the resulting vacuum.

Their youthful leader Ismail (1500–23) succeeded in re-establishing the unity of all of Persia, and converting nearly all of its inhabitants to his creed. The fanatical adherance to the "Twelver" Shia has ever since characterized Persians, and separated them from their Sunni neighbors. Thus they regained a sense of national identity, which they had lacked since Sassanian times.

Ismail became soon too successful for his own good. The rapid spread of his creed in Anatolia brought about the invasion of Persia by the Ottoman Sultan Selim I, who defeated Ismail in 1514, and would have conquered most of Persia if he had not been forced in 1516 to turn against the Mameluks instead. Persia was, however, very much weakened, and Ismail's heir was no real threat to the Ottomans in their heyday.

The real fusion between Turcoman tribesmen and Persian agri-culturalists was brought about by Abbas the Great (1587–1629), the most important of the Safawid rulers. The Ottoman Empire had by then passed its prime and he was able to regain parts of western Iran and eastern Iraq, previously lost. He reorganized his army and, with the help of two Englishmen, strengthened its artillery.

European merchants and Armenian artisans were induced to settle in Abbas's new capital of Isfahan. Silk manufacture was a royal monopoly and the export of silk was one of the main sources of income. The 16th century is the classical period of Persian carpets, which, too, were produced in state-run workshops. Their colorful richness and refined design have never been surpassed. Also the illumination of manuscripts (mostly of the Koran) and book-binding reached new peaks. The best known artist was Behzad. His pupils spread his methods throughout Persia and Central Asia. Isfahan served from the later 16th to the 18th century as the main center. Its fame rests even more securely on its Safawid architecture. There is nothing in Persia to compare with its palaces and mosques, with their wide-pointed gateways and richly colored faience tiles. The town planning of Isfahan, by Shah Abbas, was far in advance of its time.

The Safawid building style survived in Persia, Iraq, and Samarra until well into the 19th century. The dynasty itself did less well. Most of Shah Abbas's heirs were raised in the harem, and were not successful later as rulers. Their power started to decline in the later 17th century. The Shia religious leaders became their main opponents. The weakness of the last rulers brought about the increased power of the feudal princes in the provinces, while industry and trade decayed. Persia was overrun by Afghan tribesmen who captured and sacked Isfahan in 1722. The Safawid dynasty reached its end.

Persia was ruled from 1729 to 1747 by a military adventurer, Nadir Shah, who attacked Afghanistan and northwestern India. The expense of keeping his large army bankrupted Persia, and high taxes caused general unrest.

After his murder various groups fought for the primacy, until one of them, the Kajar dynasty (1796–1925), was victorious. The capital was moved to Teheran. The great days of the Safawids were, however, definitely over, and during much of the 19th and 20th centuries Persia was little more than a target for European cultural, economic, and political penetration. What ultimately ensured her survival as an independent state was the rivalry between Great Britain and Russia.

Of some relevance is perhaps the origin of the Baha'i religious movement. Its founder was put to death in 1850 and so were many of his followers in the years after. Some of those who survived were exiled and their leaders moved to Acre, and later to Haifa, in Palestine. Their great missionary success took place in the United States, where their Shia roots are usually played down.

In the economic field Iran became the first Muslim country to cash in on its oil riches. Oil was first struck in 1908. The British fleet, under Winston Churchill, converted in 1912 from coal to oil, and two years later England bought the majority of the shares of the Anglo-Persian Oil Company.

Colonel Rezah Khan Pahlavi tried between the two world wars to become the Persian Attaturk, but with limited success. In 1941 he was dethroned by Great Britain and Soviet Russia because of his pro-German leanings. His son, Mohammed Reza (1941–79), was ultimately no more successful. His Western reforms proved only skin deep. When the Ayatollah Khomeini displaced him in 1979 it turned out that the Safawid heritage of the "Twelver" Shia was still the most potent force in Iran. Under his tutelage it became more extreme and fanatical than ever before and evoked a widespread echo throughout the Islamic world.

46   The Ottoman Empire

After the battle of Manzikert (1071) Byzantine rule had collapsed in most of Anatolia and the country had been overrun by
Turcoman tribes. Most of the local, Greek-speaking, Christians
had adopted Islam, or had emigrated to those coastal areas which
were still controlled by Byzantium. Many Armenians moved from
eastern Anatolia to Cappadocia, in southeastern Anatolia, where
the principality they set up was called "Lesser Armenia." Over a
two-hundred-year period they co-operated with the Crusader principality of Antioch. Muslim Kurds moved into the areas vacated
by them. Seljuk princes were the overlords of newly Muslim
Anatolia. As the Seljuk central power in Baghdad and Isfahan
declined in the early 12th century, their Anatolian branch (the
"Seljuks of Rum") became independent, with its capital at Konya.
Their architecture is of enduring interest – monumental tombs;
mosques with elaborate doorways; calligraphic decorations and
tile-faced minarets; fortress-like caravanserais and massive castles;
religious school-buildings with innovative cupolas; fine faience
and mosaics, and early carpets.

After the mid-13th century the Sultans of Konya came under
Mongol suzerainty and some of their outlying marches became
independent. As so often happens in history (Macedonia, Rome,
Prussia, Quin) the most outlying of them was to become powerful
and famous. It was far in the west, facing Constantinople itself.
It was founded by Turcoman chieftains, the second of whom,
Osman (1281–1326), gave his name to the later Ottoman state.
Its rulers dedicated themselves to fighting the Byzantine infidels,
and a fanatical Muslim spirit became typical of their principality.
They were joined by refugees from the Mongols, by displaced
countryfolk, by Turcoman tribesmen, and by fanatical holy men
and dervishes, attracted by the "Holy war" waged on its border.
Byzantine rule was pushed back to the sea. Brussa was captured
in 1326 and became the Ottoman capital. Its surviving mosques
form a connecting link between the architecture of Konya and that
of imperial Istanbul.

The ample manpower which was at the disposal of the Ottoman Sultans enabled them to venture further afield. In 1344 their soldiers crossed into Europe, first as Byzantine auxiliaries, but from 1355 onward, on their own. Bulgaria had just then been weakened by the rising power of Serbia, which was now defeated by the Turks. By the end of the 14th century Macedonia, Thrace, Bulgaria, and Serbia had mostly been incorporated into the Ottoman Empire. Edirne (Adrianopol) became their European capital. Constantinople was cut off from Europe, and the Byzantine Empire was reduced to a city-state. Other Byzantine enclaves survived until the second half of the 15th century in Trebizond and Mistra. Repeated European attempts to drive the Turks back were defeated by the superior manpower, organization, and fighting spirit of the Turkish levies.

Constantinople would have fallen earlier, but the Ottomans were repeatedly defeated, between 1386 and 1403, by the great Mongol warlord Timur. His ferocious cruelty cowed his more civilized opponents. The European powers failed to make use of their opportunity to eliminate the Turkish menace, and soon after Timur's death in 1405, the Ottoman forces resumed their advance. Because of the great number of Muslim refugees who had escaped before Timur to the Balkans, the Turkish potential there had actually increased. Throughout the 15th century the Turks battled Serbs, Greeks, Albanians, Hungarians, and various expeditions of "crusaders" from Central Europe, until by its end most of the Balkans were securely in their hands.

Their most famous feat of arms took place far to the rear of their advancing forces. Sultan Mehmet II (1451–81) had the rare good fortune to make his mistakes as a ruler and a general early in life, when his father tried twice to retire to a monastery, but had each time to resume control. By the time he died, Mehmet was ready and made his mark in history by laying siege to Constantinople (6 April–29 May 1453). The city, which previously had housed over a million inhabitants, had been reduced by that time to barely a tenth of that number. Large parts of it lay in ruins and some areas were again worked as agricultural land. There were not sufficient soldiers to man the many miles of walls which surrounded the city. The Turks constructed heavy siege canons to breach the walls and transported their ships overland into the city's famous harbor of the "Golden Horn." When they broke into the city its defenses collapsed and the last Byzantine Emperor perished. The year 1453 has been regarded therefore by many historians as the end of the Middle Ages and the beginning of the Modern Era. Others have preferred 1492, in which Columbus discovered America. No one year can, however, be singled out for what was a protracted process.

Constantinople was renamed Istanbul. Justinian's famed Hagia Sophia, and many other churches, were turned into mosques. Luckily, some of the beautiful mosaics were unintentionally saved for posterity by being covered by whitewash. The muezzin's call to prayer supplanted the tinkling of the small Byzantine church bells. The Ottoman Empire entered its great age. Conquests continued in Europe, eastern Anatolia, and around the Black Sea. The various Christian principalities of the Aegean were incorporated and so was Trebizond (1461).

The army was reorganized. The Janissary regiments were based on the forced recruitment of one child from each Christian family. The boys were brought up as strict Muslims, in a somewhat similar way to what had been the practice with the Mameluk slave-soldiers in early Islam. They were of Greek, Slav, Armenian, or Vlach origin and formed the Sultan's crack regiment of guards, and the nucleus of the Ottoman army. When stationed in the provinces they represented there the central authority of the Sultan.

The administration in Istanbul became more centralized and autocratic, but the provinces were partly divided into feudal fiefs, controlled by senior military commanders. Ottoman feudalism differed from its European counterpart by the fiefs being used mostly as a source of revenue, but not as a territorial base of personal power to be passed on to one's heirs. While the day-to-day control of Turkey's affairs was handled by the Grand Vizier, the Sultan ensured his ultimate authority by retaining direct control of the Janissaries, and a certain measure of direct control of financial matters and the judiciary. The latter was based on Koran law, and handled by Kadis and Muftis versed in religious matters. Christian and Jewish subjects were allowed recourse to their own religious courts.

The Ottoman Empire tried to put an end to the privileged position of Venice and Genoa in the economic life of the country. It abolished their previous immunity from taxes and customs and encouraged their Muslim, Greek, Armenian, and Jewish competitors. Their previous control of the Mediterranean was challenged by Greek sailors such as Barbarossa and Dragut, who embraced Islam, and captured in the 16th century some of the main ports of North Africa. Barbarossa served also as commander-in-chief of the Ottoman navy in its heyday.

The 15th and 16th centuries were a period of relative prosperity throughout the empire. Strong government, efficient administration, and safe roads facilitated the growth of local textile industries (cotton in western Anatolia, silk in Istanbul and Brussa, mohair in Ankara, carpets in eastern Anatolia) and of international trade. Annual caravans carrying spices and silk reached Brussa from Arabia and India, and the merchandise was distributed from there to the Balkans and beyond. European woolens were sold in Brussa, or transported onward to Syria and Persia.

In late Byzantine times Constantinople had been like a head without a body. Now, as Istanbul, it regained its previous importance as the main gateway between Europe and Asia, and the main link between the countries of the Black Sea and the Mediterranean. Its incomparable covered Grand Bazaar was established in 1455, the imperial palace, later named Topkapi, in 1464. It was beautified by countless mosques, many of which mirror the architectural concepts of the Hagia Sophia, built a millennium earlier. The greatest Turkish architect was Sinan (1497–1588) whose name has been connected with 477 buildings, which he is supposed to have erected or repaired. Even if this number is inflated, no other architect in history can make any similar claim. His Süleymaniye Mosque in Istanbul and Selimiye Mosque in Edirne belong to the most beautiful Muslim buildings anywhere. Some of his other mosques are richly decorated with the beautiful blue tiles, typical of Ottoman art at its best. To the modern viewer the early 17th century Sultan Ahmet's "Blue Mosque" might seem to be not only the biggest but also the most impressive.

Flourishing arts are not always compatible with warfare and conquest. And indeed in the early 16th century the Ottoman inclination for expansion seemed to have flagged. However, the Janissaries decided then to take a hand and forced the elevation of a war-like younger son, Selim I (1512–20), to the throne. In the eight short years of his reign he changed completely not only the extent but the very nature of the Ottoman Empire. From a state limited to Anatolia, the Balkans, and the Crimea, he transformed it by the conquest of western Persia, of Iraq, Syria, Palestine, and Egypt, and the conquest of the Mameluk state, into the largest and strongest empire of his day. He made possible, during the next reign, the further conquest of Hedjas and Yemen to the south, Hungary to the north, and North Africa to the west. The Ottoman Empire thus reached a size not seen around the Mediterranean since the time of the Roman Empire.

During the reign of Süleyman the Magnificent (1520–66) it seemed for a moment that it had no real rival. It looked as if Islam was to deliver a right hook into the heart of Christian Europe, where it had failed at Poitiers with its left hook in 732. It did not succeed, however, in 1529, in capturing Vienna, the eastern gate to Central Europe, and one of the capitals of the Habsburg Empire of Charles V. Emperor Charles V spent most of his time in the Netherlands, but his most important base was in Spain. From there he created a counterweight to the Ottoman Empire by the exploration, occupation, and settlement of great parts of Mexico, Peru, and the adjacent areas. Much of the great wealth coming from South America was channeled into the naval struggle against the Turks in the Mediterranean.

In 1522 Süleyman had captured the stronghold of the Knights of St. John on the island of Rhodes. The knights were removed by Charles V to the island of Malta. Süleyman's naval forces continued to be successful, and occupied one great port of North Africa after the other. The coasts of Spain and Italy were raided by Muslim corsairs. In 1535 the tide turned for the first time, and Charles V captured Tunis and destroyed Barbarossa's fleet. It turned again, however, when in 1541 he failed to capture Algiers and his fleet was destroyed by a winter storm. After this disaster he turned his back on the Mediterranean and devoted his time to the service of the Counter Reformation.

During the first twenty years of the 16th century the Portuguese ruled the Indian Ocean and routed its trade round the Cape of Good Hope. After that Ottoman sea power overcame their advantage, and most of the trade of the Far East returned to the Mediterranean. Thus Venice was never richer than in the 16th century, when it continued to transport most of the spices of Indonesia to the kitchens of Central Europe. The struggle for the Mediterranean entered a new phase in 1543, when Barbarossa burnt Reggio di Calabria, captured Nice, and wintered at Toulon. In 1551 Dragut captured Tripoli from the Knights of St. John. The tide turned again when the Ottoman fleet failed in 1565 in its attempt to capture Europe's southern bastion, the island of Malta. Its last great success was the capture of the island of Cyprus, held by the Venetians, in 1571. The Turkish advance was stopped the same year at the Battle of Lepanto. While they consolidated in the follwing years their possession of North Africa, by the end of the 16th century the struggle for the Mediterranean lost its substance because by 1600 Dutch and English ships entered the Indian Ocean and finally rerouted its trade round the Cape of Good Hope.

The Mediterranean trade had been the lifeblood not only of Venice and Genoa, but also of the Ottoman Empire. By the end of the 16th century we reach the great divide in Turkish history. What had been an aggressive great power turned all too quickly into what was called in the 19th century "The sick man on the Bosphorus." Efficient administration failed first in the distant provinces. Local kadis and governors began to line their own pockets, internal security broke down, highway robbery stopped the free movement of goods, local industry decayed, and high inflation was caused, surprisingly, by the import of great amounts of Spanish silver from America.

Süleyman the Magnificent was followed by a nearly uninterrupted line of weak sultans who no longer led their armies in the field and instead spent most of their reigns in the harem. The queen mother, the chief eunuch, and some favorite wives became the real powers behind the throne. The Janissaries became more and more involved in court intrigues, instead of in the defence of the realm.

There were some military successes: the Turks captured the

island of Crete (1669), they completed the conquest of Podolia (1676), and besieged Vienna for a second time (1683). But after their failure in Austria there was no stopping the rout: Austrian armies captured Hungary; in the 18th century Russians captured the northern coasts of the Black Sea, and menaced Istanbul itself throughout the 19th century; Greece, Serbia, Montenegro, Romania, and Bulgaria revolted in the 19th century and with some help from Christian Europe obtained their independence.

Local chieftains wrested some measure of freedom from the central government. Often they were defeated in the end, but not always. Egypt enjoyed a short period of independence already in the 1770s and finally became virtually self-ruling under Muhammad Ali in the early 19th century.

Sometimes European colonialism intervened: Algiers was captured by France between 1830 and 1842, Tunis in 1881, Egypt by Great Britain in 1882 (Cyprus had been ceded "voluntarily" four years earlier), Libya and the Dodecanese were taken by Italy on the eve of World War I.

It is surprising not that the Ottoman Empire eventually collapsed at the end of World War I, but that it survived for so long. This was due first of all to repeated strenuous efforts at reform. Such Grand Viziers as the Koprülis in the late 17th century tried but failed. Some measure of success was achieved by Sultan Selim III (1789–1807), who organized an army on European lines, and especially by Mehmet II (1808–39), who in 1826 annihilated the reactionary corps of Janissaries and initiated a period of reforms on European lines, which his sons continued to implement throughout most of the 19th century. The administration became more effective, security improved, and some outlying areas were reclaimed.

The survival of the empire was also due to Great Britain, which throughout the 19th century defended it against all comers – from Napoleon, to Muhammad Ali of Egypt (1840), and repeatedly against the Russians, who wanted to capture Istanbul and Jerusalem for religious reasons even more than for political ones.

The Sultan Abdul Hamid II (1876–1909) tried to strengthen the ties between Turks and Arabs by a deliberately Islamic religious policy. It was wrecked by the "Young Turks," who took over in

1908 and stressed instead Turkish nationalism. As a result also, Arab and Armenian nationalism were strengthened, and the last ties holding the old empire together, snapped. Their misguided alliance with Germany in World War I only accelerated the inevitable end. After the war Turkey was reconstituted by Mustafa Kemal Atatürk (1881–1938) as a much smaller, secular national state, with Ankara as its capital.

Unfortunately it is not the brilliant empire of the 15th and 16th centuries which has left much of a legacy (except in the fields of architecture and carpet manufacture), but the decrepit later empire. Many of the social, ethnic, and political problems of the present-day Balkans and Middle East can only be understood against the background of centuries of Turkish misrule.

Part XII

The Great Age of European Civilization

By the end of the crusades western Europe was still a less civilized area than, say, Byzantium, or parts of the world of Islam, or late Song China. Even Muslim Granada, on the very soil of Europe, seemed more advanced than its rude neighbors in Christian Spain.

From the 14th century onward a complete metamorphosis occurred. Europe started moving ahead in all fields, in art and literature, in science and industry, in the use of firearms, and the building of ocean-worthy ships. In the 12th and 13th centuries the might of Western Christianity could not make a real dent in the Muslim countries of the Middle East. In the early 16th century a handful of Spaniards sufficed, with their more advanced weapons and war craft, to bring down the empires of Peru and Mexico. By that time it was European ships which crossed the oceans. European art, which during much of the Middle Ages had been little more than a Byzantine province, suddenly leaped ahead, to produce Giotto, Leonardo, and Michelangelo. The Reformation brought diversity to religion and freed the minds of men from medieval shackles. Nation states made the medieval struggle between Emperor and Pope seem irrelevant. Science showed the existence of new worlds by the use of both the microscope and the telescope. Finally, the Industrial Revolution changed the whole fabric of society. Europe had moved ahead, leaving all the other civilizations far behind.

47   The Early National States

Western Civilization is basically different from all others because of its diversity. The great ages of Egypt or China are monolithic: One big empire represents its civilization. When there is a multiplicity of states in China, for instance, it signifies a period of weakness. Not so in Western Civilization. Many different national states are its mainstay and the very symbol of its strength. Thus the great age of Europe starts with the birth of the true national state, and of national consciousness.

Frenchmen started to become conscious of being French during the long and stable reign of the Capetian kings. When King Philip IV, the Fair (1285–1314) had the Order of Templars quashed and its wealth sequestered, there was no public outcry. When he collided with Pope Boniface VIII (1294–1303), the papacy which had just recently won its epic struggle with the German Emperors, proved weak when faced with a national state. Philip took his dispute to a General Council and had it supported by the whole body of his subjects. His agents held the Pope prisoner, and Boniface died a month later. The papacy soon came completely under French control, and even its seat was removed from Rome to Avignon (1308).

French nationalism was further strengthened by the outcome of the Hundred Years War (1338–1453) and Joan of Arc's heroic part in it. All of France was united under the French crown. On the other side of the channel, the very loss of the French territories and the renewed use of the English language by the court and nobility strengthened English feelings of nationalism, which reached full bloom under the Tudor kings (1485–1603). In the Iberian Peninsula the slow and bloody struggle to recapture the country from the Muslims brought forth a strong feeling of Spanish nationalism, which was further strengthened by Spain's pre-eminent role in European politics in the 16th century.

Nationalism continued to grow and become deeper and stronger in these western European countries, without having at first any great impact elsewhere in Europe. The exception was 15th century Bohemia, where the Hussite religious reformation and the constant wars with her German-speaking neighbors produced a short flowering of Czech nationalism, to be finally uprooted in 1619 by the Habsburg victory and occupation.

There were, of course, also very different developments, such as that of Switzerland, from the 13th century onward, where one state successfully encompassed different cultural strands, and people speaking four different languages.

By the 17th century, nationalistic tendencies were prevalent in the Scandinavian countries, where Swedish nationalism received a great boost by her rise to become a major power. Nationalistic feelings were also given expression by the revolt of the Netherlands and their rise to a position of power and cultural and economic bloom. Nationalism was "exported" to central and eastern Europe by the Napoleonic wars, as a result of the national resistance the French increasingly met.

The 19th century was a period of great nationalistic fervor in Europe, culminating in the unification of Italy and Germany. The countries of eastern Europe and of the Balkans all sought national independence. The collapse of the eastern empires – Austria, Russia, and Turkey – created in 1918 the new states of Czechoslovakia, Poland, Yugoslavia, Finland, and the Baltic states.

European imperialism in the 20th century brought with it the rise of nationalist resistance movements in most of her colonies. Nationalism ceased to be a European phenomenon and became a worldwide one. It has become the most potent political ideology of modern times.

48 The Renaissance

The Renaissance was one of the great moments of the human spirit, comparable perhaps only to Athens in the times of Pericles.

It was also the time when Europe moved ahead of all other contemporary civilizations.

As usual, its background was economic. The Italian trading cities, especially Venice and Genoa, had taken the lead in international trade since the crusades. After the fall of Acre in 1291, Venice received its share of the goods from the Spice Islands and the Far East through the ports of Egypt, while Genoa plied more the northern route, through the Black Sea ports. This trade was profitable also to other towns in Italy. The Medicis of Florence, for instance, were important bankers and textile merchants, with branches from London to Venice, who handled the papal finances and loaned great sums of money to other rulers. They did so well that they became the rulers of Florence. The court of Lorenzo the Magnificent (1469–92) was the most important center of the 15th century Renaissance. Nor were the Medicis alone. The German Fuggers had by the early 16th century an even bigger banking and trading business, centered in Augsburg. In 15th century France, Jacques Coeur (*c.* 1395–1456) developed a similar business empire. The new wealth created a new middle class, first in Italy, later beyond the Alps. New tastes, a desire for comfort and for the finer things of life, replaced simpler medieval standards. Town houses and country mansions were built, with glass windows, elaborate ceilings, paintings on the walls, or shelves with books, which from the middle 15th century were mass-produced by the new printing process. Furniture and clothing became more elaborate. Artists, architects, and highly-skilled craftsmen were needed and appreciated.

Italy became the school of Europe, just as Athens had been the school of Greece. She produced great poets and writers – such as Dante, Francesco Petrarch (1304–74), Giovanni Bocaccio (1313–75), and Ludovico Ariosto (1474–1533); great thinkers – such as Niccolò Machiavelli (1469–1527) and Pomponazzi (*On the Immortality of the Soul*); important composers – such as Giovanni Pierluigi da Palestrina (*c.* 1525–94) and Claudio Monteverdi (1567–1643); innovative architects – such as Filippo Brunelleschi (1377–1446), Donato Bramante (1444–1514), and Andrea Palladio (1508–80); some of the greatest sculptors of all times – such as Lorenzo Ghiberti (*c.* 1378–1455), Andrea

Verocchio (1435–88), Donatello and, of course, Michelangelo; and above all, an unequalled group of painters – such as Giotto, Masaccio, Perugino, Botticelli, Mantegna, Leonardo da Vinci, Raphael, Giorgione, and Titian. Leonardo and Michelangelo were true "Renaissance Men," proficient in many fields.

The Renaissance created a new self-reliance. Until the 15th century, Europe had been the docile pupil of Greece and Rome. Now its thinkers dared to strike out on their own.

Italy was similar to ancient Greece, in being divided into many small independent states. The courts of many of them accommodated gifted thinkers, writers, and artists. None more so than in 15th century Florence. But the court of the Popes in Rome outshone all the others in the last stage of the Renaissance. Here were created the most important masterpieces of Raphael and Michelangelo. Its only real rival in the 16th century was rich Venice, where a sophisticated culture and innovative art continued to flourish, even when they had been stifled in the rest of Italy.

These small states developed in their interrelations some of the conventions later used in most of the world, such as the inviolate status of diplomats. Some of the intrigues and infighting actually going on between them was less edifying, as described by Machiavelli in *The Prince*: the Borgia family (two 15th century popes and their progeny), with its wide use of assassination by knife and poison, demonstrated the extremes to which such conduct could lead.

But these small states were not allowed to continue their pampered existence uninterrupted. The French kingdom, under some of its Valois rulers, invaded Italy several times from 1494 onward. The most famous attempts were those of King Francis I (1515–47). In the end they all failed, and it was their opponents, the Habsburg rulers, based in Austria and Spain, who controlled Italy for the next 350 years. In the process the Italian Renaissance culture was destroyed (except in independent Venice), but its legacy influenced and enriched the intellectual and artistic life of central and western Europe. Sixteenth century architecture, from Seville to Poland, showed its influence. Painters such as Lucas Cranach, Albrecht Dürer, Albrecht Altdorfer, Hans Holbein, Jean Fouquet, François

Clouet, and Pieter Bruegel developed its traditions north of the Alps. But its most decisive influence was, perhaps, in the fields of thought and religion.

49   Reformation and Counter Reformation

Nothing characterizes medieval Europe so much as its uniform adherence to the Catholic Church. Yet this unity was perhaps not quite as monolithic as is generally assumed. Heresies flourished in some of the very regions marked by the speediest economic growth, such as northern Italy, the South of France, and the valleys of the Meuse and the Rhine. In 1209 a crusade had to be launched against the Cathars of Provence. The Franciscan and Dominican orders were established in 1209 and 1215 respectively, in order to channel religious enthusiasm into directions acceptable to the Church. John Wycliffe (1329–84) in England and John Huss (c. 1369–1415) in Bohemia, demanded a reformation of the Church and threatened secession. Great Church Councils assembled in 1409, 1414, and 1431 in order to reform the Church from within, but accomplished little.

Renaissance thinking greatly influenced religious attitudes. Piety continued, but now it was often "learned piety" in Petrarch's phrase. Theologians were much better educated, many knew Greek, and a few even knew Hebrew. They pondered the ethical teachings of the Bible and discussed freedom of will. Erasmus published a critical edition of the Greek New Testament. He and other Humanists raised the intellectual inquisitiveness of many members of the new middle classes.

Many found it difficult to relate the behavior of the hierarchy of the Catholic Church to the teachings of Christianity. The love of pomp of many popes, their intrigues, wars, and illegitimate progeny, the dissolute lifestyle of many members of the clergy, the public sale of indulgences, stood in too great a contrast to the assumption of papal infallibility and priestly authority.

As a result, when Martin Luther affixed his 95 theses against indulgences to the doors of a church in Wittenberg in 1517, he opened the floodgates of change. Luther and many of the "Reformers" did not aspire to reform, but to a complete change. He came to regard the Pope as Antichrist, and much of the Church and its teachings as lacking scriptural foundation. He wanted to restore Biblical Christianity. Until his death in 1546 he fought for his ideas in sermons and in tracts. He translated the Bible into German to make it accessible to all those able to read, thereby incidentally creating one common German language. His ideas found a wide following in all strata of society throughout Europe.

Others preached different solutions, such as Ulrich Zwingli (1484–1531) in Switzerland, John Calvin (1509–64) in Geneva, and the Anabaptists in Switzerland and Munster. Calvin, for instance, stressed predestination and the necessity of ecclesiastical discipline. The Anabaptists preached adult baptism and literal observance of the commandments, but were too extreme and anarchic in practice to be very effective in the long run. The main stream of the Reformation swept, however, through most countries of Europe and completely shattered within half a century the previous unity of Western Christianity.

Many of the German princes eventually embraced Protestantism. But Emperor Charles V proved in his later years a stout, though not always successful, champion of the established Church. In England, Henry VIII (1509–47) attacked Luther in print, but broke with Rome in order to marry Ann Boleyn. In France the strong Huguenot party was crushed in the St. Bartholomew's Day Massacre (1572). A Spanish attempt to return England to the Catholic fold by force failed, when the Armada went down to defeat (1588).

The Catholic Church attempted to reform itself from within. Many of the previous mispractices and complacency disappeared and were replaced by a harsh fighting spirit. Previous toleration was replaced by intolerance. The Church tried sometimes to move back to medieval models and discipline. It also made use of such new tools as the Jesuit Order (founded in 1540) and the inquisitional "Holy Office" in Rome. Pope Paul IV (1555–59) directed the efforts of the Counter Reformation with great energy. The central leadership of the Catholic Church gave it, once fully mobilized, a distinct edge over the diffuse forces of Reformation.

In the later part of the 16th century most traces of Protestantism were eradicated from Italy, Spain, and France. Early in the 17th century Austria and Bohemia were forced back into the Catholic fold by Emperor Ferdinand I (1612–37). His Czech campaign turned into the opening move of the Thirty Years War (1618–48). At first the Habsburg armies were successful, under such leaders as Graf von Tilly and the enigmatic Albrecht Wallenstein, but a complete defeat of the Protestant cause was avoided, at first by the intervention of a Swedish army under King Gustavus Adolph II (1611–32) and eventually by the entry of Catholic France into the war on the Protestant side, so as to avoid a Habsburg victory. In the course of the war Germany was devastated.

The outcome of this war was the present religious–geographical configuration, with most of Scandinavia, England, the Netherlands, central Germany and northern Switzerland in Protestant hands, surrounded west, south and east by a wide crescent of Catholic countries, reaching from Ireland, Spain, and France to Hungary and Poland.

By the middle of the 17th century the old issues had become irrelevant. National power politics were back in fashion. Catholic France under Cardinal Richelieu was successfully fighting equally Catholic Spain for the dominant position in Europe. The Austrian Habsburgs had to fight the Ottoman Turks. Prussia was trying to become the predominant power in Germany. Russia was steadily enlarging her territory.

Only in Great Britain the issue was not yet dead, and the last male Stuart king was expelled because he was too active a Catholic (1688). In Northern Ireland the struggle between Protestants and Catholics continues today, nearly 350 years after the Peace of Westphalia, which concluded the Thirty Years War.

50   The European Powers in the 17th and 18th Centuries

In the later Middle Ages Europe had lacked one dominant power. When Charles V (1519–55) united Austria, Spain, the Netherlands and great parts of Italy, he was once more emperor not only in name. He spent most of his resources in his early years in wars for the domination of the western Mediterranean and in his later years in wars against the German Protestants. As a result King Francis I of France (1515–47) could serve as his opponent on nearly equal terms. The religious wars in France later in the 16th century reduced her power, and Habsburg Spain continued to be the dominant European power until the middle of the 17th century. She was helped by the riches of her vast dominions in America, but saw their economic resources dissipated by the absence of a commercially active middle class in Spain, as a result of the expulsion of Jews and Moriscos. The Castillian system of taxation made the creation of a new middle class near-impossible, by freeing the aristocracy from taxes and pauperizing the lower classes. The expensive foreign policy of the Habsburg rulers, and especially of Phillip II (1555–98), with his wars against the Turkish infidel, the English Protestants, the uprising in the Netherlands and the help to the Catholics of France, overstrained Spain's financial resources and accelerated her decline.

Next it was the turn of France. Under the guidance of two cardinals, Richelieu (died in 1642) and Mazarin (died in 1661), the French kingdom was reorganized and strengthened. Spain was defeated decisively (at Rocroi, 1643) and lapsed into passivity. Along France's other frontiers the cardinals assiduously cultivated the particularism of the tiny and harmless states of Germany and Italy. France was thus left a sole colossus among pygmies. For 230 years she was most of the time the pre-eminent European power (1640–1870). Sometimes overambitious rulers, like Louis XIV or the two Napoleons, gambled away her natural advantages; and at other times weak rulers, like Louis XV and Louis Philippe, were not up to making full use of them. Most of the conflicts and wars of Europe during this long period hinged on French ambitions – just as those from 1864 onward hinged on German ones.

The wars between 1648 and 1789 were usually "civilized" ones, fought by small armies of mercenaries, with few battles and low casualties. It has been the advances in technology and the great enthusiasms – revolutionary, nationalistic, fascist, communist, democratic – since the French Revolution, which have made war so vast and frightening as to be unsupportable within a mature society.

In this chapter we are concerned with Louis XIV (1643–1715) and Louis XV (1715–74). Louis XIV's reign is the longest on record in Europe – 72 years; hence part of his enormous influence on the Europe of the 17th and 18th centuries. French became the new international language of Europe, supplanting Latin. Kings and princes everywhere tried to copy the court of Versailles. French literature, architecture, and art became the prototype of much of the European style. French thinkers and philosophers dominated the 18th century. Paris became the cultural capital of Europe, and, surprisingly, has usually continued as such, whatever the political fortunes of France.

During his long reign Louis XIV conducted several wars and expanded the frontiers of France westward (Franche Comté and Alsace), northward (Artois), and southward (Roussillon). With some slight changes (Nice, Savoy) these are still the borders of France today. When he tried in his later years to obtain for his grandson all of the Spanish Empire, England and the Austrian Habsburgs combined forces, and their two great generals, Marlborough and Prince Eugene of Savoy, defeated the French in battle after battle. France was badly shaken and weakened, and Austria got the Spanish Netherlands (present-day Belgium) and the dominant position in Italy. The Bourbons got Spain, but on condition that it would not be united with France.

Louis XIV had reduced the aristocracy to docile courtiers. His great-grandson, Louis XV, had thus little to worry about either at home or abroad, but his reign is a list of missed opportunities, bungled wars, and inattention to the serious business of ruling. This was a pity, as in the cultural sphere the 18th century was certainly a "French Century." No Continental power arose seriously to contest France's position, but little Prussia, under Frederick the Great, was able to defy her with impunity.

The most important defeat was inflicted on France by Great Britain, who captured her colonies in North America and India. Under the Tudors, England had become an important power. But her real interests were now the expansion of her overseas trade and her colonial empire. She was drawn into European continental struggles only when the balance of power was dangerously upset, as indeed it was under Philip II of Spain, Louis XIV and Napoleon of France, and Wilhelm II and Hitler of Germany. In each case her intervention proved decisive.

Other powers had appeared in central and eastern Europe. The Austrian Empire was created by the Habsburgs, who had been ruling in Vienna ever since 1278. Usually they were also emperors of Germany, but their real power stemmed more and more from the territories under their direct rule: Austria, Bohemia, Croatia, Hungary. Leopold I (1658–1705) organized them into a closely-knit state and recaptured most of Hungary from the Turks. Thus an empire was created which ultimately reached deep into Poland in the north, deep into the Balkans to the southeast, and also into northern Italy. After 1804 the Habsburgs were emperors of Austria and no longer of Germany. Around 1715 this empire had some 11 million inhabitants (as against 19 million in France, 9 million each in Spain and Great Britain, and 13 million in Russia).

Let us turn now to Prussia, or Brandenburg, which had been ruled since 1415 by the house of Hohenzollern. The "Great Elector" Frederick William I (1640–88) first established her as a power of the second rank, in wars with France, Sweden, and Poland. His son, Frederick I (1688–1713), obtained the royal title; his grandson Frederick William II (1713–40) assembled a strong army, but used it very little.

Frederick II, the Great (1740–86), captured Silesia from Austria and defended it in several wars. His greatest success was in the "Seven Years War" (1756–63), in which he took on all the greatest powers of Europe – France, Austria, Russia – and defeated them repeatedly. Later he participated in the partitions of Poland. The result of his interventions was Prussia, which became a major

European power and was poised to play, in the following century, the central part in the unification of Germany.

Sweden, the main power in Scandinavia, which also held Finland, Estonia, and Latvia, had become during the reign of Gustavus Adolph II (1611–32) also a European power. Gustavus defeated Denmark, Russia, and the Habsburg armies. Sweden obtained parts of northern Germany in the Westphalian Peace, dominated the Baltic Sea, and influenced events in Poland. In the "Northern War," Charles XII (1697–1718) defended these lands ferociously, invading Denmark, Norway, Poland, and Russia; but was defeated at Poltava (1709) by Peter the Great. Sweden's limited resources were not up to this imperial policy, and after Charles's death it was abandoned.

Since the 15th century Poland had controlled vast territories, but played usually a passive role in European conflicts. In the late 18th century it was divided three times (1772, 1793, 1795) between Russia, Austria, and Prussia, and disappeared from the map until 1918.

Around 1650 Europe had about 100 million inhabitants (at the same time India had some 130 million and China some 170 million). By 1815 Europe had doubled its population, to some 200 million, India had about the same number, and China about 320 million.

51   The Scientific Revolution

The Renaissance created an atmosphere in which men started to look around at natural phenomena and to ask questions. Church-inspired answers were no longer accepted.

Geography was the first field to be revolutionized. The Age of Discovery proved conclusively that the Earth is round, revealed the existence of the American continent and of the Pacific Ocean, and the outlines of Asia and Africa.

Astronomy came next. Copernicus first stated the heliocentric theory in 1543 (but Aristarchus of Samos had reached the same conclusion around 250 BC). Gallileo (1564–1642) constructed a telescope and proved Copernicus's contention by observing the phases of the planet Venus. He also developed a theory of mechanics. Kepler worked out the planetary orbits. The work of these scientists was promptly proscribed by the Catholic Church, but progress could no longer be stopped. Isaac Newton (1642–1727) worked out a general law of dynamics and explained gravitational pull. Laplace (1749–1829) predicted celestial events by mathematical deduction, and advanced a theory of how the planets had originated.

Medical science, too, moved ahead. William Harvey (1578–1657) discovered the circulation of blood. Anton van Leeuwenhoek (1632–1723) first used the microscope and discovered microbes and male spermatozoa. Louis Pasteur (1822–95) identified the microbes as one of the main carriers of illness.

In chemistry, Antoine Lavoisier (1743–94) discovered the nature of chemical combustion (and was guillotined by the French Revolution), Cavendish (1731–1810) explored the nature of gases. In physics, Volta (1745–1827) developed the first electrical devices, including the battery; Faraday (1791–1867) discovered the connection between magnetism and electricity; J. C. Maxwell (1831–79) laid the theoretical foundations for the development of electronics.

Charles Linné (1707–78) gave botany an organized system and described the sexuality of plants. Jean Lamarck (1744–1829) explained the development of species among animals. Charles Darwin (1809–82) widened this theory, to include the human race. Philosophers such as René Descartes (1596–1650), Gottfried Wilhelm Leibniz (1646–1716), and Immanuel Kant (1724–1804) formulated theories in the physical sciences. Since then science in all fields has developed further and further. Scientific thought has become the cornerstone of modern culture, and science has permeated all of our civilization.

Some of the earlier scientists had no affiliation to universities. But since the 19th century science has been mainly institutionalized. Such luminaries as Max Planck (1858–1947), Albert Einstein (1879–1955), and Ernest Rutherford (1871–1937) have been associated, as a matter of course, with a seat of higher learning.

In the 20th century universities have expanded enormously and most present-day scientists spend nearly their whole adult life in the academic world. A special lifestyle has evolved, with yearly migrations to meetings and congresses, with tenured positions as the goal, with sabbaticals and pressures to publish. But as the third millennium approaches, science is threatened by overspecialization – scientists who can only see the trees and not the forest.

52   The Industrial Revolution

The leisurely tenor of agricultural life started to speed up from the time of the Renaissance, as the result of increasing urbanization and trade. More goods were needed than could be produced by hand and by simple tools. Increasingly machines had to be invented and built to supply this need.

Already in the 13th century gunpowder had been introduced from China. Soon it revolutionized the conduct of war. A gun is first mentioned in 1327, in Florentine records. This was followed by innovations in shipbuilding, which opened the Atlantic Ocean to navigation. Printing with movable metal type was developed around 1450 by Johann Gutenberg in Mainz. The making of porcelain, so long a Chinese monopoly, was tried in 16th century Italy, but the real breakthrough came early in the 18th century in Meissen, Saxonia.

The Industrial Revolution took off in the 18th century, and that mainly in England, where conditions were particularly favorable. England possessed ample deposits of iron and coal, and her long coastline, never very far away from any inland site, ensured easy access and transport. Agriculture developed rapidly, by the introduction of enclosure, replacing the previous system of open fields. Crop rotation and improved stock breeding resulted. Incomes rose, cities grew, and so did the total population. Taxes were reasonable, and the government did not interfere excessively (as it did in most Continental countries). England was the largest free-trade area of Europe.

The breakthrough came in the textile industry. For thousands of years yarns had been spun and been used for weaving by simple manual devices. The great demand for cotton cloth changed all this within a relatively short period. In 1733 James Kay invented the flying shuttle for weaving; in 1769 Richard Arkwright produced the water-powered spinning frame; in 1770 James Hargreaves patented the spinning jenny; in 1785 Edmund Cartwright came out with the power loom. Thus the whole process of cloth production was mechanized and moved into factories.

It was helped by inventions in other fields. James Watt developed a steam engine, which first was used to power steam hammers, but when he converted its lateral motion to a circular one, it could be used to drive machines, such as looms or spinning frames. Textile factories could, as a result, move away from sources of water power, and relocate in towns.

James Watt later patented a locomotive, but only in 1829 did George Stephenson start to build workable steam locomotives. The first railway was opened between Manchester and Liverpool in 1830. Thus passengers and goods could be moved speedily from town to town.

Great Britain gained handsomely by the Industrial Revolution. By the middle of the 19th century her per capita national income was about twice that of France or Germany. It had also other ramifications: it is doubtful if England could have survived the Continental Blockade and the Napoleonic wars in general, unless she had already been a semi-industrialized nation, which France was not.

Important inventions were also made elsewhere. In 1793 the American Eli Whitney invented the cotton gin, bringing mechanization also to the earliest stage of cotton preparation, before spinning. In 1798 he built a factory for the mass-production of firearms. In 1811 the first rolling steel mill was opened in Pittsburgh. In 1869 the first transcontinental railway across the United States was completed.

Frenchmen, too, were active. Marcellin Berthelot developed chlorine for textile bleaching; Joseph-Marie Jacquard built the dobbies (named after him), for the weaving of complicated patterns; Louis Robert developed a process for making paper in continuous strips. But most of the energies of the French nation were spent in other directions during the Napoleonic period.

In Belgium industrialization proceeded quickly early in the 19th century, mainly in such heavy industries as iron, coal, and the construction of machines and weapons. The resulting wealth and self-confidence were one of the main reasons for Belgium's successful struggle for independence in 1830.

In Germany, northern Italy, Austria, and Sweden the Industrial Revolution hit its stride only later in the 19th century.

The Industrial Revolution has not reached its end. The inventions of the automobile, of the airplane, of the electrical bulb, of the radio, of television, of nuclear power, of the computer – are only different facets of the same process. It has revolutionized life more than any other event in ancient or modern history.

Its results in other fields have been staggering. The population of the world has multiplied. Cities have grown larger than ever before. About half the population of the world today lives in urban centers. The social structure has changed completely. New areas of occupation have opened up, while many old ones have disappeared. The economy of Planet Earth has been revolutionized. Modern capitalism, modern banking, have arrived. The standard of living has risen – but not for everybody and not everywhere. In some areas a process of proletarization of large segments of the population has taken place. New social and political theories have been formulated. New pressures on the individual have built up, undreamed of in the agricultural society of previous times. And, of course, weapons of war have become much more murderous. Pollution resulting directly or indirectly from industry threatens cities and countryside, and might soon endanger our very lives. New, industry-related maladies have appeared. But science has moved ahead too, to help overcome some of these, and other threats.

Part XIII

European Imperialism

European cultural, economic, and martial superiority, from the late 15th to the early 20th century, brought about a unique occurrence in the annals of mankind – the actual, physical conquest of most of the planet by one civilization, and the economic and cultural domination of the remainder. This was, of course, a gradual process, which reached its fullest extent only late in the 19th century.

It started in the 15th century, with the Portuguese, Spanish, and English voyages of discovery. At first it was a haphazard process, but the riches gathered by Portuguese naval dominance and trade in the east, and by the Spanish conquest of the Americas in the west, gave it a new and worldwide impetus. By 1600 Dutch, English, and French traders and freebooters had taken over from the Iberian powers the domination of the oceans, and during the 17th and 18th centuries they colonized North America, India, and much of Indonesia, and discovered Australia and much of the Pacific Ocean.

The Industrial Revolution gave a new impetus to European imperialism. Overseas countries were targeted as an enormous market for mass-produced manufactured goods. While the conquest of America by the Spanish had been to a certain degree an accident, the conquest of India, and later of Africa, and of parts of southeastern Asia, were often the outcome of a conscious act of creating captive markets for European manufactured goods. The later 19th century brought British and French interests into sharp conflict and introduced also such newly unified nations as Italy and Germany to the race for colonial possessions, which, as a result, grew even more hectic.

During these centuries, Europe spilled over, and some of her most daring, most avaricious, most cruel and most idealistic sons dispersed to the ends of the world in order to find adventure, to become rich and powerful, or to serve their God in the process of discovery, conquest, settlement, and administration of their new possessions. There seemed to be two sides to their endeavor.

On one hand, was the brilliant achievement of unifying all of the planet under one civilization; of bringing the accomplishments of their science, technology, culture, and administrative ability to areas which could not match them and stood in need of them; of settling vast tracts of nearly uninhabited land, like Australia and most of North and parts of South America; of creating a worldwide economy, with the specialized products of one civilization introduced to all the others; and of eradicating such old scourges of mankind as the plague and cholera by introducing modern medicine to their central seats, such as India.

On the other hand, in this process, a great part of the native population of the Americas was killed directly or indirectly already in the 16th century, and the same happened later also elsewhere, for instance in parts of Oceania, or on Tasmania; European diseases were introduced to foreign countries, and exotic ones were brought back to Europe; the scourge of the slave trade was imposed on black Africa; an inferiority complex was induced in many foreign civilizations, the consequences of which are particularly virulent in present-day Islamic society; the use of alcohol and of drugs such as opium was forced, for commercial reasons, on the Chinese and on American Indians; and nation was set against nation by colonial administrators working on the time-honored principle of "divide and conquer."

No other event in history seems to have turned mankind so upside-down as this European eruption and consequent century-long colonial rule and general Western preponderance. Even in China, which was never really conquered by Europe, such Western ideologies as the 19th century pseudo-Christian Tai Ping movement, or 20th century Communism, got a complete hold over its inhabitants; in India, even though English rule is long past, the English language still rules supreme; the Japanese were so good at imitating Western Civilization that first they outsoldiered the Europeans, and when this did not work, they outperformed everybody else in the economic field; Islamic society is mostly still deep in the throes of a fanatic xenophobic reaction to Western past superiority; African tribal society has been uprooted by European colonial rule to such an extent that the sub-Saharan part of the continent is today in a state of upheaval, trying to find its bearings.

Europe itself became at the end of this process so involved in colonial rivalries that this was one of the reasons for World War I, and consequently, for Europe's subsequent decline in global importance.

53   The Portuguese Empire

While the German and Italian colonial empires endured for only some tens of years, the Belgian one for less than a century, and many British colonies in Africa, Malaya, and elsewhere, too, had short histories, the Portuguese overseas empire lasted for more than 500 years – more than any other.

It was also launched earlier than any of the others, in 1415, with the conquest of the North African stronghold of Ceuta. It continued, earlier than any other, with the voyages of discovery around West Africa under Prince Henry the Navigator (died 1460), the discovery and settlement of the Azores, Madeira and the Cape Verde Islands, and the capture of Tangier in 1471, and reached its triumphant culmination when Diaz rounded the Cape of Good Hope in 1487, and Vasco da Gama reached India in 1498.

The early 16th century was the great period of the Portuguese empire. The naval domination of the Indian Ocean diverted the trade of the Far East and of Indonesian spice to Lisbon, by a route around Africa. Under such captains as Almeida and Albuquerque the Portuguese established naval bases and trading points in Goa

(India, 1510), Malacca (near Singapore, 1511), Ormuz (at the entrance to the Persian Gulf, 1515), and Diu (South India, 1515). In 1517–18 Ceylon was occupied and in 1528 the Molucca islands. The first European settlement in China was founded by them in Macao.

The reign of King Manuel I, "The Fortunate" (1495–1521) was later regarded as the great age of Portugal and her colonial enterprises. It was also celebrated in Luis de Camoes' (1524–80) "Lusidas," the great national poem of Portugal, describing Vasco da Gama's voyage to India.

The very outpouring of manpower to the colonies had, however, weakened Portugal. The number of its inhabitants was further reduced from about 2 million to 1 million, by a plague epidemic in 1521, and by the expulsion of the most productive part of the population, the Jews and Muslims.

Weakened Portugal could not retain its hold on the Indian Ocean, and Ottoman sea power achieved, from the 1520s onward, an equal, and sometimes more than equal status there, diverting much of its trade back to the Mediterranean. This was the reason for the Indian summer of Mediterranean greatness, in which participated both the Turkish Empire and its Catholic adversaries – Spain, Venice, Genoa, and Italy.

Portugal's rulers after Manuel were weaker, they became ever more influenced by the Jesuits and the Counter Reformation, and their policies were no longer in the best interest of her colonial empire. In a fatal crusade against Morocco the Portuguese king and his heir lost their lives and their country was taken over, two years later, by Spain (1580–1640). Her colonial empire was neglected and her trade in the Indian Ocean fell around 1600, becoming easy prey to English and Dutch traders. They achieved a decisive naval superiority, occupied most of the Portuguese strongpoints, and took over her trade.

This was not, however, the end of the Portuguese colonial empire – far from it. Let us look now at Portugal's main colonies – first those in America, and afterwards those in Africa.

Brazil was accorded to Portugal by the Treaty of Tordesillas (1494), before it had even been discovered. It was first reached in 1498, by Diarte Pacheco, and in 1500, by Pedro Alvares Cabral.

Initially it only served as a port of call on the way to India. Later its brazilwood was utilized. Its settlement began in 1532; Bahia was founded in 1549 and served as the capital until 1763. Rio de Janeiro was built in an enclave, which had been in French hands from 1555 to 1567.

The Indians were baptized, or killed, or driven out. They were found not to be ready and suitable for the hard work needed on the local sugarcane and cotton plantations and therefore black slaves, in great numbers, were imported from Africa.

When Portugal was taken over by Spain in 1580, the Treaty of Tordesillas became invalid, and Portuguese settlers expanded the borders of Brazil to the Andes in the west, way beyond the old frontier. All of the Amazon basin was occupied, though only sparsely settled. A great increase in immigration and settlement resulted from the 18th century discovery of gold and diamonds.

In the 17th century prolonged hostilities resulted from Dutch attempts to take over the north of Brazil. In the 18th century the Spanish fought the Portuguese for what is today Uruguay in the south. In 1807 Portugal herself was attacked by the French, during the Napoleonic wars. Although it was in the end successfully defended by Wellington, the court moved to Brazil (1808). Under direct government the huge country developed much quicker. When the king had to return in 1820 to Portugal, his son Pedro joined the revolutionary forces in Brazil and became emperor of the country. The ties to Portugal were thus cut in a quick and relatively easy way.

In Africa the Portuguese had first deeply influenced a kingdom near the Congo, which they had reached in 1483. Its king adopted Christianity and ruled from 1506 to 1543 as Don Alfonso I. Priests, artisans, and even printers were settled there, and the local nobles traveled to Portugal for their education. Even the court etiquette was modeled on that of Lisbon. But this interesting experiment was not seriously followed up – the slave trade proved much more profitable.

Areas of Portuguese influence developed originally along the coasts, in West Africa from Senegal to Sierra Leone; further southeast, on both sides of the Niger delta, and including the islands of Principe and São Tomé; south again, on both sides of the Congo; and along great stretches of the coast of East Africa, from Sofala in the south to Somaliland in the north.

When, later, other colonial powers arrived, Portugal held on only to her islands and Portuguese Guinea in the northwest, and concentrated on the development of Angola and Mozambique in the south. Luanda, the capital of Angola, was founded in 1576. The main interest there was in the thriving slave trade. Luanda was the greatest slave port in Africa. From 1580 to 1836 some three million slaves were exported from Angola alone, mostly to Brazil. As the slaves were led aboard ship, they were usually baptized wholesale. The principal trader was, by custom, the governor. Some Dutch observers of the 17th century claimed that the Portuguese slavers were more humane than others; nevertheless, some 20 to 30 percent of the slaves embarking in Angola usually perished during the voyage.

In Mozambique the trade in the Indian Ocean was at first the main item of economic interest; then there was also some mining of gold and silver at inland Manica. Both declined during the 17th century, and by the 18th century the slave trade had become the major local industry also in Mozambique. Until 1800 some 10 000 slaves were exported yearly, and some 15 000 afterwards. In the years 1840–50 their number even reached 25 000.

Reforms introduced by Pombal in Portugal in the third quarter of the 18th century were echoed also in the colonies; for example, Angola was properly organized and administered for the first time. The slave trade was officially prohibited in 1836, but this had no real effect in the colonies. It took much British pressure before it really disappeared, as late as the early 20th century.

When, by the second half of the 19th century, the partitioning of Africa went into high gear, Portugal stood in danger of being pushed out of Africa by stronger rivals. This is, indeed, what happened to some of her claims around the mouth of the River Congo. But further south, the great powers found it in the end convenient to enable Portugal to develop the interior of Angola and Mozambique, in order that they should not fall into the hands of more consequential rivals. For a moment it looked as though she would be allowed to link up her two colonies, but this would have stopped Great Britain from realizing her

Cairo to Cape axis, and it was eventually not allowed to happen.

It is questionable whether Angola and Mozambique were greater assets or greater liabilities to the mother country, which remained throughout one of the poorer countries of Europe. The Portuguese hung on to their colonies in the middle of the 20th century, even after the rest of Africa had been decolonized. In the meantime Portugal herself had, in 1910, become a republic, and in 1926 a dictatorship. Colonial disengagement did not sit well with the imperial mentality of Salazar's authoritarian regime (1932–68), but local uprisings in both Angola (from 1961 onward) and Mozambique (from 1964 onward) forced Portugal eventually out of Africa in 1975, to be replaced by quasi-communist regimes.

In Portugal itself the dictatorship was replaced by increasingly left-leaning regimes, but a Communist take-over was forstalled in 1975, and a sufficiently democratic government introduced to enable the country to join the EEC in January 1985.

54   The Spanish Empire

In the late 15th century the Spanish state was a new creation, brought about by the marriage (1469) of Queen Isabella of Castile (1474–1504) to King Ferdinand II of Aragon (1479–1516). Castile was basically a Continental country, the history of which was inextricably bound up with the Reconquista, the recapture of the Iberian Peninsula from the Muslims. Its last stage was the capture of Granada in 1492. Aragon, on the other hand, had an old tradition of Mediterranean trade and involvement, having ruled Sicily since 1282, Sardinia since 1324, and the Kingdom of Naples since 1442. Some Andalusian traders had competed with the Portuguese in the early ventures to West Africa. When Columbus discovered America, this was something of a lucky fluke, opening by pure chance a complete continent to nascent Spanish colonialism.

Its conquest is an amazing saga, achieved by a handful of tough Castilian soldiers, led by a few younger sons of the gentry. Hernán Cortés (1485–1547) overthrew the Aztec Empire of Mexico (1519–22) with the help of only 600 soldiers and 16 horses; Francisco Pizarro (1476–1541) annihilated the Inca Empire of Peru (1531–8) with only 180 men and 37 horses. Other hidalgos and their men completed the task elsewhere, from northern Mexico, to Chile in the south. Vasco Nunez de Balboa (1475–1519) was the first Spaniard to reach the Pacific, in 1513 – a further area for Spanish expansion, where the Philippine Islands were occupied from 1564 onward. An attempt to capture also the Molucca islands (held already by the Portuguese) failed.

Spain was ruled after 1516 by the Habsburgs. Charles V (1516–56), who was also German Emperor, ruled the Netherlands and parts of Italy, and had his brother deputize for him in Vienna. Never before had Spain been the center of so vast or complicated a system. Wars were conducted against the Turks in the Mediterranean, against the Pope in Rome, against the Protestants in Germany. There was great prestige in Spain's new imperial posture – but also great financial expense. Much of what happened in America after the conquest has to be understood against the constant need of the Habsburgs for great sums of money for their imperial policies.

The "Conquistadores" established new towns in America, divided parts of the country among themselves, and tried to enslave the Indians. The rights of the Indians were, however, defended by Spanish monks, who came out to America from 1523 onward, and were sometimes (for instance in Mexico) surprisingly successful in imposing a new pattern of civilization on the Indians. Las Casas and other clerics devoted their lives to the task of securing fair treatment for the Indians. Two royal decrees backed them up, and their endeavors were partly successful.

The Spanish crown was surprisingly efficient in eventually imposing its authority on the vast territories conquered, in avoiding the establishment there of large holdings of land by individuals, and also in making sure that there would develop no local hereditary feudal aristocracy. But the incomes from the silver mines and from the taxes imposed on the local plantations were essential in order to fill the Habsburg coffers, thus for both, the cheap labor needed had to be provided by the import of great numbers of black slaves from Africa. Their fate did not disturb the conscience of the Spanish leadership – the need for money was too acute.

Modern research assumes that the total population of the Americas must have counted tens of millions of Indians by 1500, a great percentage of whom died during the 16th century, partly as a result of the mistreatment by the colonizers, but mostly from such illnesses as influenza, tuberculosis, pneumonia, and smallpox, against which the Europeans had some immunity, but the Indians had very little. This meant a demographic catastrophe unequalled in human annals. Only a few million Indians were left by the end of the century.

As the conquerors were accompanied by only a few women, soon various racial mixtures developed, between whites and Indians ("mestizos"), and whites and blacks. The total number of inhabitants seems, after the first, enormous reduction of the number of Indians, barely to have increased in the first 130 years of colonial rule, but to have doubled in its final 175 years. While there was a huge preponderance of Indians until 1650, they became a minority of barely more than one-third of the total by the end of colonial rule; and by that time blacks, mestizos and mulattos were actually the majority.

The 16th and early 17th centuries represent the high-water mark of Spanish history. Spain was the dominant power of Europe, and her soldiers were often victorious in their wars. A feeling of euphoria accompanied the reign of the early Habsburgs. This is also the great age of Spain in architecture, art, and literature – the age of El Greco, Velázquez, Zurbarán, and Murillo among painters and of Lope de Vegas, Calderón, and Cervantes among writers. To walk through the halls of the Prado in Madrid is to enter a wonderland of art, which does not fall short of Florence or Rome. Cervantes' Don Quixote is a towering figure in the world of literary creations, unequalled elsewhere.

There were some conspicuous points of weakness in Spanish society. The country lacked, outside of towns like Barcelona, a real middle class. The expulsion of the Jews in 1492, and of the Moriscos in 1502 and 1570, deprived Spain of the very social strata she would have needed most. As a result the riches of the New World did not remain in Spain, but speedily moved

on to her economically higher developed neighbors. The same
Catholic extremism which was responsible for these expulsions
involved Spain later, in the time of Philip II (1556–98), in wars
with Protestant England, and caused (in 1566) the uprising of the
Netherlands. As a result the country was over-extended politically,
and lived economically beyond its means. In the 17th century the
caliber of its leaders was unimpressive, and finally Spain was
defeated by Richelieu's France and relegated to a secondary role
in Europe and the world. In the War of the Spanish Succession
(1702–13) she had become a mere plaything in the hands of
stronger and more vigorous powers. The outcome was Bourbon
rule in Spain (as questionable a blessing in Spain as later in France)
and the loss of her possessions in Italy and Belgium.

In the 19th century Spain's history was reduced to a comic opera
procession of incompetent kings, libidinous queens, rebellious
royal uncles, and military strongmen. Spain continued to rule her
colonies in America and the Philippines by a centralized system
from Madrid. No measure of local self-determination was granted.
The enormous area from southern Chile to northern Mexico was
governed uniformly, without local variations. The same laws and
the same administrative principles applied everywhere.

The increasing numbers of Creoles (locally-born whites) in
America brought about in the 18th century the growing aliena-
tion of the colonies from the motherland. The mainland colonies
became independent, after lengthy struggles, early in the 19th
century. And in 1898 Spain lost the Philippines and Puerto Rico to
the USA, and Cuba eventually became independent. Only Spanish
Morocco and Rio de Oro, in northwestern Africa, remained
Spanish until the second half of the 20th century.

55   The Netherlands and Their Empire

Since the 14th and 15th centuries the Low Countries had
formed an alternative center of economic prosperity and cultural achievement to Renaissance Italy. Flanders, Brabant, and
Holland belonged to the most urbanized and most advanced

regions of Europe. Their banking system and cloth manufacture were the most highly developed of the continent. Painters such as Jan van Eyck, Rogier van der Weyden, Pieter Brueghel, and Hieronymus Bosch rivaled the great names of Italy. During the 14th and 15th centuries these towns, provinces, and privileged groups were brought, step by step, under the unified rule of the Dukes of Burgundy. The Dutch language was spoken in most of the country, but French was the language of the Walloon south, and of the court. The Habsburgs were perhaps not great conquerors, but they were certainly the greatest inheritors of history. They inherited not only Spain, but also the Netherlands. Charles V conducted from there the affairs of his world-spanning empire. He organized the Low Countries into seventeen provinces and cut their old ties to the Holy German Empire, of which he served as Emperor. His intention was to form them into a strong, separate state, to serve also in future as the cornerstone of the Habsburg possessions.

This plan was thwarted by the penetration of the Reformation into this area, and especially into its northern part. Charles V and Philip II tried by every means to exterminate the new creed. And in this way the previous loyalty of the population was alienated. The nobility was also critical of Philip because he had removed the center of his government to Spain (1559). From 1566 onward there occurred widespread revolts against king and Church. The Duke of Alba was despatched from Spain to re-establish Habsburg rule, and did indeed succeed, albeit with ample use of force. William of Orange organized from abroad the nobility and bourgeoisie, and with the help of the "Seabeggars," his naval arm, gained a foothold in the country, from which in 1572 he occupied the provinces of Holland and Zeeland. By 1576 most of the country was in his hands. But the Catholic aristocracy of the south co-operated only half-heartedly, and Spain succeeded between 1579 and 1585 in weaning the Catholic south from the Protestant north. This split became, in the years after, irrevocable, and two separate states evolved – the "Spanish Netherlands" (later Belgium) in the south, and the Dutch Republic in the north. Spain tried, until an armistice was reached in 1609, and again throughout most of the Thirty Years

War, to revoke this outcome and reconquer the north, but the efforts were in vain.

While previously the south had been more advanced economically and culturally, throughout the 17th century it was the independent north which took the lead. In its great period it was anything but a unified state – it remained a loose confederation of provincial estates, each of which had a stadtholder of its own, who was, though, usually a prince of the House of Orange. Under this unlikely and unwieldy political structure, the most brilliant of national accomplishments in 17th century Europe was achieved. The Dutch Republic became the most advanced banking, trading, and industrial nation of the continent, and the richest as well.

When one asks nowadays where modern capitalism was born, one can claim that it arose in the Florence of the 15th century, or in the London of the 19th. But a very good case can also be made out for the traders and bankers of the Amsterdam of the 17th century.

The wealth was held no longer by a tiny group of aristocrats, but by a large bourgeoisie. Their taste can be admired in the pictures of the great artists of this period – Franz Hals, Rembrandt, Vermeer, and a host of others. The country's free atmosphere enabled such thinkers as Spinoza to work unimpeded.

As a result of their struggles with Spain, there originated the Dutch trading ventures, mostly to the Indian Ocean and Indonesia, but partly also to America. Since the middle of the 16th century ships from Antwerp had transported many of the eastern goods from Lisbon to the ports of northern Europe. During the Dutch wars with Spain much of the commercial organization of Antwerp was evacuated to Amsterdam. When Philip II closed the port of Lisbon to them (Portugal was then under Spanish rule) they developed their direct trade around the Cape of Good Hope, to the Indian Ocean. In 1596 their ships called for the first time on the main ports of Indonesia, and from then on this trade increased enormously. Spices – such as mace, nutmeg, and cloves – were the main cargo. The Dutch developed alliances with several of the local Muslim rulers, initially against the Portuguese, and defeated them in several naval encounters between 1597 and 1602. The various commercial groups handling these expeditions were amalgamated in 1602 to form the East India Company. The Portuguese were quickly eliminated and the main competitors thereafter were the British. By 1619 the British attempt to drive the Dutch from Indonesia had been defeated, and thereafter this area remained the mainstay of Dutch trade and colonialism, with its capital at Batavia (Jakarta).

This was not all, however. The Dutch drove the British out of Malaya (1623), held Taiwan from 1624 to 1662, and Ceylon from 1658 to 1795, established in 1641 a trading point near Nagasaki in Japan, and discovered Australia in 1605.

In the north of South America the first Dutch settlement dates back to 1580; later settlements were added in 1596 and 1626, and helped to create their colony of Surinam. During the 17th century large areas of northern Brazil were captured from the Portuguese, but later had to be evacuated. In 1634 the Dutch captured the island of Curaçao. Further north they explored the area of present-day New York (from 1609) and settled it in 1614, but lost it to the British in 1664.

While Europe was mired in the Thirty Years War, the United Provinces grew richer than ever by their trade with Southeast Asia. At home there were continuous struggles between the republican and the Orangist factions. When neighboring France, under Louis XIV, grew too strong at the end of the 17th century, and threatened the continued existence of the independent Netherlands, the Orangists obtained the upper hand, and were indeed successful in defending their country and in forming a coalition which eventually defeated France. But, with the beginning of the 18th century, the great era of Dutch history reached its end.

Because of its too narrowly monopolistic attitude, the East India Company became less successful by the end of the 18th century. In 1798 it was dissolved. During the Napoleonic wars the Netherlands were occupied by France, and their colonies by England. In 1814 the French withdrew from the Netherlands and in 1816 Indonesia was returned to them. During the 19th century Indonesia was extended to its present frontiers. The main center remained in Java, which the Dutch wisely developed as a source of valuable tropical products, rather than as a market for imported goods. Sugar cultivation and tea, tobacco and rubber production increased greatly. Later this policy was followed also in the other islands. The roots of the present-day rise of Indonesia to prosperity, as one of the Pacific Rim nations, go back to this late colonial period. By 1900 the Dutch colonial empire of Indonesia was, with 65 million inhabitants, the third largest in the world.

The Dutch never tried to assimilate Indonesia culturally (the way this was done in French colonies, for instance) and did not force Christianity upon her subjects. As a result Indonesia has remained a mainly Muslim country.

The Netherlands were occupied by Nazi Germany between 1940 and 1945, and Indonesia was occupied by the Japanese between 1942 and 1945. Dutch attempts to regain full control of their colony after the end of the war were not successful, and in December 1949 Indonesia became officially independent. With 200 million inhabitants, Indonesia is the fifth most populous nation on earth.

The Netherlands themselves had in 1897 five million inhabitants. Less than a century later this number had increased to 16 million, at which point they became (together with Bangladesh) the most densely populated major state in the world.

56   The French Empire

Some nations are lucky to have experienced one period of creativity and greatness, but the French have had several. There was the medieval France of the crusaders and troubadours, the France of the struggle against England and of Joan of Arc, and the Renaissance France of Francis I and of Rabelais.

There were also periods of decline and dissent among Frenchmen. One of them occurred in the later 16th century, when Protestant Huguenots were pitched against the Catholic majority. The Huguenots represented the commercial and seafaring part of the population, led by Admiral Coligny. If they had won, they might have turned France a century earlier towards sea trade and colonialism, and might later have won the race against English sea-power. But they were massacred on St. Bartholomew's day, 24 August 1572.

There had been some early colonial ventures to Canada, such as the foundation of Quebec in 1608 and the arrival in 1625 of the first Jesuit missionaries. Serious attempts at colonization started in the second half of the 17th century, another time of creativity – the period of Pierre Corneille, Jean Racine, and Jean-Baptiste Molière in French literature. The initiator of the colonial ventures was Colbert (1617–83), the superintendent of finance and minister of naval affairs of Louis XIV. His mercantile theories caused an active colonial policy in America, Asia, and the Pacific Ocean, supervised by the government.

In 1673 French explorers reached the Mississippi and followed it to the Gulf of Mexico in 1682. The French possessions in the interior of the American Continent were named after the king, Louisiana. By 1750 the French colonies reached from Labrador in the north to the Gulf of Mexico, and were secured by a chain of forts. They thus encircled, in a wide crescent, the English settlements along the coast. This looked impressive on maps in Paris, but in reality this enormous area was but thinly held, except for the province of Quebec. French woodsmen and Jesuit missionaries roamed the forests and tried to keep up friendly relations with the Indians. Animal pelts were the commercially most valuable products.

French freebooters settled several of the islands of the West Indies during the 17th century, which had been only weakly held by the Spanish. Tortuga was their first naval base. Later they moved to the larger Haiti, which has remained French-speaking. After 1680 they transferred some of their activities to the Pacific Ocean, and operated there mainly from the Galapagos Islands. During the 18th century their activity lessened. Now explorers were sent there by the French government. Bougainville crossed the Pacific Ocean in 1767–9, reaching Tahiti and the Solomon Islands. Other Frenchmen crossed in the opposite direction, from west to east. In the early 19th century they mapped the Melanesian Islands.

During the 17th century the French founded several naval stations along the western coast of Africa. In 1642–3 they occupied a base in the island of Madagascar, and used it afterwards as a starting point for their operations in India. Colbert founded in

1664 a French East India Company. In 1672 Pondicherry, near Madras, was occupied and subsequently served as their main station in the Indian sub-continent. Another fort was planted at the Ganges estuary. During the 18th century the French–English rivalry reached its peak both in India and in North America. In 1746 the French succeeded in capturing the English base in Madras. Afterwards, during the Seven Years War (1756–63), the French lost all their possessions to England, both in India and in North America. The reason was mainly the superiority of British naval power; in America there was also the much greater number of British settlers, and in India the ability of Robert Clive, the British commander.

France had to start in the 19th century nearly from scratch, in building a new colonial empire. While previously America had been the main area of colonial endeavor, in the 19th century Africa became the coveted prize, to be carved up by the great powers. France did very well for herself in this process, eventually capturing a larger slice of the Black Continent than any other power.

The French started early with a drive up the Senegal Valley, to control the gum trade; captured Algiers from 1830 onward; later created a base north of the Congo; and from these points of departure drove inward, capturing more of West Africa than all her rivals combined. But when she tried to drive also a west to east axis through Africa, she was stopped short at Fashoda (1898) in the Sudan by much superior forces under Kitchener, who led a British attempt to build a north to south axis through the continent. But this did not stop the French expansion. In 1881 Tunis was taken over, and between 1907 and 1911 Morocco was occupied.

Another center of French endeavor was Indochina, the occupation of which started in 1852 with the seizure of Saigon, and was completed, thirty years later, with that of Laos. At the other end of Asia, in its southwest, France received Syria and Lebanon as Mandated areas, after World War I.

The total size of the French Empire, between the world wars, was nearly 12 million square kilometers, 10 750 of which were in Africa. This fell short only of the British Empire and of Soviet Russia.

Originally the French administration tried to rule its colonies directly. Before 1870 it confiscated a large percentage of the land owned by Algerians, to make possible widespread French settlement there. Later, more sophisticated methods were preferred. In Morocco, Tunis, Anam, Cambodia, and other colonies, the old established dynasties were allowed to continue to rule – but under close French supervision.

France was more conscious than the other colonial powers of what she called her "civilizing mission," which meant mostly the introduction of the French language, the teaching of French history and literature to the upper classes, and the imposition of French ideas and institutions on native populations. The French purpose was to assimilate their possessions culturally.

As a result, when France had to withdraw, after World War II, from nearly all of her empire, the use of French continued to be widespread in many of her previous colonies. Among the dominant Maronite community of Lebanon, for instance, French was used as the first language well into the 1980s. In some of the African colonies remnants of French culture have perhaps been more prominent and more beneficent than the absence of such European vestiges proved to be in many of the non-French ex-colonies.

57   The British Empire – the Largest of Them All

The English had always been a seafaring nation. Alone among the non-Iberian nations of Europe they participated in the great early voyages of discovery. John Cabot reached Newfoundland in 1497 and New England in 1498. The Newfoundland fisheries were exploited in the 16th century.

Henry VIII (1509–47) founded the Royal Navy, with ships specially commissioned to fight, and specially built for service in the Atlantic Ocean. This gave England an advantage over her rivals, who, initially, either had no professional fighting navy, or had one of rowing galleys intended for service in the Mediterranean. This early advantage was never quite overcome by the other

European powers, and explains much of England's later success as an overseas trader and colonial power.

Under Elizabeth I (1588–1603) the energies of England, which in previous centuries had been turned, somewhat profitlessly, to conquests in France, found their true outlet, by turning away from Europe and towards the oceans and overseas trade. Threatened by the Catholic Spain of Philip II, England reacted by attacking Spanish harbors, shipping, and colonies – especially in America – under such captains as Hawkins and Drake. The latter also circumnavigated the world, and attacked the undefended Spanish ports along the western coast of South America (1577–80). Trade followed piracy and brought prosperity to England. The euphoria of the Elizabethan age cast its light also on the cultural scene, and ushered in her greatest period of literary creativity – the times of William Shakespeare (1564–1616), Ben Jonson (1572–1637), and Christopher Marlowe (1564–93).

Colonial ventures were the outcome of English naval superiority under the Tudors, but were actually carried out only from Stuart times onward. While the capture of bases in the West Indies had but few consequences, the planting of colonies along the shores of North America were of the utmost importance for the future. They became one of the most important parts of the British colonial empire, and later were the foundation stones of the United States of America.

In 1607 Jamestown in Virginia was founded; Plymouth Colony followed in 1620, set up by Separatists; in 1630 Massachusetts followed and drew a large number of Puritan settlers; in the 1630s Rhode Island and Connecticut were settled; and in 1633 the colonization of Maryland began. Thus the two main centers of English settlement – one in New England, of religious dissidents, and one in the south – were set up. In the middle, between them, Swedish and Dutch colonies were planted, but they were captured in 1664 by the British. In 1682 William Penn founded Pennsylvania, and in 1733 Georgia followed. Thus nearly all of the eastern coast of the future United States had been settled within little more than one century. Everywhere the settlers started their slow expansion westward.

While French colonization was mostly planned from Paris, the

English variety was largely a private affair, run by chartered companies, and propelled onward by private enterprise. This, and British seapower, were the reasons for its eventual success.

In 1600 the East India Company was founded in London. English traders entered the Indian Ocean about that time, but soon found the access to the lucrative spice trade with Indonesia barred by the Dutch. Therefore they turned to India and from 1611 onward, planted stations on its east coast. The main one, at Madras, was founded in 1641. The main interest was in saltpeter, pepper and other spices, which were not bulky, yet high priced enough to make their transport in the small ships of that era profitable. Bombay, on the west coast, was transferred to the Company in 1668, and soon became a large and important trading center, especially with the Moghul Empire. By the end of the 17th century Bombay and Madras were strongly fortified, and what had been a trading venture only, began to develop political aspects. Calcutta was established as a fortified station in 1698.

In the 18th century in India, like in America, the competition with France became dominant. Each country developed there ties to local rulers, raised local levies, and soon client-states and outright colonies were established. During the Seven Years War the French were decisively defeated and driven out of India. Subsequently, English rule spread over all of the sub-continent. Among all the numerous colonies acquired by Great Britain during the 18th and 19th centuries, India stood out as by far the most populous and important.

After the 1857 mutiny, the East India Company handed over the rule of India to a Viceroy, appointed by London. Some twenty years later the Queen of England became Empress of India. A separate administration and army were set up. New Delhi served as capital. Some of the maharajahs continued to rule their principalities, but under British supervision. The vast area from Baluchistan to Burma and from Kashmir to Ceylon was for the only time in history under one rule, though not one administration.

A further important region of British expansion was, in the 18th century, the Pacific. Captain Cook's wide-ranging discoveries (1768–79) opened this region up to trade and colonization. After he had ascertained much of the coastline of Australia, a first settlement (of convicts) was made at Sydney Cove in 1788. From there settlements spread out, at first mainly along the coastline. The raising of sheep for high quality wool promoted the utilization of much of the inland country. Several separate colonies were established, but these were eventually united under one government.

Some of the islands of the Pacific were settled or colonized from Australia. But most of the early settlers of New Zealand were carefully selected in England and brought out and settled in an organized way, from 1840 onward. In the second half of the 19th century there were several bloody conflicts with the local Maori population. But the Maoris were culturally advanced enough to later become a well integrated part of the community, while this has been very difficult for the aboriginal population of Australia. The inhabitants of Tasmania were completely wiped out.

In North America, French Quebec was captured during the Seven Years War and incorporated in the British Empire. French continued, however, to be spoken there. After the American Revolution, Canada became the main British colony in North America. It was opened up by British and other settlers until the population spread all the way to the Pacific Ocean. The closely settled regions were all in the south, near the US border, while the cold northern territories were barely touched.

Great Britain had learned from the American Revolution that some measure of self-rule had to be granted to colonies dominated by white settlers. This was tried out in 1867 by the establishment of the Dominion of Canada. Similarly, Australia formed a Dominion in 1900. In 1909 South Africa, where the original Cape Colony went back to 1806 and the Boer Transvaal and Orange Free State had been conquered only after a protracted and difficult war (1899–1902), was granted Dominion status too. All the Dominions (including New Zealand) reached complete independence, though the nominal position of the Crown was retained (except in South Africa).

After the elimination of the French competition during the Seven Years War, and again during the Napoleonic wars, England ruled the waves worldwide, and her seapower enabled her to establish colonies wherever she wanted to. The Industrial Revolution put at her disposal a sufficient quantity of products to sell on a worldwide basis, while other nations started to catch up only late in the 19th century. It was mainly the reluctance of successive governments in London which kept her from spreading her empire even faster and wider. In 1715 Gibraltar was occupied, in 1800 Malta, in 1806 Sierra Leone in Africa and some of the islands of the West Indies, in 1819 Singapore was founded, the Falkland Islands were occupied in 1833, Aden in 1839, and Hong Kong in 1841. But late in the 19th century England participated wholeheartedly in the carving up of Africa.

Such explorers as Mungo Park, who sailed the Niger in 1795–7, and 1806–7; David Livingstone, who traveled in Central Africa between 1853 and 1873; John Hanning Speke, who discovered the sources of the Nile (1858–64) – and many others – served as the spearhead of eventual colonization. The actual occupation followed. The Gold Coast (Ghana) became a colony in 1874; Egypt was occupied in 1882; most of the other colonies were established between 1886 and 1892. In 1898 Horatio Herbert Kitchener captured the Sudan and eliminated the French attempt to prevent the establishment of a British Cairo-to-Cape axis. After World War I most of the previously German colonies were added, which made this axis a reality, and Palestine, Transjordan, and Iraq (previously Turkish provinces) were then included in the British Empire.

The British Empire had thus become by far the biggest in the history of mankind. Between the world wars its spread was nearly 40 million square kilometers (double that of the runner up, Soviet Russia), and the number of its inhabitants was some 500 million (10 percent more than those of China, the second most populous state). Over a quarter of the dry land of the globe was held by Britain, and nearly a quarter of the Earth's population.

During the later years of the Empire, opposition to colonial rule was widespread, and Great Britain was forced out of nearly every one of her previous colonies. Was this justified? The record of Africa after the end of colonialism indicates that in some countries, especially sub-Saharan ones, it might well have been better if colonial rule had been terminated later. In one case, that of Hong Kong, Great Britain might have found it profitable to terminate the colonial status earlier, before it bankrupted the cotton industry of Lancashire in the 1950s.

In one sphere British government proved very successful – that of running an efficient administration, with a minimum of expense. In nearly every ex-colony the quality of the administration has gone down, in many cases catastrophically so. In the political sphere, colonial administration was less successful. In order to rule, without undue expense, in many colonies the old principle of "divide and rule" was employed. Usually not officially, but in an underhand way, more by intelligence officers than by administrators. The outcome has in some cases been tragic. Let us mention only three examples: the use of the Muslim minority in India to fight the Hindu majority in a vain attempt to keep India British; the setting of Arab against Jew in Palestine; and the use of the tiny Turkish minority in Cyprus to fight the preference of the Greek majority for Enosis (unification with Greece). The resulting tragedies are still with us today.

What was the influence of the enormous empire she had created on Great Britain herself? As a result of her worldwide trade, and of the Industrial Revolution, she had become by the 19th century a very prosperous country indeed, with her wealth spread around a relatively numerous middle class. Many members of this class could find employment in the administration of the colonies, with a high standard of living, and an impressive position. The colonies were captive markets for her exports. The center of worldwide banking was in London's City.

Surprisingly, at the same time as so much energy was poured into the creation and upkeep of the Empire, in Great Britain itself a no less relevant development was taking place: the creation of democratic institutions, and of popular representation. Just as the British Empire had been created not by design but by accident, the same is true in this field. The personal limitations of the Stuart kings of the 17th century caused the initial strengthening of Parliament against the Crown. The foreignness of the early Hanoverians in the 18th century brought about the development of governments headed by such strong prime ministers as Sir Robert Walpole (1676–1745) and Pitt the Elder

(1708–78), ultimately dependent more on a majority in the House of Commons than on royal approval. The attempt of George III (1738–1820) to reverse this trend failed as a result of his failure in America. The House of Commons, though, was often not truly representative, as small groups of aristocrats could manipulate it with the help of the "rotten boroughs" controlled by them. It was, however, reorganized, and these boroughs eliminated, by the Reform Bill of 1832. From now on the two parties, renamed Liberals and Conservatives, competed for the vote of the middle class. The result was a strong and stable system of government, at a time when most European countries were trying, with the help of recurring revolutions and crises, to find a suitable solution. The British parliamentary system became in the later 19th century the model for the liberals in the rest of Europe. Such strong prime ministers as Sir Robert Peel, Henry John Temple Palmerston, Benjamin Disraeli, and William Gladstone showed that a government based on the parliamentary system could act no less decisively than kings. The system itself was adapted to changing social reality by widening the franchise, to include, first, the working classes (1867, 1884), and later, after long and bitter agitation, also women (1918, 1928).

Another facet of Great Britain at the height of its power was the flowering of literature. While in other countries – such as Napoleonic France, or Bismarck's and Hitler's Germany – periods of great power usually meant a silencing of the literary muse, this was certainly not the case in England between the 18th and 20th centuries. Such names as Daniel Defoe, Jonathan Swift, Alexander Pope, Samuel Johnson, James Boswell, Robert Burns, William Blake, Lord Byron, Percy Bysshe Shelley, John Keats, Jane Austen, Charles Dickens, William Makepeace Thackeray, Alfred Tennyson, the Brontë sisters, George Eliot, Thomas Hardy, A. E. Housman, Arnold Bennett, D. H. Lawrence, Bernard Shaw, T. S. Eliot, Virginia Woolf, William Butler Yeats, are the prime examples of the amazing scope and quality of the literary creation of that period.

This literary outpouring had its effect also on the development of English into the main international language. In the 20th century, English is not only spoken in America, Canada, Great

Britain, Ireland, Australia, New Zealand, and South Africa, but it has remained the language of government even in India and is the universal second language worldwide. It is also the language of technology, of international congresses (except for those held in Paris), and of air traffic control, to name but a few aspects of its dominant position.

To sum up: The outstanding success of Great Britain in so many different fields, at more or less the same time – in initiating the Industrial Revolution, creating the modern parliamentary system, sustaining a long period of outstanding literary creativity, and putting together the biggest empire ever – is an amazing and otherwise unequalled performance by a single nation, in the annals of mankind.

58   The Russian Empire

Russia has been something of a stepchild of European Civilization. Many historians regard her as an outsider, not belonging to Western Civilization at all, and that because of her roots in the Byzantine and Greek Orthodox past, and because of later Mongolian and Turkish influences, which may indeed have inclined her towards autocratic rule and widespread serfdom. In her struggles, from the late Middle Ages onward, against Catholic Poland, she represented the alien east.

Her beginnings were modest. The early principality of Kiev was destroyed by the Mongol invasion of the early 13th century. The principality of Muscovy emerged in the later part of that century into the light of history, but was still a dependency of the Mongol successor state. In 1326 the Metropolitan of the Church moved to Muscovy, giving it a special status. In the 16th century its Great Dukes took the title of Tsar, or Emperor. At the time of Ivan the Terrible (1533–84) its territorial expansion started to justify the new title. Ivan defeated the Tartars and tried in vain to reach the Baltic Sea. But he ruled already over most of the territory of European Russia, from the White Sea to the Caspian, though not over White Russia and most of the Ukraine.

Not long before Ivan's death the decisive step in the creation of the Russian Empire was taken. He had granted lands on his eastern borders to a merchant family, named Stroganov, which became the nucleus of a private commercial empire. Russian settlers penetrated Siberia on their behalf, in order to collect furs, work salt mines and extract iron deposits. Their further way was barred by the Tartar Khanate of Sibir, one of the successor states of Genghis Khan's Mongol Empire. In 1582 a force of 800 Cossacks, under Yermak, opened up Siberia by defeating the Tartars, greatly helped by their firearms. Yermak's feat can be compared to those of Cortés or Pizarro in America, and had even greater results as measured by the size of the territory conquered. All of Siberia fell to Russia. It was slowly settled throughout the 17th to the 19th centuries. Tobolsk was founded in 1587, Tomsk in 1604, Krasnoyarsk in 1628, Irkutsk on Lake Bajkal in 1652, but Vladivostok in the Far East only in 1860. Western Siberia was administered from Tobolsk, eastern Siberia from Irkutsk.

Deshniev sailed around the eastern tip of Siberia in 1648. The Danish explorer Vitus Jonassen Bering headed an expedition in 1740 which mapped the sea, now named after him, and the shores of southern Alaska. Alaska itself was settled by the Russians in the 19th century, but was sold to the United States in 1867 for 7 200 000 dollars.

Siberia remained for a long time a region of little interest to the central Russian administration, used for deporting criminals, and later political dissidents.

Russia was forced into closer contact with Europe by two rulers, Peter the Great (1682–1725) and Catherine the Great (1762–96). Their reigns are the watershed between old Muscovy and imperial Russia. Peter defeated Sweden and captured an outlet to the Baltic Sea and the West. There he built his new capital, St. Petersburg (later Leningrad), facing toward Europe. Catherine defeated the Turks, captured most of the Ukraine and White Russia, and participated in the partition of Poland. Russia reached suddenly deep into Europe, and has remained one of Europe's great powers ever since. The armies of Tsar Alexander I even reached Paris in 1814.

Some members of the Russian aristocracy shared the interest of the great tsars in European civilization, studied French, traveled to western Europe and acquired Western tastes. But most of the population was barely touched by these influences. The first printing press set up in Moscow was destroyed by the local mob. Interest in literature remained limited to the upper classes. In spite of this, Russian literature has achieved much since the early 19th century. The poems of Aleksandr Pushkin (1799–1837) and Mikhail Lermontov (1814–41), the social satire of Nikolay Gogol (1809–52), the novels of Ivan Sergeyevich Turgenev (1818–83), Fyodor Mikhaylovich Dostoyevski (1821–81), and Count Lev Nikolayevich Tolstoy (1828–1910), and the short stories of Anton Pavlovich Chekhov (1861–1904), belong to the greatest accomplishments of European letters. In the field of music Russia has produced such great composers as Pyotr Ilich Tchaikovsky (1840–93), Modest Petrovich Mussorgsky (1839–81), Nikolay Andreyevich Rimsky-Korsakov (1844–1908), Sergey Sergeyvich Prokofiev (1891–1953), and Dmitry Shostakovich (1906–75).

These achievements are the more remarkable as they were accomplished against the background of a backward country, where serfdom was abolished only from 1861 onward. The absence of a wide middle class, the poor state of schools and education, the low yield of agriculture, the sloth of workers, the widespread addiction to vodka, proved nearly insurmountable obstacles to social and economic progress.

Russia succeeded in the 19th century in expanding the frontiers of her empire even further. Georgia was occupied in 1801; Finland in 1809; Bessarabia in 1812; Azerbaijan was acquired in 1813 from Persia; central Poland was taken in 1814; Muslim Central Asia was conquered between 1868 and 1881; and in 1860 China surrendered the entire lower course of the Amur; and Japan the island of Sakhalin in 1875. No similar single landmass of anything like that size under a single regime existed anywhere else. Great Britain regarded Russia as the main threat to her Indian Empire and supported repeatedly the ailing Turkish Empire against her. Russian hopes of realizing far-reaching pan-slavistic dreams, and of conquering Constantinople and Jerusalem, of taking over the Balkans, Anatolia and Persia, all foundered on British opposition.

The weak social fabric of Russia undercut her imperial ambitions. She was defeated in the Crimean War by England and France (1853–6) and by Japan in 1904–5. The new intelligentsia became increasingly radical and turned against the autocratic rule of the Tsar. The 1905 uprising and Russian defeats in World War I prepared the way for the Russian Revolution.

The Russian Empire was, however, weakened only temporarily by the outcome of the war and the Revolution. Under Stalin all the old European and pan-slavistic ambitions of the czars were realized after World War II. The states of eastern Europe and the Balkans became satellites, under close Soviet control. The more surprising has been the complete collapse of the Soviet Empire since 1989.

Part XIV

The Great Revolutions

The tectonic plates underlying the surface of the Earth cause in their slow movement from time to time, great earthquakes and volcanic eruptions. The same can be said of the history of mankind. New developments, such as the Industrial Revolution, or the Age of Enlightenment, necessitate adjustments, which, from time to time, turn out to be violent.

The immediate causes of revolutions are often similar: a weak or unwise ruler, such as Charles I, or James II, or George III of England; Louis XVI, or Charles X, or Louis Philippe of France; or Nicholas II of Russia – in a place and at a time which necessitate a strong and wise one.

The outcomes can differ widely: the setting up of a new state, like the United States of America; or the setting up of a personal dictatorship, like that of Cromwell in England or that of Napoleon in France; or the setting up of the dictatorship of an ideology, like that of Marxism in Russia.

The final result is rarely final – the dictatorship of neither Cromwell nor Napoleon, nor of Communism in Russia, lasted very long – though the latter certainly outlasted the former.

All revolutions have one characteristic in common – they are all chaotic, unexpected, and highly wasteful of human life. They are interesting to read about and difficult to live through.

59   The English Revolution

The habit of obedience to the crown had been inherited from the Tudor age. So what went wrong so soon after, under the Stuarts? As usual in English history there are few grand causes, and the reasons for the outbreak have to be understood from the accidents of events and personalities. The outcome was to be the more clear-cut and momentous.

The basic reasons were twofold – religious in Scotland and social in England. James I (1603–25) inherited both crowns and both problems. In Scotland the newly-established Presbyterian Church wished to control the state. In England the gentry was increasingly well educated and regarded a strong Parliament as an outlet for their talents. Both problems need not have led to a revolution, but their mishandling by James and especially by his son Charles I (1625–49) had this effect, which had initially not been desired by anybody.

James I regarded the conduct of foreign policy as his prerogative, but the money needed for it had to be voted by the House of Commons. As Parliament was not co-operative the king raised money by various expedients, which were criticized by the public, but were not critical during his peaceful reign. Charles I was more venturesome, but not very successful. He needed larger sums of money for his unlucky wars with Spain and France, and Parliament, led by such men as Edward Coke, John Eliot, John Hampden, and John Pynn, became ever more unco-operative. In the 1628 Petition of Right it was declared illegal to collect money without parliamentary consent. Charles dissolved Parliament and tried to rule for eleven years without it, but found himself ever more on a collision course with the gentry and the merchant class. His advisors, first Buckingham and later Strafford, on the secular side, and on the Church side Archbishop Laud (who initiated what later was called the High Church tradition), were thoroughly despised and hated by ever-wider sections of the populace.

On Laud's advice the Anglican prayerbook was imposed on Presbyterian Scotland. Scotland revolted. The king needed money so badly that he had to reconvene Parliament in 1640. Its members first turned on Strafford, who was declared guilty of treason and executed in 1641. The House of Commons declared that it could not be dissolved without its own consent, and declared the various royal expedients for raising money to be illegal. Charles I tried in 1642 to arrest five leaders in the House of Commons, failed, and the Civil War broke out. Most of the nobility, the army and the rural districts of the north and west, supported the king, while the wealthier south and east supported the Parliament.

At first the king's more experienced armed forces had the upper hand, but in Oliver Cromwell his opponents found a gifted commander, who organized the "New Model Army" and soundly defeated the royalists. The religious enthusiasts, such as the Puritans, who made up most of the army's manpower and high command, gave it its high fighting morale.

Charles escaped to the Scots, who, in their turn, were defeated by Cromwell. Charles was convicted of high treason, and executed on 30 January 1649 – the first in the line of royal personages to pay the ultimate price in the great revolutions of Europe.

Parliament soon found that it had exchanged an ineffectual ruler against a much stronger and more formidable one. It was closed down by force by Cromwell (1653), who proceeded to rule as Lord Protector, thus avoiding the pitfalls of a return to the trappings of royalty, which proved later so detrimental to the good name of Napoleon in a similar situation.

Cromwell was highly successful in the fields of foreign policy and of war. He suppressed the resistance of Ireland and of Scotland, defeated Spain (gaining the Island of Jamaica), and fought successfully against the Netherlands. He tried to impose his vision of a Godly Commonwealth on England – with mixed results. Puritans were to remember this time with satisfaction for a century and a half, and to celebrate it in such works of literature as John Bunyan's *Pilgrim's Progress* and John Milton's *Paradise Lost*. But ordinary men were increasingly disillusioned with his Puritanism, militarism, imperialism, and heavy taxation. After his death in 1658 his regime collapsed, and in 1660 Charles II was recalled from exile.

Charles II proved to be the one exception among male Stuarts;

he was an able ruler, popular, and his colonial policy was successful. The great problem was the Catholic persuasion of his brother
and heir, James. Over the question of whether to exclude him from
the throne, opinion was divided, resulting in the formation of the
two great parties of the later British parliamentary system – Tories
and Whigs (redefined as Conservatives and Liberals in the 19th
century).

The Tories won, James II ascended the throne (1685) and
quickly threw away his and his house's chances by resolutely
trying to impose Catholicism on England. The Tories joined
the Whigs in inviting William of Orange, the stadtholder of the
Netherlands (and husband of a Stuart princess), to take over the
crown of England. James II had to leave the country (but fought
on, unsuccessfully, in Catholic Ireland).

The "Glorious Revolution" of 1689 signifies the successful
completion of the English experiment in revolution. It was that
rarity, a revolution which ended in compromise, and, as a result, a
successful revolution. England remained Protestant and Dissenters
could practice their religion openly. Parliament had gained much,
but not everything. The crown was retained, but it was now generally agreed that its power was no longer absolute. A nascent party
system had been born, which, from the 18th century onward,
became the main foundation of parliamentary government. The
Habeas Corpus Act guaranteed the liberty of individual subjects.
Soon after, the Bank of England was founded, and England and
Scotland were merged in 1707 into the United Kingdom of Great
Britain.

If in the 17th century England had been an example of revolution and violence, it became in the 18th one of stable government
and of liberty, an example to be admired and imitated.

60   The Enlightenment

The fires of the Counter Reformation had burned themselves out
by the end of the 17th century. The 18th century turned its back
on matters of religion and tried to cope with more mundane

affairs. Much of Europe was still bound by medieval shackles, which to widening circles looked like an anachronism. The high aristocracy of France had been drawn by Louis XIV to the royal court, and had ceased to run the army and the administration. The bourgeoisie moved into the vacuum left by the aristocracy, but felt insufficiently appreciated and rewarded. The artisan class was hemmed in by remains of medieval guilds, and farmers were often only nominally better off than serfs. Much of the tax load was shouldered by the lower, weaker classes, while the nobles were mostly exempt, without, however, contributing any longer any real service to society.

Such a situation had to give rise to thought and cause criticism in the relatively well educated, rationally thinking, western Europe of the 18th century. Public opinion was prepared by the work of such English thinkers as John Locke (1632–1704), the contemporary of the English Revolution, who wrote about tolerance and was one of the founders of English Empiricism. In France, public opinion was greatly influenced by such works as Pierre Bayle's *Critical and Historical Dictionary* (1690s), and especially by Denis Diderot's *Encyclopedia* (1750–72), which tried not just to inform, but to convert by implication to a more enlightened attitude, to reason, to toleration, to liberty and to equality. The idea was to educate in order to reform.

The direct assault was led by Voltaire (1694–1778), in innumerable philosophical, historical, and political books, articles, and pamphlets. He attacked the Church, the aristocracy, and the monarchy itself, in a veiled way (because of censorship), but with biting sarcasm. And became the generally recognized leader in the fight for enlightenment.

Voltaire was backed by such philosophers as Montesquieu (1689–1753), whose *Esprit de lois* explained the laws of nations as stemming from their character and historical background, and demanded a balancing of powers between executive, legislative, and judiciary. The youngest of the great thinkers of the 18th century was Jean-Jacques Rousseau (1712–78), who moved on from rationalistic thought to a more emotional attitude, foreshadowing romanticism. The human heart was to him of much greater importance than the mind. Honesty and sincerity were to be preferred to mere intellect and outward show. His influence was immense in the 19th and 20th centuries. Even the roots of some of the fascist theorizing can be traced to him.

The Physiocrats in France and Adam Smith in England demanded a revised set of values in the administration of the economy. To free production, farming, and mining from taxes, and to have free trade, were regarded as the cure-all. The reform of criminal law was demanded with great passion by the Italian Beccaria.

In the last third of the 18th century, theory was often applied in practice. Pombal introduced a more enlightened attitude to the government of Portugal and drove out the Jesuits; Frederick the Great in Prussia was a friend of Voltaire's; Joseph II of Austria tried to carry out a liberal revolution from above, and failed; in Geneva the burghers carried out a successful coup d'état; Belgium and Poland rose in revolt. France was growing more prosperous, but its antiquated laws and vested interests caused its government nearly to go bankrupt.

What in the earlier 18th century had been original thought, had become by the end of the century mere commonplace. Almost everybody believed by then that all men were equal and that the medieval remains in the social structure should be swept away. The stage was set for revolution.

61   The American Revolution

The American Revolution was the opening shot in a round of revolutions which eventually spanned the globe and continued for 170 years. It was a national and not a social revolution, yet for the first time egalitarian and republican principles proved successful, and it became thus an ideal and a prototype to be followed by others.

The American colonists had been keen on the protection of the mother country as long as there were Frenchmen, and Indians equipped by them, to threaten them. After the Seven Years War this was no longer the case. All of Canada and all the land to the Mississippi had been conquered, or ceded by the French. In 1763 the British lost much popularity by reserving the land west of the Appalachians for the Indians. The government in London grew even less popular in America when it asserted its rights to legislate for the colonies, when various taxes were imposed and armed forces were kept on American soil. The colonists denied London's right to tax them without representation.

The American colonists were armed and clashes occurred of increasing severity: from the 1770 "Boston Massacre," to the 1773 "Boston Tea Party," and the 1775 clashes at Lexington and Bunker Hill. In the meantime London had passed the "Intolerable Acts" and Boston harbor was closed as a punitive step. These measures brought about unexpected unity among the Thirteen Colonies. On 7 September 1774 a Congress met at Philadelphia, led by such men as Thomas Jefferson, Alexander Hamilton, and John Adams, which declared the colonists' right to "Life, liberty and property" and nominated George Washington as commander-in-chief. His forces were small, and not sufficiently trained, but they knew the country and how to use the terrain to best advantage. The English war plans were often too elaborate and unrealistic. Their soldiers were mostly German mercenaries, who had less motivation to fight well than the colonists. In 1776 Washington drove the British from Boston and from New York (battles of Trenton and Princeton).

On 4 July 1776, Congress endorsed the Declaration of Independence, and the war became official and widespread. The British tried first to attack New England, but were defeated, and General Burgoyne surrendered at Saratoga. Next they tried to attack in the south, but in the meantime France had joined the nascent United States, in order to take revenge for her defeat in the Seven Years War, and Lord Cornwallis surrendered in 1781 at Yorktown. That ended land operations in America. A definitive treaty was signed on 3 September 1783, by which the independence of the United States was recognized, and all land south of Canada was transferred to them, up to the Mississippi.

This was not yet quite the end of the American Revolution. A constitutional system, based on the principle of the consent of the governed, had still to be adopted. A Convention was commissioned, which decided on a balanced system of power between executive, legislative, and judiciary. The legislative was to be of two branches, with equal representation for each state in the Senate, while the seats in the House of Representatives were to be awarded according to population. The powers of the national government were exactly defined, so that all other authority would be left to the States.

This system was highly complicated, yet has worked surprisingly well, with only minor changes, for over two hundred years.

62   The French Revolution

Some of the long-term reasons for the outbreak of the French Revolution have been discussed in the chapter on the Enlightenment. Others have been voiced by historians such as Louise-Adolphe Thiers, Auguste Mignet, Jules Michelet, Alexis-Charles de Tocqueville, and so many others that in the 20th century it is customary to organize them into such schools as "Marxists," "Revisionists," etc. But history is not always as neat and accommodating as historians would like to have it. One can also make out a good case that the revolution might just as easily not have happened at all, and did happen less because of long-term reasons, and more as a result of pure chance. De Tocqueville claimed, for instance, that "The social order destroyed by a revolution is almost always better than that which immediately follows it, and experience shows that the most dangerous moment for a bad government is generally that in which it sets about reform."

And indeed, had Louis XVI been stronger, more determined, and less well meaning and bungling, things might have developed quite differently. He summoned the 1789 meeting of the Estates General on the advice of an Assembly of Notables, the aristocratic members of which tried, this way, to hold on to their fiscal privileges, in spite of the fact that the government was steadily pushed toward bankruptcy, as a direct result of its inability to tax those who possessed the money. The weakness of the king and the shortsightedness of the aristocracy quickly met with their just desert. The confused proceedings of the Estates General (the assembly of representatives of the three estates – clergy, nobility, and the Third Estate or commons) caused those of its members who represented the middle classes to proclaim themselves a National Constituent Assembly (17 June 1789), and to swear later not to disband until France had a written constitution. The king himself forced the aristocracy and clergy to join this body.

As there was some doubt as to whether the King might change his mind, the Parisian mob captured the Bastille prison in order to arm itself (14 July 1789), an event which gained symbolic value out of all proportion to its modest intentions. The king lost control, while the Assembly found itself more and more in charge of affairs. The feudal system was abolished by the Assembly, church land was taken over, and a "Declaration of the Rights of Man and the Citizen" was promulgated. A new constitution was worked out, providing for a limited monarchy, and for a Legislative Assembly, to run the government.

Louis XVI was forced to move from Versailles to Paris; later he tried to escape, with his family, but mismanaged this operation as badly as everything else (1791). When calm returned to Paris, the possibility of a republican solution had suddenly become a reality.

The French Revolution passed through several stages. At first liberal members of the aristocracy co-operated with the middle classes. Later the men controlling the Revolution became more and more radical. The moderate Girondists were ousted by the radical Jacobins, led by such men as Jean-Paul Marat, Georges Jacques Danton, Louis Antoine Saint-Just, and Maximilien de Robespierre. The vote was first given to property-owners only, but later practically to all citizens.

This radicalization was, in part, the outcome of the war which broke out between France and Prussia and Austria. It was felt that the Girondists had not handled it successfully, and the Jacobins were certainly more determined and ruthless. The Prussian invasion had been stopped at Valmy, and Belgium had been conquered. But this caused Great Britain, Holland, and Spain to join the coalition. The French were in a difficult situation, and this contributed to the radicalization of the Revolution.

On 10 August 1792, the Tuileries were occupied and the monarchy was overthrown. The following month came the "September Massacres," during which 1100 of the inmates of the prisons of Paris were killed by the mob – partly as a result of panic, because of the capture of Verdun by the Prussians. The period of terror was inaugurated. Louis XVI was executed on 21 January 1793. As a result royalist Vendée, Bretagne, and Lyon revolted. When the Girondists were executed, their strongholds of Marseilles and Bordeaux revolted. The harbor of Toulon fell into British hands.

In this hour of crisis the Revolution took extreme measures to fight back. Military service was made compulsory. Lazar-Nicholas Carnot organized the French armed forces, much as Leon Trotsky was to do in the Russian Revolution. A Revolutionary Tribunal was created, to deal with suspected traitors at home. A Committee of Public Safety was inaugurated, which eventually usurped many of the functions of government. The extreme measures had the backing of the populace of Paris. But there was little patience with theoretical extremists, such as Jacques René Hébert and François-Noël Babeuf, who developed theories foreshadowing later socialism.

The towns which had revolted in the south were recaptured with great bloodshed (3000 were guillotined or shot in Lyon, for instance). Bloodshed was even worse in 1793 – four royalist risings in the Vendée – some 400 000 are believed to have perished.

The Jacobins introduced some revolutionary measures, such as a new calendar, starting, rather immodestly, with their accession to power in 1792, as "Year 1"; a Cult of Supreme Being, to take the place of the abolished religion; and regulations to call everybody "Citizen" or "Citizeness," instead of "Monsieur" or "Madame."

The reign of terror lasted until the summer of 1794. About 2600 aristocrats and other potential "Enemies of the Revolution" were guillotined in Paris, but many more were killed in the provinces (for instance 2000 in Angers; hundreds were drowned in Nantes). Soon the Jacobin leaders fell out. Marat was murdered in his bath by a woman. Hébert and Danton were executed. Robespierre and Saint-Just ruled supreme – but only for a short time.

Many of their colleagues were afraid for their own lives –

the Revolution seemed to be devouring her own sons – and the population of Paris was no longer prepared to take up arms on their behalf. They were guillotined on 28 July 1794.

The French Revolution was a chaotic affair, and it has been interpreted in too many ways to repeat here. Yet, of all the revolutions mentioned here in Part XIV, it has become the classical revolution, from which many others stem, and with which other revolutions are compared.

The Terror was over and the suspects were released from prison. The moderates were back in the saddle. They formed the Directory (1795–99), usually dominated by Paul Barras, but threatened by risings of the left and the right (which were put down with the help of young General Bonaparte and one of his deputies). Their 1795 constitution provided once again for a middle-class electorate.

The Directory was neither efficient, honest, or popular – but it was better than the Terror had been. One would not have thought that it would be able to deal effectively with the severe challenge of the war. But blind chance, which had such a prominent part in all the developments of the French Revolution, once more took a hand.

63   Napoleon

To the historians of the 19th century Napoleon Bonaparte (1769–1821) was one of two things: the greatest soldier ever, or a war criminal; a genius, or an ogre; a true French patriot, or a careerist without conscience. But one thing was held in common: he was a superman. Twentieth-century historiography has changed that image. Newly-found diaries, letters, and other sources have been found to contain different slants and unexpected insights. Detailed research has focused on every step in his career. More than a quarter million books and major articles have been written about him – more than about any other figure in history. Even more important: many of the sources of the Restoration period have been discredited, and their piquant stories are no longer used by serious historians.

The result has been the emergence of a different Napoleon, but no less fascinating. He was born in 1769 in Ajaccio in Corsica. His mother tongue was Italian and not French. Corsica had just been annexed to France and he could therefore attend military college there. He was taught the latest theories of war there and commissioned as a lieutenant of artillery. While many of the aristocratic officers left France during the Revolution, Napoleon, like other penniless young officers, joined the Revolution. At first he tried to make his way on his native island. Although he gained much valuable experience, all his military and political exploits there failed. After his expulsion, he landed in southern France and joined the expedition for the relief of Toulon. As no other professional artillerist was available he was appointed to head that department and suddenly showed his gift for military tactics. His was the main initiative which brought about the capture of the harbor. After a few months he was advanced from captain to brigadier-general, and became the Chief of Staff of the Army of Italy. There he had time enough to study the army's problems at leisure. As a friend of the Robespierre brothers he was jailed at their fall. When released he was in Paris, looking for employment, when Barras needed a general of anti-monarchical inclinations to put down a royalist uprising. He did so with a few cannons, and was rewarded first with the command of the Army of the Interior, afterwards with the command in Italy, and in addition with the hand of Josephine, the discarded mistress of Barras.

Among all the meteoric careers of the Revolution, Napoleon's was the most meteoric. But he delivered on his promise. On arrival in Italy he proceeded to win the war for France. He was very lucky to be assigned to the theatre of war which he had studied in detail, and where he could put into effect plans which he had prepared as chief of staff there. He and his fellow generals were young and energetic, while the Austrian generals he opposed were usually twice his age. He defeated them in battle after battle in 1796 and 1797, until he had captured all of northern Italy and was on his way to Vienna. Austria was forced to sue for peace.

Another stroke of luck: he was left to govern northern Italy, the problems of which he understood thoroughly, being an Italian himself. He gained there much valuable experience in matters of civil government.

He also gained experience in Egypt, where he had himself sent, mainly for political reasons – to remain in the eyes of the public until the time was ripe to replace the Directory of France. The directors sent him there willingly, in order to be rid of him. They nearly succeeded for good: he conquered Egypt, then a Turkish province, without difficulty (1798), but was cut off when Nelson sank all of his fleet at Abukir.

As a way out Napoleon tried early in 1799 to embark on an Alexander-like expedition to Syria and Persia, apparently hoping to conquer an empire of his own there. Some of his French officers were none too enthusiastic about his personal plans, and the expedition failed to capture the provincial harbor of Acre. Napoleon showed himself to be rather weak in siege warfare and had to withdraw back to Egypt. There he left his soldiers in the lurch and returned to France. He was preceded by the news of a last victory over a Turkish expedition, also at Abukir, while the failure at Acre was explained away.

Another piece of luck: he was just in time to join in a conspiracy against the by now thoroughly discredited Directory and on 18 Brumaire (9–10 November 1799) seized control of France. He quickly disposed of his fellow conspirators and became First Consul. These were his great years. He surprised everybody by his grasp of civilian affairs, but with his previous experience this was hardly surprising. His great and lasting deed was to consolidate the achievements of the Revolution. The administration of France was reorganized, the economy strengthened, a compromise was reached with the Catholic Church, and the codification of laws, which had begun already before, was brought to its successful conclusion (the justly famous *Code Napoléon*). The middle classes became the real support of the state. These achievements have stood the test of time and have survived Napoleon and his regime.

Napoleon was highly popular – perhaps too much so for his own good. For the appealing, slim figure of the young First Consul, so peace-loving, hard-working, and efficient, is replaced now by the much less sympathetic one of the Emperor (1804), forever campaigning in distant lands, surrounded by a few mistresses, by a court, by a new aristocracy, and, worst of all, by his large and squabbling Italian family.

First he embarked on his most famous exploit, the conquest of Europe. He and his marshals were at the peak of their military abilities and had developed just the right type of offensive battle, which they did best. At Ulm he defeated the Austrians, at Austerlitz the Austrians and Russians (1805), at Jena the Prussians (1806), at Friedland (1807) the Russians. Europe was his, to a degree unprecedented in Western history. Many of the achievements of the French Revolution were transplanted to the other countries of Europe. His dream of a unified Europe is of great relevance today, when the same ideal is being achieved by very different means.

For Napoleon the years after 1807 were a road leading relentlessly downward. He had nobody to blame but himself. He appeared to lose touch with reality and over-reached himself. To crush his sole remaining adversary, Great Britain, he tried to close Europe's markets to her, with the help of his Continental System, but only lost the goodwill of Europe's (but not yet France's) middle classes. To impose his blockade everywhere he first invaded Spain (1808) and later Russia (1812), and in both found primitive conditions which did not allow him to solve his logistical problems in his usual way, by living off the country, nor did he find there a sympathetic middle class. His armies grew larger, but their size outstripped their organization and they were no longer the finely-tuned instrument of his earlier campaigns. Although he managed to win his battles, he started to lose his campaigns. Altogether he won 59 of his 65 battles and sieges, but only seven of his fourteen campaigns – both figures never equalled by any other general in history.

Pictures show him late in his reign as a fat, small man. The light had gone out of his eyes. He was surrounded by his sycophants, and when contradicted broke into outbursts of rage, shouting, kicking his subordinates, and overturning tables. His empire was crumbling after his withdrawal from Moscow, the Church had been offended, the economy was in a shambles, and his popularity was slipping even in France.

In 1813 he fought all over Germany, but was finally defeated at the battle of Leipzig, and had to withdraw to France. In 1814 he put up a great campaign in France itself, with much smaller and more manageable armies, but was finally crushed by the vastly stronger Prussians, Russians, and Austrians and had to abdicate. The Bourbons returned, but were soon as unpopular as ever. In 1815 Napoleon returned, and seized all of France again – only to be defeated at Waterloo by the British and the Prussians, who by now had learned to counter his tactical moves.

His remaining years were spent on St. Helena, quarreling with the local governor, and dictating his memoirs, in which he reinterpreted his life and reign in a way which would confuse historians and help his nephew to regain the crown of France.

64 The Liberation of Latin America

It is questionable if Latin America was really ready for independence early in the 19th century. But the Napoleonic wars more or less forced it on her.

Haiti ensured its independence after a lengthy insurrection (1791–1804); during which Napoleon's brother-in-law, who commanded the French forces, succumbed to fever. French has continued to be its official language.

When Napoleon's armies neared Lisbon in 1808, the Prince Regent, with some 15 000 courtiers, fled to Rio de Janeiro, and set up there the central government not only of Brazil, but of all of the Portuguese Empire. The old mercantile monopolies were abolished, and trade and manufacture flourished. Cultural life became livelier, accompanied by the setting up of a printing press, the opening of a public library, and of an Academy of Fine Arts. The Regent returned in 1821 to Lisbon, taking with him most of the cash in the Bank of Brazil. Under Crown Prince Pedro, Brazil declared herself independent (1822) and he declared himself emperor. In 1831 he went into exile, and his son Pedro II followed him as emperor (1831–89). He gave Brazil a period of stability and tranquility, nearly unique in the annals of Latin America.

In 1806 and 1807 the British Navy tried twice to capture Buenos Aires, and was twice repulsed, not by the Spanish, but by the local inhabitants. This military achievement resounded throughout Spanish America. When Napoleon invaded Spain in 1808, there were repeated demands to emulate the United States and fight for independence. The agitation was led by the Venezuelan Francisco Miranda, who was thinking of one unified country, called Colombia, stretching from the Mississippi to Cape Horn. In reality, in each of the provincial capitals local juntas were set up to run affairs, while Spain was occupied with her struggle against the French.

In Mexico a local priest, named Hidalgo, led an uprising of Indians in 1810; but he was defeated and executed by the local aristocracy. The country's actual independence was achieved by a second revolution, under Augustín de Iturbide, in 1821.

In South America the royalists, reinforced from Spain after the end of the Napoleonic wars, managed to reimpose their rule in all provincial centers, except for Buenos Aires. In Caracas, Miranda capitulated (1812). His lieutenant, Simon Bolivar, continued the revolution from what is today Colombia. In 1813 he recaptured Caracas, but lost it again a year later. In 1816 he tried once more, and this time, with the help of some 5000 British volunteers, succeeded in liberating Venezuela, Colombia, and Ecuador. Then he marched on Peru, where he met up with General San Martín, who had crossed the Andes from independent Argentina into Chile, and then turned north. Lima had been the seat of the Spanish Viceroy, and with its capture and the pacification of Peru by Bolivar (1825) the liberation of South America was complete.

Bolivar could not, however, impose his rule on the various countries he had liberated and soon South America split up into nine separate Spanish-speaking countries. Their development has not been a happy one. We can mention here only a few especially significant episodes. Even the basic organization of these new states was often problematic. In the Argentine it took until 1880 to have the provinces agree to Buenos Aires serving as the capital. Uruguay had to fight all her neighbors to secure her independence (1828). Between 1865 and 1870 the Paraguayan dictator López fought the combined forces of Brazil, the Argentine, and Uruguay, until the male population of his country had nearly been wiped out.

Most of Latin America was ruled by dictators, called caudillos. Mexico's dictator, Santa Ana (1821–55), fought the United States over Texas (1846) and had to cede to her the enormous territory that now makes up California, New Mexico, Arizona, Nevada, and Utah. Napoleon III tried in 1863 to impose on Mexico the Austrian Archduke Maximilian as emperor, but the Indian president Juárez defeated and executed him four years later. Mexico was ruled from 1876 to 1911 by one of the most tenacious of caudillos, Porfirio Díaz (1830–1915). He brought stability to the country and as a result also some economic progress.

Another foreign conflict broke out over Panama. The United States was keen to build a canal there to connect the two oceans. They forced Colombia to grant Panama independence (1903) and pushed through the building of the canal, which was opened to traffic in 1914. They are to withdraw from the Canal Zone by the year 2000.

Argentina and Chile developed their economies faster than the other countries. Meat and wool became the staple of Argentina's exports to Europe and the foundation of her wealth. By 1895 she had four million inhabitants. English loans and technology helped her develop. By 1912 she had 20 000 miles of railroads. Tramways were installed in Buenos Aires. Chile's economy was based on the export of nitrate, used for fertilizer, and copper. Between 1879 and 1883 she defeated Peru and Bolivia in order to extend her nitrate mining areas northward.

Brazil's exports consisted first of rubber and later of coffee, but she remained basically a poor country. This was the fate also of the remaining republics of Latin America, nearly all of which had economies controlled by small oligarchies.

An exception was Venezuela, which, since the days of the dictator Juan Vicente Gómez (1908–35), has derived big revenues from the oil found there. Severe problems were encountered by neighboring Colombia, where some 300 000 persons were killed between 1946 and 1957 in clashes between right-wing and left-wing factions. Later, fabulously rich drug producers corrupted much of the country's administration and had opponents killed.

The 1899 war between the United States and Spain brought independence to the island of Cuba; while Puerto Rico has been retained by the United States. In the second half of the 20th century Communist rule was tried out by Fidel Castro in Cuba and – none too successfully – by the Sandinistas in Nicaragua.

In Argentina the populist dictator Juan Perón (1943–55 and 1973–4) demonstrated how a basically healthy economy could be ruined by inexpert tinkering. Inflation rose from 30 percent to 950 percent annually, and the 1945 foreign currency surplus of 5000 million dollars turned into a 1951 deficit of 2700 million. In Chile the left-leaning President Salvador Allende (1970–3) tried similar measures, but was removed and killed by General Augusto Pinochet (1973–90). Pinochet, like the army in Peru, in Argentina, and elsewhere, employed death squads to silence the opposition. General Galtieri of Argentina occupied the Falkland Islands (Malvinas) in 1982, but was speedily driven out by the British and subsequently removed from office. Bolivia contrived to ruin its thriving export of tin, by attacking Paraguay, and losing the ensuing Chaco War (1932–5).

Most of the Andean Indians used to remain outside the monetary economy, but in recent years Peruvian smallholders have grown about 60 percent of the coca leaves which Colombian dealers turn into retail drugs.

It is questionable whether the proletariat of Brazil is better off than the Andean Indians. In such towns as São Paolo and Rio de Janeiro, abandoned children are only too numerous and much of the poor population lives in shanty-towns lacking even the simplest hygiene facilities. Brazil's foreign debt used to be the largest in the world. Mexico City and São Paolo are two of the largest cities in the world today, but seem in their poorer sections to have become completely unmanageable. In some South American cities students and workers mounted an urban guerrilla warfare against authority. Their sympathies have been often more anarchist than Marxist. In Montevideo these guerillas are called the Tupamaros, who started operating in 1967.

This pessimistic tale is, however, only part of the truth. In nearly all the countries of Latin America a middle class has been growing and education has spread widely. Economic conditions are improving. The best indication of the ongoing change for the better is that in nearly every Latin American country the once prevalent dictators have disappeared during the second half of the 20th century, and some sort of democratic government has been introduced instead.

The impact of South America on the rest of the world has been small, relative to its high numbers of population. Nevertheless, there have been some interesting novelists, and some great painters in Mexico – such as Diego Rivera, José Orozco, and Alfaro Siqueiros – and some innovative architects, such as Brazil's Oscar Niemayer. But the best known contribution of Latin America has been in the field of football. Names like Pellé and Maradonna are household words everywhere.

65   Classicism and Romanticism

In Spain and Great Britain the times of greatest political and colonial activity coincided with the greatest achievements in literature and art. This did not apply to Germany and France. Germany, from the times of Bismarck to those of Hitler, was in many fields unoriginal and barren, and so was the France of Napoleon I. German literature, philosophy, and music flourished, however, in the very time that those of France declined.

Gottfried Ephraim Lessing (1729–81) was the first giant of German literature, modeling himself on Shakespeare. His plays *Minna von Barnhelm* and *Nathan the Wise* are still performed.

The greatest name in German literature is Johann Wolfgang von Goethe (1749–1832). His lyric poetry, his novel *Werther*, his play *Götz von Berlichingen*, and above all his *Faust* are only the best known of his many and varied works. He also headed the administration of the small principality of Weimar.

His contemporary was the most important German philosopher, Immanuel Kant (1724–1804). In his *Critique of Pure Reason*, Kant accepted the failure of speculative reason to establish truth and reconciled idealistic and materialistic viewpoints. Building on Kant's foundations, there later came other German philosophers, such as Arthur Schopenhauer (1788–1860). Among writers, the dramatist Friedrich Schiller (1759–1805) and the poet Heinrich Heine (1797–1856) are worthy of special mention.

Far beyond the reach of the German language spread the fame of her composers. The work of Johann Sebastian Bach (1685–1750) comprises mainly church music. He achieved a synthesis of the previous polyphonic music with the then new Italian harmonies. Among his best lines of work were his chorales, cantatas, and Passions. His contemporaries knew him mainly as a great harpsichord and organ player.

Wolfgang Amadeus Mozart (1756–91) played a major role in establishing the classical style of composition. He wrote much church music, piano concertos, and symphonies, but is perhaps best known for his operas. Joseph Haydn (1732–1809), too, developed the classical style, and wrote 104 symphonies, nearly 80 string quartets, over 50 sonatas, 31 piano trios, and the Austrian national anthem.

Ludwig van Beethoven (1770–1827) made the decisive step of no longer addressing a limited rococo-court audience, but humanity at large. He combined the use of classical forms with great depth of personal expression and expanded the concept of the symphony so that it has become the medium of most composers' profoundest musical ideas. He stretched the sonata form to its limit, relied to a great extent on the use of modulation and dissonance, and has remained the world's most popular classical composer.

After the age of Classicism came that of Romanticism. This was a reaction against rationalism and mere intellect, an attempt to project feeling rather than thought. Nature and post-Classical history were its inspiration. Its theoretic foundations had been laid long ago by the philosopher Baruch Spinoza (1632–77). In the 1760s there appeared a taste for wild gardens and Gothic architecture. Gothic tales of horror became popular.

Romanticism's first appearance in literature was in England, and it was evident in the works of such poets as Thomas Gray (1716–71), Robert Burns (1759–96), William Blake (1757–1827), Samuel Taylor Coleridge (1772–1834), William Wordsworth (1770–1850), Lord Byron (1788–1824), Percy Bysshe Shelley

(1792–1822), and John Keats (1795–1821). Sir Walter Scott (1771–1832) was an adherent of neo-medievalism.

In France the Romantic Movement made the leap from literature and art to politics. Chateaubriand (1768–1848) and Alphonse Lamartine (1790–1869) were not only writers, but also politicians, and both served as Ministers of Foreign Affairs. Lamartine was one of the main leaders of the Revolution of 1848. The novelist Victor Hugo (1802–85) spent many years in political exile. Thus was created the tradition of political involvement, which is still in vogue among French writers. It might be questioned, however, if exile did indeed improve their work. Such less involved writers as Stendhal (1783–1842), or Honoré de Balzac (1799–1850), have been preferred by posterity. Influential German romantic writers include Friedrich Hölderlin (1770–1843), E. T. A. Hoffman (1776–1822), and Heinrich von Kleist (1777–1811).

Elsewhere, the Italian Manzoni (1785–1873) and his *I Promessi Sposi* (The Betrothed); the Russian poet Alexsandr Pushkin (1799–1837), a true romantic; and the Polish novelist Adam Mickiewicz (1798–1855) were influential.

There existed Romantic schools in historiography, represented by Thomas Carlyle (1795–1881); in aesthetics, represented by John Ruskin (1819–1900); and even in economics, in early 19th century Germany.

Among the main painters of the Romantic were Jean Louis Théodore Géricault (1791–1824) and Eugène Delacroix (1798–1863). But the greatest painters of that age, Goya (1746–1828) in Spain, and William Turner (1775–1851) in England, did not belong to the Romantic school.

Music is even more amenable to romantic feeling, as witnessed by such composers as Franz Schubert (1797–1828), Robert Schumann (1918–56), Felix Mendelssohn-Bartholdy (1809–47), Gaetano Donizetti (1797–1848), Vincenzo Bellini (1801–35), Hector Berlioz (1803–69), Frederic Chopin (1810–49), and Franz Liszt (1811–86).

Romanticism strengthened in central and eastern Europe nascent nationalistic feelings. This was especially true of Germany, Italy, Poland, and Hungary, but also of other countries. The collecting of folk tales was used to make people more aware of their past. This new awareness later became the motive force behind the political nationalist movements of the 19th century.

66   The Revolutions of 1830 and 1848

The allies who had vanquished Napoleon met in 1814–15 at the Congress of Vienna, which redefined Europe's frontiers and principles. The latter were the legitimacy of dynasties, the containment of France, and a new balance of power. The victors were thoroughly reactionary; they did not take into account such novel forces as nationalism, which were to dominate Europe. Yet they were highly successful, for their actions banished universal wars in Europe for a century. The Austrian Metternich was the main architect of the peace and he was to remain in office until 1848.

France was returned to the rule of the Bourbons, who were forced to retain many of the most important achievements of the Revolution. For some years the population was glad enough to have peace and quiet, but soon a new generation was captured by the Napoleonic legend, and the unheroic new rulers became thoroughly unpopular.

Liberal ideas became increasingly popular all over Europe. The current vogue of Romanticism made the reactionary settlement of 1815 seem outmoded. The "Holy Alliance" organized by Tsar Alexander seemed pointless to the rising middle classes of western and central Europe. The repressive legislation did not sit well with the newly affluent classes. New radical newspapers attacked the French government.

Nationalism first raised its head in an unexpected quarter. The Greeks rose in revolt against Turkish dominance and misrule. They proclaimed their independence in 1822, but were nearly crushed. Torn between the principles of legitimacy and the fashionable admiration of Ancient Greece, the great powers of Europe finally did come to Greece's assistance, and annihilated the Turkish fleet at Navarino (1827). Russia then invaded Turkey on her own account, occupied Romania, and captured Adrianople.

At that stage (1829) the Turks had to agree to the independence of Greece and Serbia, and the autonomy of Romania. Their retreat from the Balkans had commenced.

In France, Charles X ascended the throne in 1824 and soon became highly unpopular because of his actively reactionary and clericalistic policy. His conquest of Algeria in 1830 seemed to strengthen his hand and as a result he published the reactionary *July Ordinances*. He had not prepared sufficient military power to enforce them. Students, workers, and some veterans of the Napoleonic wars rose in Paris in revolt, and barricades of cobblestones were thrown up. Some of the troops deserted and Charles X had to abdicate. Memories of the 1793 regime of terror were too fresh, and therefore no republic was declared. Instead, Louis-Philipe, of a liberal Bourbon sideline, was crowned King (1830–48).

The revolution did not become universal, but Belgium revolted, and succeeded in throwing off the Dutch rule, imposed in 1815. Poland revolted too, but was recaptured by Russia and treated very harshly. Some disturbances in Italy were suppressed by Austria. But the general scenario had been tried out, to be repeated in 1848.

In the following years France continued to be the central problem. Louis-Philipe tried to play the part of the nice, constitutional monarch, but it turned out that this was not what the French wanted. Glorification of the Napoleonic campaigns grew ever stronger, as the memories of what they really had been like grew dimmer. The return of Napoleon's remains from St. Helena in 1840 turned into a vast Bonapartist rally.

Nationalistic sentiments grew ever stronger throughout Europe. National roots were rediscovered by Czechs and Magyars, and more energetically followed up by Italians, Germans, and Poles.

The 1815 settlement seemed less and less to fit the new, wealthy Europe, in which the Industrial Revolution was making steady progress, and the old reactionary ideology seemed unrelated to the new situation. For the first time not only the interests of the middle class were mentioned, but also those of the workers, who were becoming more numerous, as Europe grew more industrialized.

The revolution broke out, as usual, in Paris, in February 1848.

Louis-Philipe escaped to England. This time a second republic was declared. In the provisional government there participated for the first time also a representative of the workers (Louis Blanc). But leftist agitation frightened the middle classes and when an uprising occurred, they backed General Cavaignac's repression. Bonapartist sentiments caused the election of Napoleon's nephew as President, and he established in due time the "Second Empire" and ruled as Emperor Napoleon III (1852–70).

Other revolutions broke out in various places, all over Europe. In Vienna old Metternich was ousted and a new Emperor (Franz Joseph, 1848–1916) was crowned. In Germany there were uprisings in Berlin and elsewhere, and a serious and prolonged attempt was made to set up a federalistic, liberal, unified Germany. Had it succeeded, the history of the 19th and 20th centuries might have been very different from what it turned out to be.

Other uprisings occurred in Hungary, Prague, and in Italy. The King of Piedmont attacked Austria, in order to drive her out of Italy. He was defeated and had to abdicate. In Rome the revolution was headed by Mazzini and Garibaldi.

The success of the revolution turned out to be ephemeral. Soon the rulers of Austria, Prussia, Russia, and France reorganized and stamped it out. The French intervened in Rome, the Russians in Hungary, the Austrians in Bohemia and Italy. The revolutionaries turned out not to be as tough as those of 1789 and 1917, and were quickly and soundly defeated. The great liberal revolution had failed. Although some of its traditions were to survive in the countries involved, new forces were to appear now, which channeled the political inclinations of Europe into different directions.

67   The Creation of National States: Italy and Germany

The leadership of nationalist movements passed in the second half of the 19th century from liberal revolutionaries into the hands of conservative statesmen.

The central figure on the European stage of the 1850s and

early 1860s was Napoleon III. In order to remain popular in France, he had to conduct an active foreign policy and to try and imitate his great uncle. The outcome of his ill thought out schemes proved in the end highly detrimental to the interests of France. Richelieu and Mazarin had based France's greatness on the political fragmentation of Italy and Germany. It fell to Napoleon III to undo their work.

Italian nationalism had awakened during the times of Napoleon I and had become an ever more potent political movement during the Romantic period. The Italian "Risorgimento" caused widespread revolts in the various small principalities of the peninsula in 1848. But after their failure, the leadership of the movement passed from republican liberals like Mazzini, into the hands of the prime minister of Piedmont, Cavour (1810–61). He showed unusual ability in his manipulation of the great powers of Europe and of the small principalities of Italy. He participated in the Crimean War in order to gain the goodwill of France and England. Later he managed to enlist France's help in a war against Austria, by bribing Napoleon III with the transfer of Savoy and Nice to France. Then he managed to provoke Austria into declaring war (1859). The Austrians were promptly defeated at Solferino (as a result of which the Red Cross was founded), and Cavour obtained rich Lombardy, with its capital Milan. Napoleon III had well-founded second thoughts at this stage, and withdrew his support, but by then he was no longer really needed. The whole edifice of tiny independent Italian states, propped up so far by Austria, came tumbling down. Garibaldi mounted a republican expedition, which overran Sicily and southern Italy (1860). To forestall him, Cavour despatched a Piedmontese army into central Italy. A great part of the Papal state was incorporated (but not Rome itself, which was held by French troops), and then Napoleon III lost what little Italian goodwill was left. All the central Italian principalities were incorporated, and in southern Italy Garibaldi had no choice but to turn over his conquests.

United Italy, with the Piedmontese king, Victor Emmanuel II, at its head, had become a fact. Turin was its first capital, Florence the second, and after 1870 Rome became its third and final capital.

Austrian-owned (since Napoleonic times) Venetia was acquired in 1866, and Trieste and South Tyrol in 1918.

Italy remained for a long time, in spite of its unification, a relatively poor country, which did not quite belong to the group of great European powers. To compensate, she built up a colonial empire in Libya, Eritrea, Somaliland, and the Dodecanese, but was defeated ignominiously when she tried to conquer Ethiopia (1896). More important was the great advance of Lombardy, the most industrialized part of Italy, where the standard of living rose to a level nearly equal to that of France and Germany. Southern Italy, on the other hand, remained undeveloped, lacked a real middle class, and appeared to belong to a different world from the prosperous north.

The unification of Germany came about in a similar way. Here, too, one dominant power, Prussia, undertook the task, and one dominant statesman, Otto von Bismarck (1815–98), handled the operation with supreme skill. His policy of "blood and iron" left a lasting mark on Germany for many years to come. He was helped by an outstanding soldier, Helmut von Moltke (1800–91), who orchestrated the victories over Denmark (1864), Austria (1866), and France (1870–1), which were the stepping stones to unification, and to the creation of the "Second German Reich." Austria had to be eliminated from Germany, in order to give Prussia a free hand. After that, Napoleon III helped Germany by his enmity just as much as he had helped Italy by his friendship. The Germans succeeded less by subterfuge and more by the force of their armies, which became predominant in Europe. In the Franco-Prussian War the French were decisively defeated at Sedan and Metz, Napoleon III was taken prisoner, the German Reich was pronounced in January 1871, with the Prussian king, Wilhelm I, becoming Emperor of Germany. Alsace Lorraine was added to Germany, thus creating a bone of contention for the future.

Germany became the dominant power in Europe, not only politically, but also economically. Her industrialization in the late 19th century was rapid and thorough. By 1900 she had overtaken Great Britain.

The German nation was fervently nationalistic, and drew the

conclusion, from the way its unification was achieved, that armed force, under vigorous right-wing leadership, was the best way for conducting diplomacy. As long as Bismarck retained control, this was tempered by experience and wisdom, but under Wilhelm II (1888–1918), Germany became the bully of Europe.

Thus, between 1859 and 1871 the map of Europe was completely redrawn. The full ramifications became clear only in the 20th century. The two World Wars can be regarded, to a certain extent, as the outcome of the unification of Germany.

68   Realism, Impressionism, Socialism

Europe changed during the 19th century more than ever before. The Industrial Revolution spawned factories; agricultural workers flocked into the cities hoping for a better life; as the cities' inhabitants increased, their old fortifications had to be pulled down and they spilled over into their suburbs; railways carried travelers from town to town with previously unimagined speed; steamships reduced the distance between continents. A new world was being born. Aristocrats lost much of their economic importance, while rich industrialists, traders, and bankers controlled the economies of their countries; the middle classes increased manyfold and the number of industrial workers increased even more. New social problems appeared, but also new technologies and new scientific advances.

It was a stimulating time to live in. And writers, thinkers, scientists, and composers were indeed stimulated as they faced new and previously unimagined challenges. Rarely, if ever, has there been a time of such proliferation of new schools and of important new works in all these fields.

In literature and art, Paris continued to rule supreme. The realist school included writers such as Gustave Flaubert (1821–80), Guy de Maupassant (1850–93), Alphonse Daudet (1840–93), and, above all, Emile Zola (1840–1902). Great realist artists were Théodore Rousseau (1812–67), Camille Corot (1796–1875), Jean-François Millet (1814–74), Honoré Daumier (1810–79), and Gustave Courbet (1819–77).

In the search for realism a sudden transformation occurred in art. It was no longer enough to paint forms and figures – the very sunlight had to be put down on canvas. The Impressionists had arrived – Edouard Manet (1833–83), Claude Monet (1840–1926), Edgar Degas (1834–1917), August Renoir (1841–1920), Alfred Sisley (1839–99), and Camille Pissaro (1830–1903). This was one of the greatest moments in the history of art, comparable to Ancient Greek sculpture or Renaissance painting. They were followed by such Neo-Impressionists as George Seurat (1860–91); expressionists such as Paul Cézanne (1839–1906), Vincent Van Gogh (1853–90), Paul Gauguin (1848–1903), and Henri de Toulouse-Lautrec (1864–1901); "Fauves" ("wild beasts") such as Henri Matisse (1869–1954), André Derain (1880–1954), and Maurice de Vlaminck (1876–1958); and cubists like Pablo Picasso (1881–1973) and Georges Braque (1882–1963).

All the previous conventions of art and aesthetics were overturned within two generations. Abstract art was tried out by Wassily Kandinsky and Piet Mondrian. In Munich, before World War I, there flowered an exciting school of German expressionists. From Russia came some of the great names of the "School of Paris," such as Marc Chagall (1887–1985) and Haim Soutine (1894–1943); and Amedeo Modigliani (1884–1920) came from Italy. But by the 1930s the great period of art seemed to have burned itself out, except for some of the weaker works by artists like Chagall or Picasso.

The great composers of this era were much more widely distributed than the artists. Some were Germans or Austrians, such as Gustav Mahler (1860–1913), Richard Strauss (1864–1949), and Arnold Schoenberg (1874–1951). Edward Grieg (1843–1907) came from Norway, Claude Debussy (1862–1918) from France, and Giuseppe Verdi (1813–1901) and Giacomo Puccini (1858–1924) from Italy.

While only relatively small groups appreciated art and literature, many more were influenced in this age by the ideas of thinkers and innovators. Comte Henri de Saint-Simon (1760–1825) in France and Robert Owen (1771–1858) in England were prophets of a new industrial order and early socialism. Hegel (1770–1831) in

Germany developed a new philosophy of history. His disciple was Karl Marx (1818–83), who wrote *Das Kapital* and developed the theory of "historical materialism." His influence on later history was immense. One step further went the Russian Mikhail Bakunin (1814–76), the father of anarchism. When during the later part of the 19th century the earliest socialist and labor parties were formed they were usually of a less doctrinaire coloring than the teachings of Marx, and went back more to the practical socialism of Ferdinand Lassalle (1825–64), who in 1863 founded the first German socialist party. The Labour Party in Great Britain was founded between 1900 and 1906, but only in 1918 became an avowedly socialist party. The earliest attempts at putting socialist theory into revolutionary practice were made by the 1871 Commune of Paris (a byproduct of the Franco-Prussian War), and in 1905 by the first Russian Revolution (after the defeat by Japan). The great moment of Marxism came after World War I.

Other thinkers prepared the way for right-wing ideologies. Arthur Schopenhauer claimed that will was the motive force of the universe. Hegel believed that the supreme leader is above the morals of ordinary man and predicted that "Germany's hour" would come and that its mission would be to regenerate the world. Friedrich Wilhelm Nietzsche (1844–1900) wrote: "The strong men, the masters, regain the pure conscience of a beast of prey; monsters filled with joy, they can return from a fearful succession of murder, arson, rape and torture with joy in their hearts" – which reads already like a description of Nazi excesses in World War II.

The composer Richard Wagner (1813–83) prepared the way for German nationalist extremism. Hitler said about him: "Whoever wants to understand Nationalist Socialist Germany must know Wagner." Which does not mean, of course, that there was not a lot more to Wagner than that.

The historian Heinrich von Treitschke (1834–96) glorified the state and war, and regarded citizens of the state as little more than slaves: "The concept of the State implies the concept of war, for the essence of the State is power ... that war should ever be banished from the world is a hope not only absurd, but profoundly immoral." The cataclysmic events of the 20th century were thus prepared by some of the thinkers of the 19th.

69   The American Dream

Few nations have been as lucky as the Americans. To have a continent to settle, to possess no powerful neighbors, to enjoy most of the time deep peace, to be a fairly homogeneous group of people with similar values – these are advantages enjoyed by few nations at the outset of their history. No wonder that the Americans have been an optimistic people expecting easy success on both the personal and the national level. By the standards of most other nations they were well paid and well fed. For a very long period theirs were the richest millionaires and the most optimistic dreams.

The main challenge of early American history was the settling of the vast country. The frontier moved steadily west. New areas were opened up by settlers, new towns were founded, new territories were organized, which became, in due time, states of equal status to the original thirteen. By 1796 Kentucky and Tennessee had been added, to be followed soon after by Ohio. In 1803 Jefferson made the "Luisiana Purchase," obtaining from France, for 15 000 000 dollars, control of the whole central river system of the continent. By 1820 Indiana and Illinois in the northwest, and Alabama and Mississippi in the southwest, had become states.

The rough spirit of the frontier has had a strong influence on the American character in its formative years. It taught self-reliance, aggressive self-confidence, and a dislike of discipline and subordination. The Indians along the way were brushed aside. An important highway to the west was the Erie Canal, completed in 1825, which also confirmed New York as the main trade and finance center of America. The settlers who traveled along it built Buffalo, Cleveland, Detroit, and Chicago. Yankees moved along it to the northern areas, while Southerners settled Alabama and Mississippi, and both currents met in Ohio, Indiana, and Illinois. The expedition of Lewis and Clark, sent out by Jefferson, first reached the Pacific in 1804–6. In their wake fur companies were set up. Settlers moved southeastward via the Santa Fe trail, and northwestward by the Oregon trail. Utah was first settled by Mormons.

Americans crossed the frontier into Mexican territory. The settlers of Texas gained their independence in 1835, and were admitted into the Union ten years later. Other Americans moved into California. As a result of the Mexican War, the southwestern territories were taken over. The 1849 gold finds in California drew so many new settlers there that it was incorporated as a state in 1850.

In the years between 1860 and 1890 the gap between the Mississippi and California was settled. The herds of buffalo were wiped out, the Indians subdued, the land cleared. Railroads were pushed across the continent from east and west, joining up first in 1869. At first these vast areas were utilized for cattle grazing and for mining. Later, farmers took over. By the end of the century the frontier was about to disappear.

Industries were founded mainly in the north, agriculture both in the north and in the south. In the south, slave labor was utilized. The struggle between Southern slave-owners and Northern abolitionists brought about, after several compromise solutions had failed, the secession of the Southern States, when Lincoln was elected as the first Republican President (1860). The ensuing Civil War lasted until 1865 and was on a much vaster scale than any previous war, both in the number of soldiers engaged and in the scale and quality of equipment. If formations of corps size had first been used by Napoleon, now army-size formations were used. The Civil War was in its characteristics more like World War I than like the Napoleonic wars.

At first the Southern armies enjoyed better leadership, under such commanders as General Robert E. Lee. But northern preponderance in men and matériel made itself fully felt, when such gifted generals as U. S. Grant and W. T. Sherman took over command. By 1863 Lincoln felt strong enough to announce the abolition of slavery and by 1865 the South had been defeated, devastated, and conquered. It took nearly a hundred years before the Southern states were again on an equal footing with the Northern ones, both in the economic and in the political fields (such as having a two-party system or nominating a president).

The war had given an immense stimulus to industry. The modern America of Big Business emerged from it. It was controlled mainly from centers such as New York. By 1890 America was producing more iron and steel than Great Britain, by 1900 more than Britain and Germany combined. New immigrants in increasing numbers were drawn from Europe. Vast industrial enterprises were developed, such as Rockefeller's "Standard Oil," or Ford's car manufacture. Vanderbilt and others combined railroads into regional monopolies. J. P. Morgan created a "money trust." New American millionaires began to outshine the old-rich of Europe. Excessively large monopolies brought about the enactment, in 1890, of the Sherman Antitrust Act.

America was isolated by two oceans from the events of the rest of the world. Her dominant economic stature involved her therefore only fairly late in global events. But later presidents such as Theodore Roosevelt (1901–8), Woodrow Wilson (1912–20), and Franklin Delano Roosevelt (1933–45) started to play an increasingly dominant role on the world stage. Although in between there were periods of withdrawal and isolationism, in the long run America could not avoid becoming one of the leading powers on a global scale.

America was materialistically orientated, and has, to a certain degree, remained so. Success in life has usually been equated with income. Yet the 20th century has also brought a wider interest in literature and art, and indeed, a flowering of American literature and painting. But America's main impact has been, perhaps, in the field of architecture. Louis H. Sullivan (1856–1924) built the first skyscrapers in Chicago in the 1890s; Frank Lloyd Wright (1867–1959) is generally regarded as one of the four most outstanding architects of the 20th century; another one of these four, the German Mies van der Rohe, built his most important buildings in the United States, and his pupils and imitators have changed the face of much of Manhattan in his spirit. Nowhere else does modern high-rise architecture look quite as convincing as in central New York.

Most of the other large towns of the United States have had a less happy fate. While everywhere else in the world, and especially in Europe, the town is the real seat of civilization, this is no longer true of America. Shrinking down-town areas are often enclosed by a wide belt of no-man's land, where any pedestrian is in danger of being mugged or worse. The real center of American life is beyond this belt, in the green suburbs, with their shopping malls and ample parking spaces. A tourist without a car finds it near-impossible even to see what the real America looks like.

The top universities of America lead the world in many fields, and especially in scientific discoveries. Americans have received many more Nobel Prizes in the sciences than any other nationals.

The economic scene has changed tremendously in recent years. For most of the 20th century manufacturing was dominated by the automobile industry of Detroit. But no longer. Steel production is regressing, and different types of manufacture and new service industries have moved to the top. IBM, Microsoft, computer technology, and electronic communications have become what General Motors and car-making used to be a few years ago. Now, approaching the end of the 20th century, America has to face tough economic competition from both Europe and the Pacific Rim. She is still predominant in the entertainments industry, but no longer in industrial production. This is perhaps the reason why "The American Dream" is appropriate at a time in which the Disney Corporation has become to America what General Steel used to be a century ago.

70   The Russian Revolution

Russia was an autocracy before the Revolution and became one again after the Revolution. It had a notorious secret police before, and an even worse one after. It suffered from a bloated bureaucracy under Nicholas II, and the bureaucracy was even bigger and less efficient under Stalin. A small group of aristocrats controlled most of the wealth and held most of the senior positions in the administration before 1917. For some years after, an equally exclusive coterie of party members had many special perks, enjoyed a better standard of living than most of the population, and had a lockhold on most senior governmental appointments. The historian can only wonder why Russia had a revolution at all if these characteristics were embedded so deeply in the Russian soul as to be immutable. No other revolution mentioned here seems to have made so little difference.

The revolutionaries could not know, of course, that in the long run they would fail. They were inspired by liberal, Marxist, and anarchistic ideologies, imported mostly from the West, and hoped to create a new Russia, very different from the old one. There was little possibility of legal agitation for change in Tsarist Russia, and clandestine activity and acts of terror were the main venue open to would-be reformers. Tsar Alexander II was killed in 1881 by terrorists. His grandson, Nicholas II, lived all his life in the shadow of a possible similar fate. As a result of one of the plots against his life, the elder brother of Lenin was hanged. Under Nicholas the Tsarist regime became weak and indecisive. As we saw in 17th century England and 18th century France, nothing invites revolution so much as a weak autocracy.

Among the earliest opposition groups were the Narodniks, who believed in "going down" to the peasants in order to create a unified opposition. From their ranks were recruited the later Social Revolutionaries. Another group was Marxist, and was led by Georgy Plekhanov. Among his disciples were both Vladimir Ilyich Lenin (1870–1924) and Leon Trotsky (1879–1940). He believed that a revolution would become possible only after Russia had been further industrialized, thus creating the proletariat, which he regarded as the proper breeding ground for socialist revolutionaries. In July 1903 a meeting of delegates was organized, first in Brussels and later in London, to discuss the question of whether the Marxist party was to be run democratically, as Mantov proposed, or as a closed dictatorship, as was Lenin's program. With the help of a trick, Lenin won by a majority of two. The party split, and his group took the name of Bolsheviks (majority), while Mantov's group has gone down in history as Mensheviks (minority). Lenin organized his followers as a team, tightly controlled by himself – the prototype of how Russia was indeed organized after he assumed power.

When Russia was defeated by Japan in 1904–5, a first revolution broke out, masterminded in Petrograd by Trotsky, who set up a central council, or Soviet. There were revolts in other cities as well, and a second Soviet was organized in Moscow. The revolt collapsed, first in Petrograd and later in Moscow. Trotsky and other leaders were arrested. But the general scenario had been tried out, to be repeated on a wider scope in 1917.

During the years of World War I the Tsarist government showed all too clearly its inability to run the war efficiently, and its armies were repeatedly defeated by the Germans. Soldiers and civilians were equally sick of war and disillusioned by the Tsar's performance. The "February" Revolution (calculated according to the Julian calendar) broke out on 7 March 1917. Petrograd was filled with industrial workers and with replacement regiments, less than eager to be sent to the front. The Tsar had just left for the front, and bread rationing had been introduced. Strikes and demonstrations took place and turned into disturbances. The vast crowd suddenly became aware of its power: bakeries were looted; the police tried but failed to keep the crowd from the city center; the Cossacks did not even try; police stations and jails were attacked. By 12 March soldiers started to join the insurgents, and arms were looted from the arsenal and distributed. The government collapsed, the Duma refused to disperse, in spite of the Tsar's command, and a Soviet was set up. Nicholas was unable to return to his capital, and abdicated on 15 March.

A provisional government was installed. Its moving spirit was Alexsandr Kerensky. Had he succeeded, Russia might have taken the difficult but more promising route to democratic government. He made, however, the crucial mistake of continuing the war.

Lenin was returned, with German help, by railway from Switzerland to Petrograd, arriving on 16 April. A large crowd was there to receive him, and he immediately demanded that the war be ended. During the summer of 1917 the war was going from bad to worse for Russia, and Lenin's insistent demand for its cessation proved to be his passport to victory.

A first attempt at overthrowing Kerensky's government failed on 16–17 July. By the end of October the Bolsheviks had some 400 000 active supporters in Russia, and many of them were organized in battalions of Red Guards. Trotsky convinced a part of the garrison of Petrograd to join them. The "October" Revolution broke out on 7 November; the Bolsheviks took over Petrograd, while Kerensky, like Nicholas, had departed for the front. The government collapsed and after several days of confused fighting, Kerensky fled and Lenin seized power (16 November).

Most of European Russia fell into the hands of the Bolsheviks, but in the Don area and in Siberia counter-revolutionary armies seized power. Lenin moved the capital to Moscow, to be out of reach of the advancing German armies. On 25 November elections were held, in which the Bolsheviks polled only 9.8 million votes out of a total of 41.7 million, while the Social Revolutionaries received 20.8 million. Lenin sabotaged the resulting Constituent Assembly and ruled Russia without it. Even at this early stage the wheel had turned full cycle, from autocracy to autocracy.

Bolshevik representatives established administrations in other key cities, workers were given control of factories, and the property of the Church and of "counter revolutionaries" was confiscated.

At Brest Litovsk the Bolsheviks signed a separate peace with Germany and Austria (3 March 1918), accepting all their harsh demands. But with the collapse of the Central Powers in late 1918, some of its provisions were no longer of importance. The border far to the west, established by Catherine the Great, was lost.

The Revolution itself was a relatively simple and unbloody affair, when compared with the Civil War which followed, from 1918 to 1921. The Bolshevik regime in Moscow had to fight opposing "White" armies, which controlled Siberia, much of the Ukraine, the Crimea, the Caucasus, and areas around Petrograd. On the initiative of Winston Churchill, an English–French force landed in Murmansk in June 1919, seizing also Archangel, but had to withdraw in October of that year. In 1920 the Red Army drove the Polish forces out of Kiev, which they had occupied, invaded Poland itself, but was repulsed.

Lenin was successful in organizing his regime in Moscow, while

Trotsky led the Red Army on the various fronts, until the White forces had been driven from Russia's soil and destroyed.

The Russian Revolution inspired some short-lived attempts at Communist take-overs in Hungary and Bavaria, but Soviet hopes for widespread revolutions, especially in Germany, were not fulfilled. Only in far away Mongolia could a Communist regime be organized.

Russia was ravaged by the Civil War much more even than by World War I. Hunger and epidemics killed further millions in its wake. Further, the promised democratization and liberalization never came. The demands of war made Lenin's regime ever more autocratic. After his death (1924) the leadership passed, not as expected to Trotsky, but to the Secretary General of the Communist Party, Joseph Stalin, a native of Grusinia. His personality and rule (1924–53) made even Ivan the Terrible look benevolent. He had some ten million kulaks (wealthy peasant farmers) deported or killed. The kulaks had been the most efficient and successful farmers in Russia, and their elimination for ideological reasons (they opposed collectivization) was a blow from which Russian agriculture never recovered.

In the 1930s Stalin had the leadership of the Communist Party and of the Red Army purged (including the chief-of-staff, Tukhachevsky, and more than half of its generals). Some seven million arrests were made; three million persons perished. Many others were exiled to forced labor camps in the Arctic and Siberia.

Nevertheless, the very energy and forcefulness of the regime helped it to survive, in spite of all its crimes, while the slightly more benevolent Tsarist regime had been overthrown, mainly as a result of its weakness and lack of decisiveness.

The regime survived for some 70 years, until Mikhail Gorbachev's "Second Russian Revolution," which has to be understood in terms of the utter failure of the first to change Russian autocracy and bureaucracy.

Part XV

The Break-Up of Empires

After 500 years, has the dominant position of Western Civilization come to an end? Not so long ago the eminent historian Arnold Toynbee believed that all other civilizations had effectively disappeared and had been absorbed by the victorious Western Civilization. But by the end of the 20th century it is quite clear that this was an incorrect diagnosis. The Islamic civilization, for instance, continues to exist, and is embarked on a very different course of its own. Western imperialism has withdrawn from practically all the colonial possessions and outposts it had occupied. Most of the Western traces which were left behind in previous colonies in Africa and southeastern Asia seem destined to disappear. Sub-Saharan Africa seems to be facing a new period of tribalism, rather than an advance to Western standards. The countries of the Pacific Rim have drawn on their own cultural resources to outproduce the West.

But the West is certainly not finished, as Oswald Spengler had assumed early in the 20th century. America and western Europe are more prosperous than ever. Out of three great economic centers of the world, two – the United States and western Europe – are part of the Western Civilization. But they certainly do not control any longer single-handedly the destinies of the world.

71 The Road to Self-Destruction

The Great Powers of Europe were not sufficiently aware of the fact that the Industrial Revolution had changed the very nature of war. Beforehand, successful wars had served as the ultimate sign of success of rulers and nations. The limited wars in Europe, since 1815, had not been too terrible, and certainly not for the victors, such as Germany in the wars orchestrated by Bismarck. The Civil War of America had already hinted how frightful a future war might become, but it had not had much of an impact on Europe. Therefore the nations of Europe and their leaders had to experience for themselves how dreadful a full-scale post-Industrial Revolution war was, before they understood that such a war might amount to near-suicide. Some nations, such as France and England, had learned their lesson after World War I, but Germany and Japan needed World War II to drive home the lesson.

The two World Wars did not destroy Europe totally, but they did destroy her colonial empires and her dominant position in the world.

Very few prophetic minds foresaw any such results before 1914. Thus the Great Powers indulged in a merry round of international intrigues, building up a net of alliances, which made sure that it would be impossible to localize any armed conflict if war actually broke out.

At the center of this web was the Germany of Kaiser Wilhelm II (1888–1918). Looking back, one can only wonder what Germany had to gain from a war – she seemed to have everything. She was rich, had very generous borders, both in the west and the east, and Bismarck had demonstrated that this could be combined with reasonably good relations with most of her neighbors.

Only France was an exception, but she was in a vulnerable position. She was the only power which had something to gain from a war – the recapture of Alsace-Lorraine. Bismarck's policy had been to isolate her as far as possible. France's industrial expansion could not keep pace with that of the other Great Powers, and her population was not growing any more.

Germany was certainly the leading nation of Europe. But this was not enough for Wilhelm II, and for his advisors and subjects. They craved world leadership. To this end as many colonies as possible were grabbed up in Africa, though their usefulness in the case of Germany seemed unclear. A big navy was built – referred to by Wilhelm habitually as "my navy," which could not but antagonize Great Britain, Prussia's oldest ally, ever since the wars of Frederick the Great and Napoleon. Wilhelm regarded himself as the "Tool of Providence" and liked to strike attitudes of arrogance, which were highly popular in Germany, but were regarded as war-mongering abroad.

The Germans felt their nationalistic juices flowing after the unification of 1871, and wanted to show the rest of Europe who the new strong man of Europe was. Had not the French done just the same for centuries, when Germany was weak and divided? The problem was that it was too late by now; there were no nice, little wars around any more, in the style of Louis XIV – war meant a holocaust.

Wilhelm II did not renew the Reinsurance Treaty negotiated in 1887 with Russia. In 1894 a Franco-Russian alliance was concluded, partly in response to Wilhelm's shenanigans. Germany had to prepare, as a result, for a two-front war, an eventuality which Bismarck had always wanted to avoid. Wilhelm and his ministers could and did complain loudly about "encirclement."

Germany's armed might seemed more than to counterbalance those of France and Russia combined. This changed when Wilhelm's aggressiveness, colonial ambitions, and especially his building of a fleet, slowly pushed England into the opposing camp. Great Britain had longstanding colonial conflicts with France, but these were settled amicably after the Fashoda incident of 1898. Her rivalry with Russia was of even longer standing, resulting from the threat Russia seemed to pose to her lifeline to her Indian Empire. Nicholas II seemed, however, less aggressive than his predecessors, and relations with Russia improved. Great Britain was disturbed by the threat to the European balance of power, and just like in the days of Louis XIV and of Napoleon, was preparing to throw her lot in with the weaker and less aggressive side. Strategic talks with France took place, but no official alliance was concluded. England was, however, one of the guarantors of Belgian neutrality, which was threatened by the German Schlieffen Plan for an overwhelming right-hook attack through Holland and Belgium, in case of war, in order to outflank the French fortress zone.

Early in the 20th century Germany found herself very much alone among the Great Powers, and therefore did her utmost to strengthen her alliance with the moribund Austro-Hungarian Empire. Further, she tried to draw the equally moribund Ottoman Empire to her side. She inherited thus the many insoluble problems of these two allies, especially in the Balkans, where nationalist forces tried to throw off the domination both of Turkey and of Austria.

In the fifteen years before World War I, crisis seemed to follow crisis. Wilhelm's visit to Jerusalem in 1898, in the guise of a "crusader," seemed to the other powers an interference by a newcomer in an area in which they had been locked in rivalry for centuries. In 1905 Wilhelm made a similar visit to Tangier, in order to support Moroccan independence, when France was trying to occupy that country. As a result, England drew closer to France. In 1908 Austria annexed Bosnia, which had been occupied by her troops since 1878, thereby threatening Serbia and angering Russia. Germany forced Russia the year after to recognize this annexation, thus making her draw even closer to France and England. The Serbs in Bosnia began a campaign of anti-Austrian terrorist acts. Several Balkan wars followed, during which Turkey was nearly pushed out of Europe. In 1911 there was another Moroccan crisis, when Germany sent her gunboat the *Panther* to Agadir, to protect her very minor commercial interest there, allegedly threatened by French expansion. But it was Great Britain which felt alarmed by this show of strength so near to Gibraltar. This crisis, too, was settled, but it brought about, for the first time, close co-operation between the War Office and the Admiralty in London, to face the possibility of war.

Thus Germany had prepared Europe for what she basically did not want, a general war. But as some of her initiatives had backfired, she felt herself more and more threatened by the very "encirclement" she had brought about, and against all reason, and her own best interests, started to regard war as a real chance to break out of the diplomatic corner into which she had maneuvered herself.

The scene was set. Europe was richer than ever and had greater colonial empires than ever. It was possible to travel without passports from one end of the continent to the other. Business relations were international. Science had come up with new discoveries, from quantum physics to relativity, from genetics to psychoanalysis. New inventions had just been made – such as the automobile, the airplane, the wireless. Everybody was so used to the one century-old deep peace, that almost no one believed that a general war could break out. But this was exactly what did happen.

72   World War I

On 28 June 1914 the Austrian heir, Archduke Franz Ferdinand, was assassinated at Sarajevo by a Serbian nationalist. Austria sent off a stiff ultimatum to Serbia, which surprised everybody by accepting most of its stipulations. Austria decided, in spite of this, to seize this chance, in order to reverse her sagging fortunes in the Balkans, and declared war. Serbia's big ally, Russia, mobilized her forces (a slow process, and therefore decided upon precipitately). Austria's big ally, Germany, not to be outdone, mobilized too, and, for good measure, declared war on Russia (1 August) and on France (3 August). The Schlieffen Plan was immediately put into effect and Belgium was invaded, upon which Great Britain declared war on Germany. Turkey and Bulgaria later joined the Central Powers while Japan, Italy, Romania, and the United States joined the Allies.

Germany's strategy was to decide the war speedily in the west, and then shift her forces to the east. But new defensive weapons, such as the machine-gun, made attack costly and the use of cavalry impossible. The German armies were too unwieldy, lacking yet an Army Group Command. Their First Army, on the extreme right, opened up a gap, into which the British Expeditionary Force blundered. The Schlieffen Plan had taken no account of a British army, and floundered rapidly. In the first Battle of the Marne (5–11 September 1914) France brought up reinforcements, partly in Paris cabs, counter-attacked, and the Germans were stopped.

This was perhaps the decisive battle of the war, marking the transition from a war of movement to a war of attrition. For the next four years an unbroken line of trenches and mined barbed-wire obstacles stretched from the Swiss border to the sea. Attacks were costly beyond anything dreamed of in previous wars. New weapons, such as poison gas, first used by the Germans at Ypres in 1916, or tanks (developed on Churchill's order by the Admiralty, as the Army command was too hidebound to do so), first used on the Somme the same year, did not manage to force the issue and only added to the gruesomeness of trench warfare.

In the east the relatively small German forces surprised everybody by repelling the large Russian forces and completely annihilating a Russian army at Tannenberg. The commanding general was the aged Hindenburg, and the real architects of the victory seem to have been his chief-of-staff, Ludendorff, and his chief-of-operations, Hoffmann. The first two moved up later to control all of the German war effort, when Kaiser Wilhelm proved to be a weak reed behind his bluster. Hoffmann controlled the later operations in the east, which eventually knocked Russia out of the war.

In the Balkans, Serbia was overrun in 1915–16. On Winston Churchill's insistence a British landing was attempted at Gallipoli in 1915, in order to take Istanbul and open a short line of supply to floundering Russia, but the Turks under Mustafa Kemal (the later Atatürk), defeated the attempt and the mostly Australian troops had, eventually, to be evacuated after substantial loss of life. Instead, two other fronts were established, one around Salonika, to threaten Bulgaria, and one in Palestine, to keep the Turks away from the Suez Canal.

Italy, which had originally belonged to the Central Powers, decided to join the Allies instead. But she was repeatedly defeated by the Austrians, with some German help, and had to be reinforced by French and English formations in order not to be knocked out of the war.

The German colonies were quickly overrun by British forces,

except for Tanganyika, parts of which were held by the Germans until the end of the war.

A decisive aspect of the war was the close blockade by the Royal Navy. The results were hunger and epidemics in Central Europe, as the war drew to its close. The Germans made but one attempt to attack, and were reasonably successful at the Battle of Jutland (1916), but for the rest of the war their expensive fleet was left to rust in its home ports. The more active were their submarines, which attacked the merchant ships supplying Great Britain. The threat was grave, but in due time they were defeated by the convoy system and other counter-measures. Furthermore, the declaration of unrestricted submarine warfare brought the United States into the war (1917). It very soon played an essential part in producing huge quantities of munitions and other war materials.

As the war neared its end the most important leaders of the Allies were Lloyd George in Great Britain, Woodrow Wilson in the United States, and Georges Clemenceau in France. All the forces of the Allies in France were commanded, for the first time, by one general, Ferdinand Foch.

In 1918 the Germans tried to force the issue once more on the Western Front, by transferring there the bulk of their troops from Russia. They managed to cross the Marne, but were repelled in the end (20 July 1915). Increasing numbers of American soldiers began to arrive in France, enabling the Allies to advance in the autumn, first slowly, then more rapidly.

At the same time the Allied forces advanced also from Salonika northward and from Palestine into Syria. Bulgaria first requested an armistice, to be followed by Turkey and Austria. The armistice with Germany came into effect at 11 a.m. on 11 November 1918 – the eleventh hour of the eleventh day of the eleventh month.

Could Germany have won the war? Probably. If Russia had been attacked first, and the French frontier held defensively until Russia had been overcome, Great Britain and the United States might not have entered the war. France would not have been able to stand up to a concentrated attack by all the German forces. But the Schlieffen Plan had the German leadership mesmerized.

The results of the war were awesome. More than 10 million Europeans had perished, not counting the further millions who died in 1918 and 1919 of an influenza epidemic, caused by undernourishment in Central Europe. Among the dead was the flower of Europe's youth. When one wonders about the mistakes made in the years between the wars, one has to remember that most of the potential leaders had been killed. France, for instance, had lost half its men between the ages of twenty and thirty-one. Also many of those who did return were changed men. The optimism of the generation before 1914 was gone for many years. America withdrew into "normalcy" and isolationism, Russia into Communism and Stalinistic autocracy.

Another result was the Balkanization of eastern Europe. Weak new states were set up, as a result of the Versailles Peace Treaty – such as Yugoslavia, Czechoslovakia, Poland, the Baltic states, and an enlarged Romania. Although this was a triumph for the nationalistic principle, they proved unable to stand up to the encroachment of Nazi Germany and Stalinist Russia. Furthermore, the harsh treatment of Germany by the Versailles Treaty ensured that the Germans would try again. The "War to end War" spawned, as a result, another World War.

73   The Years between the Wars

The years between the wars were a time of ideological struggle between Communism and Fascism, and between these totalitarian ideologies and democracy. The battleground was worldwide.

In Hungary the Communists, under Béla Kun, swept a Democratic regime aside in March 1919, only to be ousted themselves in November of that year by Admiral Horty, the last commander-in-chief of the Austro-Hungarian navy, in World War I. His was the first postwar dictatorship in Europe, and it lasted until 1944, when he was arrested on the order of his erstwhile ally, Hitler.

Another military strongman was Marshal Pilsudski (1867–1935), who drove the Soviet armies out of Poland (1920) and served as virtual dictator of his country from 1926 to 1935.

The first real Fascist regime was set up in Italy, by Benito Mussolini (1883–1945). In his youth Mussolini had been a socialist journalist and agitator. The war changed his ideas and he formed right-wing radical groups which merged into the Fascist Party. The name was taken from the bundles of rods borne before ancient Roman magistrates, and was first used in 1919. Some of its ideology was derived from the poet Gabriele D'Anunzio (1863–1938), who had led a band of volunteers to occupy the city of Fiume in 1919, and introduced the raised hand salute, later adopted by Fascists, Nazis, and Falangists.

As formulated by Mussolini, Fascism stood for national pride, hostility to Marxism, contempt for democracy and the old order, and obedience to one leader. In Italy there was often a bit of cheap theatre about it. But the middle classes favored Mussolini as they were afraid of a Marxist take-over. In 1921 there were serious riots in Milan, Bologna, and Florence. Mussolini staged his "March on Rome" in October 1922, but in reality he traveled by express train, and his followers did no more than stage a parade in Rome, after he had been entrusted by King Victor Emmanuel III (1900–46) with forming the government.

Gradually Mussolini turned Italy into a Fascist dictatorship and assumed the title of Duce (leader). His regime relied in part on force, on the ruffians of the "Black Shirts," on censorship of the press, on destruction of the trade unions, and repression of all dissent. But outwardly Italy looked more efficient, "the trains ran on time," and the Catholic Church was placated by the 1929 Concordat, which established the independent state of the Vatican.

Mussolini's image demanded an aggressive foreign policy, and in 1935 he invaded and conquered, with some difficulty, Abyssinia. The League of Nations proved unable to stop him. In 1939 he annexed Albania. In 1936 he formed the "Axis" with Berlin.

Germany passed through a runaway inflation in 1923, in which the savings of much of the middle classes were wiped out. The Weimar Republic was fatally weakened by the economic chaos of the 1920s. Left- and right-wing parties came to the fore, at the expense of a stable democracy. Adolf Hitler (1889–1945) was an Austrian, who had served in the German Army in World War I. In 1919 he joined the new "National Socialist German Workers Party," and became its undisputed leader. He made his name with anti-Semitic tirades and attacks on the Treaty of Versailles. In 1923 he staged the "Beerhouse Putsch" in Munich, but failed and was arrested. In prison he wrote *Mein Kampf* (My Struggle). The depression of 1929 and the following world slump made his party the second largest in Germany, and led in 1933 to his appointment as Chancellor by President Hindenburg. Hitler immediately established a one-party system, eliminated possible rivals in the 1934 "Night of the Long Knives," and took over also as head of state and Führer (leader).

Propaganda was used intensively to mold public opinion; the intellectual values which had been so prominent in Germany were rejected; modern art was condemned as degenerate; Jews were persecuted and packed off to concentration camps; "Racial Purity" was proclaimed with much fanfare; and "Brown Shirt" rowdies terrorized the opposition.

In 1934 Hitler had Dolfuss, the dictator of Austria, murdered. He then began an intensive program of rearmament, which improved Germany's economic position and increased his popularity.

Let us look now at some of the remaining democracies. In France the Third Republic (from 1870) did not prove much of a success. The party structures were weak; there was a multiplicity of factions and a lack of responsible politicians; governments were short-lived – forty-four cabinets between 1918 and 1940, headed by twenty different prime ministers! Nevertheless, the democratic tradition in France was strong and no real threat materialized from either Communism or Fascism. Paris continued to be the cultural capital of the West, with more writers and painters than ever before competing for attention. Many were politically involved. Pablo Picasso painted his *Guernica* as a protest against Fascist bombings in Spain.

In England, too, there was a lack of able politicians, as shown by prime ministers of the modest caliber of Stanley Baldwin and

Neville Chamberlain. The Liberal Party split and ceased to be an alternative to the Conservatives, to be replaced by the Labour Party. There were several years of industrial unrest, culminating in the General Strike of 1926. The Depression years in the 1930s had a negative influence on public morale. The belief in her democratic system seemed sometimes less sturdy than it later proved to be in World War II. Soviet spymasters were able to enlist a surprising number of Cambridge students, who later infiltrated the British secret services. In 1936 Great Britain was shocked by the Abdication Crisis, in which Edward VIII preferred his twice-divorced American lady love, Mrs Wallace Simpson, to his crown.

After the end of World War I the United States withdrew into isolationism, and refused to join the League of Nations. By collecting the War debts in full, and by raising tariff barriers, America contributed her share to the postwar economic chaos of Europe. In the 1920s government was reduced to a minimum, and a free hand given to the great business corporations. Between 1921 and 1929 industrial output nearly doubled. Such products as automobiles, radios, vacuum cleaners, and refrigerators swamped the market. The entertainment industry came of age, with Hollywood films being distributed worldwide. Newspapers gave pride of place to the marital problems of such stars as Jean Harlow and John Barrymore, over the newsflashes about Fascist or Nazi outrages in Europe. Prohibition (1919–33) did little to stop the use of alcohol, but gave the Mafia and gangsterism in general a head start, which the forces of law have still not been able quite to make up.

The 1929 stock market crash pushed the economy into an unprecedented depression. By 1932 the output of industry and the national income had both been reduced by half. Fifteen million persons were unemployed. The poor performance by President Hoover put a question mark to the continued existence of the traditional democratic way of life. America might, just possibly, have turned to a populist agitator like Senator Huey Long of Louisiana, if it had not been saved by Franklin Delano Roosevelt (1933–45). Within a hundred days he had fifteen proposals enacted by Congress. His decisiveness and his "New Deal" returned a spirit of confidence to the United States. The national government became much stronger than it had been before. But it was only World War II that once again brought full prosperity back to America.

Spain was run by a Fascist-type dictator, Primo de Rivera, from 1923 to 1930. His son founded the Fascist Falange party in 1933. The monarchy had been abolished in 1931 and the Republican government was weak and divided. The army generals revolted in 1936 and for three years the Spanish Civil War drew the attention of all the world. Ideological differences were fought out here, weapon in hand. Germany and Italy came to the assistance of General Franco, and the Soviet Union helped the Republicans. Many well-meaning Europeans enlisted in the International Brigades, finding out too late that they were effectively controlled by the Communists. When Soviet Russia withdrew its support in 1939, the Republican forces collapsed and their last strongholds were captured in Barcelona and Madrid. Franco continued to govern Spain until his death in 1975. Spaniards are in debt to him, though their historians will as yet not admit it. He, alone among the 1939 leaders, was able to keep his country out of World War II. Further, he gave his nation nearly forty years of quiet, peace, and efficient government, which had been sadly absent from Spanish history for the previous quarter millennium. Thus he made the growth of a large middle class possible, which became the sound foundation of the democratic way of life ushered in after his death.

In the last years before World War II Hitler had become the central figure of Europe. In 1936 he remilitarized the Rhineland, and in March 1938 he absorbed Austria in the "Anschluss." He managed to browbeat and convince Neville Chamberlain and Daladier, at Munich in September 1938, to let him occupy the German-speaking Sudetenland of Czechoslovakia. But Chamberlain's belief in appeasement and "Peace in our time" soon proved short-sighted: Hitler occupied Prague in March 1939 and the Memel region of Lithuania soon after. In the Nazi–Soviet pact of August 1939 Hitler paved the way for the occupation of Danzig and the attack on Poland (1 September 1939). When England and France declared war on Germany (3 September), World War II

had commenced. Russia occupied her share of Poland, and also
the Baltic republics and Bessarabia.

74 World War II

It is somewhat amazing to note that Hitler and his advisors had
not understood the basic lesson of World War I – that full-scale
war had become prohibitively expensive in life and property. The
result was a second gruesome conflict, which devastated Europe
– no country more so than Germany and Russia, its two main
instigators.

Poland was overrun in 1939 by the German armies within a
month, while England and France did nothing to help. In April
1940, Denmark was occupied and Norway captured by the Germans, with ineffective English interference. Neville Chamberlain
was ousted and the veteran Winston Churchill took over as
Prime Minister. In May 1940 the Germans invaded Holland
and Belgium, sending the British fleeing from Dunkirk, and,
wheeling south, knocking the French out of the war. Most of
France was occupied by them and Marshal Pétain was installed
as their puppet.

Hitler's first setback came in the late summer of 1940, when his
air force was defeated in the Battle of Britain, and England could
not be invaded. Italy joined in the war, sure that the Germans had
won, but her army in Libya was promptly defeated by the British
based in Egypt, and her attack on Greece was repulsed. Germany
came to her aid in the spring of 1941, occupying Yugoslavia, and
capturing Greece and the Island of Crete. But the German war
machine lost precious weeks in these campaigns.

Hitler invaded Soviet Russia on 22 June 1941, with help from
Finland (which had repelled a Russian attack in 1939–40),
Hungary, Romania, and Italy. This unprovoked and eventually
suicidal attack on Russia illuminates Hitler's inability to learn
from history. He was involving himself in a two-front war,
which had lost Germany World War I, and he was invading
Russia, which neither Charles XII of Sweden, nor Napoleon

had been able to carry out successfully. And indeed, in spite of all the German blitz-advances, the mere size of Russia, the winter conditions there, and the fierce resistance of her soldiers, stopped the Germans before they could capture either Moscow or Leningrad.

There is another parallel between Hitler and Napoleon – Hitler, too, ruled for a short period over nearly all of continental Europe. However, his barbarian behavior to conquered nations, and especially to the Russian civil population, which he regarded as sub-human, did not exactly recommend his rule to his new subjects. In Russia, there existed, for instance, a very real potential in the enemies of Stalin and Communism who would have been prepared to throw in their lot with the Germans, and might have helped decide the war on the eastern front. One army was indeed formed from Russian deserters, under General Vlassov. But when the Russians witnessed the full measure of German barbarity and disdain for them, they quickly lost any illusions they might have harbored.

Behind the frontiers the German SS was occupied in liquidating the Jewish population of Europe. No similar case, on such a scale, of cold-blooded genocide of a people who had not even fought the Germans is recorded by history. This Holocaust brought death in concentration camps and gas chambers to some six million Jews, men, women and children – nearly two-fifths of all the Jews in the world. In most occupied European countries the local population helped the Nazis in rounding up the Jews, though there were some exceptions, most notably in Denmark.

On 7 December 1941, the Japanese joined in the fray by attacking Pearl Harbor (they had been already at war with the Chinese ever since 1937). While the United States had been hopelessly divided until then isolationists and interventionists, the Japanese managed to unite them overnight behind President Roosevelt's war policy. Germany, to keep her hand in, declared war too. Both Axis powers made a fatal mistake, as they did not appreciate sufficiently America's enormous potential for war production. When fully geared up, the US industry was able to produce tens of thousands of tanks and airplanes and hundreds of ships per year. Germany and Japan could not even try to match this production. Further, alerted by scientists like Einstein, America began building the Atomic Bomb, which would have decided the war anyway. But, as it was, the issue was decided in Europe before the bomb was ready.

Until the middle of 1942 the Axis was victorious everywhere. The Japanese overran Burma, Malaya, Indonesia, Siam, Indochina, and the Philippines, and captured Singapore, Hong Kong, and most of the islands of the western Pacific. Only at Bataan did General MacArthur put up a spirited defense, and parts of New Guinea were successfully defended by the Australians.

The Germans attacked southern Russia in 1942, and reached Stalingrad and the Caucasus. In Libya, General Rommel intervened, and in the summer of 1942 penetrated deep into Egypt. But then the hinge of fate turned, to use Churchill's phrase. Large amounts of American weapons, tanks, and other matériel of war began to arrive. Rommel was defeated by Montgomery at el-Alamein (23 October–4 November 1942) and began his retreat to Tunis, where what remained of his army, was taken prisoner in May 1943. The Americans and British landed in North Africa, under the command of General Eisenhower (8 November 1942). The Russians encircled the German Sixth Army at Stalingrad (5 September 1942–31 January 1943) and the long German retreat from Russia commenced. In the Pacific the Japanese were defeated in the naval battle of Midway Island (4 June 1942), and from then on were pushed backward.

Roosevelt and Churchill decided to give precedence to the European theatre of war, but American resources were so vast that even as a secondary theatre of war the Pacific war was kept nearly abreast with the war against the Germans. In several important meetings between Roosevelt, Churchill, and Stalin, in Teheran (28 November–1 December 1943), Yalta (4–11 February 1945) and Potsdam (16 July–2 August 1945), the great strategy of the war and the general outline of the postwar settlement were thrashed out. The compromise solution between divergent opinions often proved successful. Thus, for instance, America's desire to launch a premature invasion of Europe in 1942, as against Churchill's desire to attack only Europe's "soft underbelly," resulted in a reasonable compromise: Sicily and Italy were attacked in the summer of 1943 (upon which Mussolini's regime collapsed), and the main invasion of the continent was launched in Normandy on 6 June 1944. The Russians protested against the delay, as, in the meantime, they had to face most of the German might, but, after all, they themselves had helped Hitler between 1939 and 1941. Stalin, the brutal tyrant, proved a very effective war leader, if only because his soldiers feared the brutality of his regime even more than they feared the Germans. The Red Army became a formidable fighting force, which defeated the Germans in the greatest tank battle of history, at Kursk (5–15 July 1943). The Russians then pushed on, through eastern Europe, until in the spring of 1945 they reached Berlin and Vienna.

Far behind the front lines, local resistance groups started fighting the Germans, from France to Russia. Perhaps most effective were Tito's Partisans in Yugoslavia.

American, English, French, and Polish forces advanced up the Italian boot between 1943 and 1945. American, English, Canadian, and French armies advanced in 1944 from the Normandy beachheads to Paris and to the German border. The Germans made a final attempt at a counter-attack in the Ardennes (16 December 1944 to 16 January 1945), but were defeated and pushed back into Germany.

Hitler committed suicide on 30 April 1945, in the ruins of Berlin, two days after the Russians and Western Allies had linked up on the River Elbe. On 7 May the Germans capitulated. The father of Fascism, Mussolini, found the end he had deserved: he was killed by partisans of his own nation, while trying to flee to neutral Switzerland. His body, and that of his mistress, were brought back to Milan, to be strung up by their heels.

The Japanese had been pushed out of Burma by the British, and then defeated in the greatest sea battle of history, at Leyte Gulf (24–6 October 1944), by the Americans, who proceeded under Admiral Nimitz and General MacArthur to advance by island-hopping northward, until they reached Iwo Jima and Okinawa. Such desperate Japanese measures as the suicide attacks by Kamikase pilots could not change the outcome. The next stage was to have been the invasion of Japan, but beforehand, on 6 August 1945, the first atomic bomb was dropped on Hiroshima.

The Russians attacked the Japanese forces in Manchuria, and Japan surrendered on 14 August 1945.

The victory was followed by the trial of war criminals, both German and Japanese. At Nuremberg, 177 persons were indicted, 25 were sentenced to death, 117 to various prison terms. Many were sentenced elsewhere. But relative to the scale of German atrocities in Europe, and especially in Russia, these numbers seem very modest.

In the last stages of the war the Soviet armies had been guided by political motives, which the Allied Commander-in-Chief, General Eisenhower, did not sufficiently appreciate. Thus all of Poland, Romania and Hungary, and large slices of Germany and Austria ended up under Soviet control, and were later turned (except for Austria) into Soviet satellites. Only Churchill's spirited intervention saved Greece from a similar fate.

In Japan, General MacArthur's control was complete, but northern Korea fell into the hands of the Communists.

In April 1945 the setting up of the United Nations was decided upon in a conference in San Francisco.

Germany and Austria and their capitals were divided each into four occupation zones, with France under General de Gaulle joining the other three allies as an outwardly equal partner.

75   The Collapse of European Colonialism

The two World Wars lost Europe her colonial empires. What had held them together was not so much the armed forces stationed in the colonies, as the great prestige of the white man, his culture, and his institutions. This prestige was heavily taxed by the spectacle of European powers fighting each other, and even more by Japan's easy victories early in World War II. They captured Dutch Indonesia, the American Philippines, French Indochina, British Malaya and Burma. After their inhabitants had witnessed the superiority of Japanese arms, they were not prepared to accept any renewed rule by the white man when the colonial powers tried to return after the war.

Sometimes there was no struggle. America, for instance, granted the Philippines full sovereignty on 4 July 1946.

In Indonesia the story was different. An Indonesian Nationalist Party had been founded by Achmed Sukarno (1901–70) in 1927. He spent thirteen years in Dutch prisons, but emerged from the Japanese occupation as the de facto President of Indonesia. The Dutch tried in 1947 to recapture the islands by force, heavily bombing Jakarta in 1948, but in the end the Netherlands had to recognize Indonesia's independence in 1949. In 1963 the Netherlands also ceded western New Guinea. Sukarno ruled as dictator until he was overthrown by General Suharto in 1967.

The British set up a "Union of Malaya" in 1946, but changed it to a more independent "Federation of Malaya" in 1948 and expanded it in 1963 into Malaysia, which also included North Borneo and Sarawak. An attempt by the Chinese to launch a guerrilla war in the jungle was suppressed by the British, with Malayan backing (1950–60). Singapore received a great measure of self-government as the "State of Singapore" (1959–63); it joined the Federation of Malaysia in 1963, but left it two years later, because of discrimination against the Chinese, and became independent. Singapore's destinies were guided, with a firm hand, by Lee Kuan Yew, until 1990. Burma was granted independence by Great Britain in 1947.

Neighboring India, the most important and populous of all colonies, had a much longer history of nationalist struggle. The Indian National Congress was founded in 1885, as an educational association. But soon such leaders as B. G. Tilak (1856–1920) were demanding political activity as well. The Japanese victory over Russia in 1905, and the decision to split the province of Bengal into two parts, intensified this line, and turned the Congress into a political party. The British responded by arrests, executions, and by an attempt to enlist the large Muslim community as an ally against the Hindu nationalists. In 1906 the Muslim League was accordingly formed. In 1909 a reform act made Indians eligible for membership in the legislative, advisory, and executive councils of India. Separate constituencies were created for the Muslims. After further agitation, sometimes with Muslim co-operation (as they opposed England's campaigns against Muslim Turkey in World

War I), a further Act established in 1919 a bicameral parliament for India, and legislative councils in the provinces, elected by Indians.

M. K. Gandhi (1869–1948) emerged as the leader of the Congress movement. He preached passive resistance – boycotting British goods, and civil disobedience. When arrested he resorted to hunger strikes. He soon gained world renown and put the British thoroughly on the defensive. His followers regarded him as a saint and called him "Mahatma," the "Great Soul." One of his associates was Motilal Nehru (1861–1931), the founder of a dynasty which has ruled India most of the time since independence. His son Jawaharlal Nehru (1889–1964) organized the more practical aspects of the struggle for independence by the Indian Congress. During World War II most Congress leaders were jailed, but the British Labour Government agreed, after the war, to give full independence to Britain's most important colony. Congress demanded a united India, but the Muslims, led by M. A. Jinnah (1876–1948), demanded partition and the creation of Pakistan. In elections after the war, Jinnah's followers won nearly every seat in the Muslim areas. While discussions about the borders between Pakistan and India were going on, Jinnah favored "direct action" and many were killed in the chaotic translocation of Muslims and Hindus, when India and Pakistan received their independence in 1948. Gandhi was one of the victims, as he was assassinated by a fanatic Hindu. Jawaharlal Nehru became Prime Minister of an independent India, to be followed later by his daughter Indira Gandhi (1966–84) and grandson Rajiv Gandhi (1984–91). Indira and Rajiv were both assassinated by Sikh and Tamil extremists, respectively. Eastern Pakistan agitated for independence and after a war between India and Pakistan in 1971, succeeded. It then became a separate state, named Bangladesh.

The decision to let India go meant that there was not much point for Great Britain to hang on to other far less important colonies and territories, if they desired independence. But in some of the more strategic localities, an armed struggle was necessary.

In Palestine, an Arab uprising had taken place between 1936 and 1939, which the British subdued with Jewish help. During

World War II Britain's anti-immigration policy sealed the fate of hundreds of thousands of Jews in Nazi-controlled Europe, who might otherwise have found refuge in Palestine. As a result, the Irgun Zvai Leumi, under Menahem Begin, began from 1943 onward to operate against British army and administration targets, joined, from time to time, by two other underground organizations. By 1947 Great Britain had to keep 100 000 soldiers in small Palestine – as many as in India – and the British administration had withdrawn into a few compounds defended by barbed wire. Britain that year returned its mandate for Palestine to the United Nations, which decided to divide the country into two states. This was enthusiastically received by the Jews, but opposed by the Arabs, who in 1948 attacked the new State of Israel, but were repelled. Neighboring Jordan took over the main part of what was to have been the Arab state.

In the nearby Island of Cyprus the Greek-speaking majority of the population demanded "Enosis" – unification with Greece. The British made use of the small Turkish minority as an excuse to withhold concessions as long as possible. The Greeks organized the EOKA movement, led by Colonel Grivas (1898–1974), which fought a guerrilla war against the colonial government. By 1959 the British decided to grant independence to the island, and Archbishop Makarios (1913–77), the Greek leader, became President (1960–74). The Turks invaded Cyprus in 1974 and carved out a "Turkish Federated State" in two-fifths of the island. Greek families had to flee to the island's Greek part. In the years since, Greek Cyprus has become economically very successful, while the poorer Turkish part was evacuated by many of its inhabitants, who were replaced by new settlers from the mainland.

In Africa decolonization went much smoother for Great Britain. Nevertheless, between 1952 and 1956 the part terrorist, part magico-religious Mau Mau movement of the Kikuju tribe of Kenya operated against the British settlers. Independence was granted to Kenya in 1963. Sudan had become independent already in 1956 and Ghana in 1957. England's other African colonies followed soon after. Problems were encountered mainly in Southern Rhodesia, which was dominated by a white minority. Its leader, Ian Smith, served as Prime Minister from 1964 to 1980 and refused to share power with the African majority. When he declared unilateral independence Britain refused to intervene by force, but imposed trade restrictions and an oil embargo. Guerrilla activity by blacks commenced, and some 20 000 people were killed. Strong international pressure was brought to bear on Smith, until he had to give in. In 1980 independent Zimbabwe was proclaimed.

The most populous British colony in Africa, Nigeria, received Dominion status in 1960 and became a republic three years later.

A particularly messy affair was the independence of the Belgian Congo. Originally it had been obtained by the explorer Stanley for King Leopold II of Belgium (1885). Much scandal about abuse of the natives implicated the king's administration, and King Leopold had to sell the Congo to his kingdom, Belgium, in 1908. The population was denied all political rights, nor was much done in order to further education in the country. In 1960 the Belgians decided to grant independence, but without proper preparations or sufficient time for a handover. Civil war broke out between the President, Kasavubu (1917–69), and his Prime Minister, Lumumba (1925–69), and between both and the leader of the rich mining province of Katanga, Tshombe (1919–69). The latter hired white mercenaries to fight his battles, and became for some time Prime Minister of Zaire, as the country was renamed. The Secretary General of the UN, Dag Hammarskjöld (1905–61), lost his life whilst trying to negotiate a settlement. In the end a previous Sergeant Major of the Belgian-controlled forces, Seko Mobutu (born 1930), seized power, ousted Lumumba, and had Tshombe condemned to death in absentia.

The decolonization of the French Empire proceeded in several stages, marked by two full-scale wars. The postwar French government was much less ready to depart from her colonies than the Labour government in Great Britain. In 1944–5 France was forced out of Syria and Lebanon by local uprisings, with some British backing. But the first great challenge was in Indochina. A Vietnamese Nationalist Party had been established there in 1925. Local revolts occurred later. But the real damage to the French position was caused by the Japanese occupation in World

War II (1941–5). The Vietminh resistance movement fought the Japanese from 1942 onward, and on their surrender in September 1945 a Vietnamese republic was proclaimed in Hanoi, under the leadership of Ho Chi Minh (1890–1969). The French returned in strength to Saigon, but a full-scale war was fought by them against the Vietminh between 1946 and 1954. The latter were commanded by General Giap (born 1912) – one of the most successful military commanders of the 20th century – who defeated the three major powers of France, the United States, and China. The main action against the French was fought in 1954 at Dien Bien Phu, near Hanoi, where 16 500 French paratroopers were reduced to some 3000 before they surrendered. Two months later France signed an armistice and withdrew from Vietnam.

After recurring unrest, France granted Morocco and Tunis independence in 1956. Guinea bolted the French Empire in 1958. In the years after, most other African colonies were granted independence, often with generous help from France. Particularly successful was the Ivory Coast, ruled by President Felix Houphouet-Boigny (born 1905), who had the unique advantage of having previously served in the French cabinet. Chad was helped by France when invaded by Libya.

The exception was Algeria, which was a part of France itself, and not a colony, and had been settled by many Frenchmen. In 1947 France promised the Algerians a full share in the political life of their country, but in view of the intransigence of the local French army, this promise was never honored. As a result, a bitter civil war ranged from 1954 to 1962 between the Algerian FLN and the French. The army in Algeria, with the backing of the white settlers, overthrew the Fourth Republic in May 1958 and installed General de Gaulle instead. Yet he, too, saw no alternative to an agreement with the FLN, and in spite of two further military revolts (in 1960 and 1961) pushed it through. Algeria became independent in 1962.

Except for some Pacific islands, British Hong Kong, and Portuguese Macao (both of which are due to be returned to China), nearly all colonies have disappeared.

Many of the newly-independent states – such as India, Indonesia, Malaysia, Syria, Israel, Singapore, and Morocco – have amply proven their ability to govern themselves. But the great majority, especially of African states, have done poorly, and chaotic conditions prevail. Local leaders often did little else but enrich themselves, while such facilities as roads, ports, and industries were left to rot. Famines and epidemics (of AIDS, for instance) are endemic. Democratic institutions were immediately abolished. Among the dictators were such bizarre figures as Idi Amin of Uganda (1971–9) and "Emperor" Bokassa of the Central African Republic (1966–79), who was later sentenced to death on charges of "murder, cannibalism and fraud."

Tribal groups often fight each other. Unfortunately it seems to be a law in poor countries that the more rational a government's economic policies, the greater its domestic unpopularity. Much of sub-Saharan Africa has reverted to conditions similar to those that existed before the white man appeared on the scene, but made worse by new maladies, deadlier weapons, expanding deserts, and the disappearance of the local fauna and flora.

76   The Cold War

Optimists, like President Roosevelt, had hoped that the close relationship with Soviet Russia could be continued after the end of World War II. They were wrong. Long before the war was over Russia started to disregard previous commitments, in order to set up Communist regimes in the area captured by the Red Army.

Some 10 000 Polish officers had been murdered at Katyn by the Soviets in 1940. The Red Army did not come to the aid of the Warsaw Rising in 1944, letting the Germans kill some 15 000 Poles. A Communist government was forced on Poland once it had been captured, with Russian Marshal Rokossovsky as Minister of War, to keep an eye on the proceedings. Such devoted Communists as Bolesław Bierut (1948–56), Władyslaw Gomulka (1956–70), and Edward Gierek (1970–80) were appointed Prime Ministers, to keep Poland in line, in spite of strikes and rioting in 1956, 1970, and 1980.

In Hungary, too, a similar procedure was followed, but in

1956 a full-scale revolt broke out, under Prime Minister Imre Nagy. Russian tanks recaptured Budapest, Nagy was executed, and Janos Kádár was installed as Prime Minister (1956–88). He succeeded in carrying out many reforms, especially in the economic field.

In Bulgaria a Communist regime under Georg Dimitrov was set up, after the country was captured in 1944. The real power was later in the hands of the secretary of the Communist Party, Todor Zhikov (1956–89). The Bulgarian secret services were used sometimes by the KGB to carry out its dirty work, such as in the case of the attempted assassination of Pope John Paul II.

Most of Czechoslovakia was captured by the Russians, but General George Patton's Third Army reached Pilsen in 1945. An uprising in Prague was supported by the previously pro-Nazi Vlassov Army. President Edvard Beneš returned from exile and Jan Masaryk (1850–1937) became Foreign Secretary. In a coup in February 1948 the Communist leader Klement Gottwald (1896–1953) seized power and had Jan Masaryk murdered by defenestration. The Soviet regime was particularly repressive, as shown in the 1953 Slansky trials. When Prime Minister Alexander Dubček tried to introduce a modicum of freedom and democracy in 1968, Warsaw Pact divisions invaded Czechoslovakia and the repressive Communist government was reimposed.

In Germany the Soviets did not participate in the establishment of a unified state by the other three occupying powers, and instead set up a Communist German Democratic Republic in the part occupied by them (1949), first under Walther Ulbricht (1949–71) and later under Erich Honecker (1981–9). Mass demonstrations were suppressed in 1953. A higher industrial output and standard of living were achieved than in the other satellites. Her greatest impact was in the field of competitive sports, where East Germany often reigned supreme.

What was happening in eastern Europe was described by Winston Churchill in a speech of 5 March 1946 as the bringing down of an Iron Curtain. The term "Cold War" was coined by Bernard Baruch in a speech of 16 April 1947.

The United States tried to check further Soviet penetration in Europe by a programme of financial aid to the Western countries of Europe (the Marshall Plan, of 1947). It totaled $17 000 million over the period 1948–52, and was very successful – especially so in West Germany, where it triggered the "Wirtschaftswunder." A German Federal Republic was set up in 1949, with Bonn as capital, and Konrad Adenauer as Chancellor (1949–63). While East Germany represented to a certain degree the continuation of the autocratic traits of old Prussia and of the Germany of Bismarck, Wilhelm II, and Hitler, new ground was broken in the Federal Republic, where a democratic regime proved, for the first time, highly successful in Germany. The Federal Republic became the economic powerhouse of western Europe. In foreign relations strong ties to France provided the foundations for the European Common Market and the European Community. The most important later Chancellors have been Willy Brandt (1969–74), Helmut Schmidt (1974–82), and Helmut Kohl (since 1982).

The other main power of western Europe was France, where de Gaulle (1890–1970) replaced the faltering Fourth Republic by the Fifth Republic, with a strong presidency, which has proved very successful, under such presidents as Georges Pompidou (1969–74), Giscard d'Estaing (1974–81), François Mitterand (1981–95), and Jacques Chirac.

The Cold War led to a number of crises. The Russians tried in 1948 to squeeze the Western Allies out of Berlin, by imposing a blockade. The Americans and British responded by organizing a successful airlift of food and fuel during the winter of 1948–9.

By 1949 the Soviets, too, had developed the atomic bomb, apparently with the help of secrets stolen from the Americans. Because of the Russian threat, the United States and her European allies formed NATO (later joined also by Greece, Turkey, and West Germany). The Soviets responded in 1955 by setting up the Warsaw Pact. Europe was divided thus into two armed camps, between whom an armed conflict seemed only too possible.

An actual war broke out, however, elsewhere. In 1950 Soviet-controlled North Korea invaded American-backed South Korea. As Russia was then boycotting the UN Security Council sessions, America succeeded in pushing through a mandate to help South Korea. Fifteen nations sent troops, which came under the command of General Douglas MacArthur. While nearly all of South

Korea had been overrun (except for the area around the port of Pusan), MacArthur launched a naval counter-invasion at Inchon, far behind the lines. The North Koreans had to withdraw, and most of their country was occupied. Communist China intervened in November 1950, and the Americans were forced back sixty miles beyond the previous frontier. A new UN offensive in 1951 established the line near the old frontier, which has divided the two Koreas ever since. The loss of life was very high, possibly four million people (including 142 000 American servicemen).

In Europe a constant stream of refugees moved from the East to the West. To stop this haemorrhage the Berlin Wall was erected in 1961 – the very symbol of the Cold War.

Fidel Castro's accession to power in Cuba in 1959 opened a threat much nearer to the United States itself. The 1961 "Bay of Pigs" attempt to overthrow Castro failed, partly because it was not given the air support originally provided for. The Cold War nearly became a hot war when, in 1962, US intelligence discovered the Russians placing missiles in Cuba, which could have reached all of the continental USA. President Kennedy imposed a naval blockade, the Russian ships with further missiles turned back, and the missiles which had been instaled were dismantled. Never had World War III seemed more imminent.

Next came the Vietnam War (1965–75). America tried to build up South Vietnam as a barrier to the spread of Communism in Southeast Asia, and had, under President Johnson, increasingly to involve her own armed forces. Some 400 000 American soldiers were deployed there by the end of 1966. But General Giap managed to utilize jungle conditions in order to neutralize America's huge predominance in weaponry. The rising resentment against the war, in the United States itself, led to a reduction of the effort under Richard Nixon (1969–74), to the evacuation of the American forces, and to the eventual conquest of South Vietnam by the Vietcong (1975).

Not to be outdone in making mistakes, the Soviets invaded Afghanistan in 1979, in order to prop up their supporters there. They were not much more successful than the Americans had been in Vietnam, and because of the increasing pressure of the

Muslim Mujaheddin ("holy warriors"), and their crisis at home, they evacuated their forces in 1988–9.

In the 1970s the Cold War expanded into Africa, where Angola, Mozambique, and Ethiopia became Soviet satellites. In Angola, for instance, some 50 000 Cuban troops, 1100 Soviet advisors, and 500 million dollars a year were needed to prop up the regime, against UNITA rebels, supported first by South Africa and later by the United States. Some 200 000 lives were lost in the fighting.

Another area in which the Cold War heated up was the Middle East. Soviet military advisors had been active since the 1950s in Egypt and Syria, and their armies were equipped with Russian airplanes, tanks, and other equipment. To counter this situation the Eisenhower Doctrine was promulgated in 1957, and put into effect by helping King Hussein of Jordan and by landing 10 000 Marines in Beirut in 1958. During the Yom Kippur War (1973) the Soviets airlifted large amounts of equipment to Egypt, and the Americans even larger amounts to Israel.

The Cold War, in an age of atomic weapons, was surely a dangerous adventure. The Soviets must bear most of the blame for it, but the great difference between them and the Nazis can be seen from the fact that it never became a hot war. Khrushchev's dangerous game with missiles in Cuba resulted in his removal by his own peers.

77   The Western Powers since World War II

After the Depression years, after the horrors of World War II, a period of unprecedented peace and prosperity came to the West. New principles seemed to guide its destinies. It was no longer the powers with the greatest armies, the largest physical areas and the richest colonies which were best off. Germany and Japan came to understand that they had been chasing a chimera, and succeeded in recouping their fortunes no longer by means of force and arms, but by hard work, efficient industrial organization, and good labor relations. The colonial powers shed their colonies and found that their rising standard of living was unaffected.

During the 1956 Suez Crisis, Great Britain and France tried, for the last time, to play the Big Power game and found that they no longer belonged in that league.

The United States was the only Great Power left in the West, and the country found this to be a rather expensive honor. The armament and prestige race with the Soviet Union nearly bankrupted the economy. The development of the hydrogen bomb, of other armaments, the race into space and to the moon, became more and more expensive. Some presidents, like Dwight David Eisenhower (1953–61) and Jimmy Carter (1977–81), preferred to get involved as little as possible in the rivalry with the Soviet Union. Others, like Harry S. Truman (1945–53), John F. Kennedy (1961–3), Lyndon Baines Johnson (1963–9), and Ronald Reagan (1981–9), seemed more aggressive in their policies. Reagan's "Star War" plans, though possibly chimerical, seem to have been the last straw which broke the will of Soviet Russia to continue the race.

For many years America continued to be the pre-eminent economic power. But in the 1980s Japan and Germany overtook her in many fields. Not having to shoulder any similar load of defense spending, their lot was easier. America found it difficult to compete with Japan and Germany in the production of cars and machines, but forged ahead in such novel fields as computer technology and electronic communications. In the 1990s her economy seemed to perform again more successfully than that of her main rivals.

Many basic changes have occurred in American society. The civil rights movement has done a lot to improve the status of the blacks. In 1954 the Supreme Court outlawed segregation in public schools, and struck this way at segregation in general. During the 1960s "sit-ins" and other forms of direct action were used, and white racism in the South was slowly overcome. The first Southern president since the Civil War, Johnson, passed the crucial acts which outlawed racial discrimination in employment, education, voting, and public accommodation. But while racism has receded, the lot of many of the blacks has not necessarily improved.

Women have achieved more equal rights, but at a price – the family as the basic unit of society has been weakened. The divorce rate stands at 50 percent; single-parent families are no longer an exotic curiosity. Whites are less dominant – the percentage of Hispanics, blacks, and Asians is constantly rising.

Some of these social phenomena apply also to Europe. But for the most part it is America that leads and Europe which follows. Hollywood and television are often the media by which American values are disseminated.

The leveling of culture has enabled Europe to embark on the novel experiment of a European Market and a European Community. The original initiative came from such French leaders as Robert Schumann and Jean Monnet. Differences between the various member nations are no longer so wide as to be unbridgeable. Also the experiences of World War II – often far from laudatory or heroic – have enabled the nations of Europe to be more flexible in their attempts at unification. If Great Britain seems so often to be the odd man out, this may derive from the fact that her conduct in the war was largely irreproachable.

Great Britain has lagged behind in productivity. While previously "Made in England" stood for quality, this has no longer been so for the last quarter century. Countries like France, Italy, and even Spain have overtaken her in the industrial field. Great Britain's main problem has been that not only her labor force tends to be less motivated, but even more so her managerial class – originally perhaps because of high income taxes. Thatcherism has had some impact, but the change for betterment is not all that great. People in the Latin countries of Europe are simply prepared to work harder.

The European Community is one of the three main centers of economic and political power and influence in the world today, on an equal level with the United States and Japan, but able to draw on a much larger reserve of manpower.

Germany has become very much the leading economic power of Europe, and since the 1990 unification with East Germany, also her political potential is vast. Sometimes the historian cannot but feel that western Europe is back to where it started out as an independent civilization a thousand years ago, with Germany very much sitting centerpiece.

78   The Advent of Women Power

The last third of the twentieth century has been a time in which more than ever before women around the world have been able to have their opportunities widened, their rights respected, and their voices heeded. One of the results of this new situation has been the impressive number of women who have taken over the leadership of their countries. While there have been successful queens ever since Hatshepsut in 15th century BC Egypt, there had previously been no female prime ministers or Presidents. This has changed now.

The first female prime minister was Mrs Sirimava Bandaranaike in Sri Lanka (1960–77), soon followed by Indira Gandhi in India (1966–84), who turned out to be the most formidable prime minister independent India has produced so far. However, they were the wife and daughter of previous prime ministers and would not have reached their position otherwise. Mrs Golda Meir of Israel (1969–74) was the first female prime minister to make it completely on her own. Both Mrs Meir and Mrs Gandhi were called upon by circumstances to run serious wars, and did so successfully.

The first female President was María Estela Perón, in Argentina (1974–6), who was far from successful (Perón's first wife, Evita, had been the real force behind her husband's rise to power).

A real mover and shaker was Mrs Margaret Thatcher (1979–90), the longest consecutively serving British prime minister in 160 years and one of the outstanding figures of her time. Her character, and her victory in the Falkland Islands War, earned her the title of "Iron Lady," and her economic and social ideas were credited with the reversal of the decline of the British economy, and entered history as "Thatcherism."

Other recent prime ministers were Mrs Gro Harlem Brundtland of Norway (several times between 1986 and 1996), one of whose cabinets consisted 50 percent of women; Benazir Bhutto in strictly Muslim Pakistan (1988–90, 1993–7); and Kazimiera Prunskiene of Lithuania (1989–91), who helped spearhead the drive for Baltic independence.

Two female Presidents, whose rise to power were world sensations, were Corazón Aquino in the Philippines (1986–92), who ousted a dictator, and Violeta Chamorro in Nicaragua, who defeated a Communist regime at the polls in 1990.

In the same year Mrs Mary Robinson was elected President of Catholic Ireland. In France Edith Cresson served as Prime Minister in 1991–2. In Bangladesh, in February 1991, both leaders in parliamentary elections were women. Begum Khaleda Zia, the wife of a previous dictator, won a handsome majority and formed the government. Hanna Suchocka served as Prime Minister of Poland in 1992–3.

The greatest achievement of these women is that in future the rise of a woman to the top political job of her country will no longer be a sensation (at least outside the United States).

79   The Revival of Islamic Fundamentalism and Fanaticism

Since the 16th century the Islamic countries had been pushed to the sidelines by Western Civilization. This has left them with a deep-seated feeling of resentment against the West, in spite of the fact that in the second half of the 20th century they have been coming into their own again. They have been affected only marginally by Western Civilization. Their own values have survived intact and are now being reinforced. From the Atlantic to the Pacific this is being proclaimed by the thousands of slim minarets which are built in their traditional style even today.

Some of the border states of Islam – such as Turkey, Malaysia, or Indonesia – are keen to co-operate on an economic level, the one with the European Union, the two others with the prosperous Pacific Rim states. Among the 190 million Muslims of Indonesia, Islam is somewhat watered down – alcohol is freely consumed, women are allowed much freedom, and Islam is not the official state religion; but this is not the case elsewhere.

The most extreme case is Iran. Extreme fundamentalism and religious fanaticism have been typical of Persia since the Ayatollah Khomeini (1979–89) assumed power. All the laws of the Koran have to be implicitly observed. Regiments of untrained teenagers were flung in the Gulf War against Iraq's modern weaponry. Hundreds of thousands of them were killed or maimed. The rationale was that as fighters in a holy war of Islam those killed would be elevated directly to paradise. Khomeini was prepared to act also beyond the borders of his own country, as he did in issuing a death sentence against the novelist Salman Rushdie because of his "blasphemy against Islam." In contravention of all accepted norms of diplomatic immunity, in 1979 he had sixty-three members of the American embassy taken hostage. International terror activities are inspired, financed, and run from Teheran.

Persia does not stand alone. Similar fundamentalist doctrines guide large and influential groups in most Islamic countries. In Jordan, Sudan, and Algeria fundamentalists have had surprising electoral victories in recent years. But in most Islamic countries there are no elections, or at least no elections which are not rigged. Most of these countries are ruled by dictators, such as Qadafi of Libya, Assad of Syria, or Saddam Hussein of Iraq.

In southern Lebanon the Hezbollah factions mount suicide operations, similar to those of the "Assassins" in the same area, in the times of the crusades. Hezbollah was responsible for the car-bomb attacks in Beirut in 1985 and for the taking of western hostages there in the 1980s. Normal humanitarian considerations do not apply.

In Saudi Arabia the code of law is the Koran – thieves have their hands amputated, alcohol drinkers are publicly flogged, and women are forbidden even to drive a car. And Saudi Arabia is one of the richest countries on Earth, with enormous holdings in foreign countries and vast international economic influence.

Islam is as intolerant regarding other religions as it was a thousand years ago. The "Assyrian" minority in Iraq, for instance, was wiped out in the 1930s by the ruling Muslims. The Kurds of that country have suffered from persecutions for a long time, and some of their villages have been attacked with poison gas by Saddam Hussein. The small, Christian-dominated republic of Lebanon has been wrecked, since 1975, by its Muslim citizens, who wanted to dominate it. In the bloody civil war (which ended in 1990), first the Palestine Liberation Organization (PLO) intervened and later the Syrian army. Conditions became so insufferable that many Christians have left the country, which today harbors a Muslim majority. When Israel tried to intervene in 1982, in order to help the Christians and eliminate PLO bases from where attacks were mounted against her, the Christian leader and president elect, Bashir Gemayel, was promptly assassinated by Muslim terrorists, and Israel had to withdraw.

Some of the Islamic countries, such as Bangladesh and Egypt, are facing a frightening threat of overpopulation. But Islam is opposed to birth control nearly as much as the Catholic Church. There is little chance of its being implemented successfully. Other countries, such as Iraq, Saudi Arabia, and the Gulf sheikhdoms, actually encourage high birthrates. The number of unemployed, from Morocco to Jordan, is vast (40 percent of the men in Tunis). The population explosion adds to the dangerous instability of the Islamic world. Life is held of little value in such a society. In a ten-day civil war in Southern Yemen in 1986, 10 000 people were killed. The number of casualties in the war between Iraq and Iran was more than one million.

Islamic fanaticism is not limited to religious matters. In the Arab world it is prevalent also in politics. Western ideas of diplomatic decorum do not apply. Such dictators as Qaddafi of Libya or Assad of Syria have been the main supporters of international terror organizations. Assad had thousands of the inhabitants of the city of Hama massacred after political disturbances there. Saddam Hussein invaded Kuwait, which had supported him financially throughout the Iran–Iraq War, when he felt that he needed the revenue of her oil-fields.

Most extreme is Arab fanaticism where it concerns Zionism or Israel. The Arabs of Palestine organized pogroms against the local Jews in 1920, 1921, and 1929, with considerable loss of life. Further attacks occurred in the period 1936–9, and again in

1948, when the British withdrew from Palestine. When the Jews proved able to stand up to them, the Palestinians were reinforced by the regular armies of Egypt, Syria, Iraq, and Jordan. These too were defeated, and the State of Israel came into being. Since then it has had to endure constant harassment by its Arab minority and threats from its Arab neighbors. President Nasser of Egypt closed the Suez Canal and the Red Sea to Israeli navigation, and in the resulting Six Day War (1967) Israel captured Sinai, and when attacked by King Hussein of Jordan, it also captured the West Bank (of the River Jordan) and the Golan Heights from Syria. When Israel proposed to return these areas in exchange for a peace treaty, she was turned down. In 1973 Israel was attacked on the religious holiday of Yom Kippur by Egypt and Syria, but succeeded again in repulsing their attacks. In 1977 President Sadat of Egypt agreed to a separate peace, and Sinai and all Israel's oil-fields were turned over to him. He was, however, promptly assassinated by a Muslim fanatic for this "act of treason." The Intifadah (1987–93) tried to cement nationalistic Palestinian feelings by attacks against Israeli civilians and soldiers, with considerable loss of life on both sides. Serious peace talks have been held since 1993 between Israel and her neighbors. Full agreement has been reached with Jordan and partial agreement with the Palestinians.

Arab and Islamic intransigence is probably the biggest danger to the peace in the post-Cold War period, as illustrated by Saddam Hussein's occupation of Kuwait in 1990. It did not pass unchallenged. It found the United States in an unprecedented position of unquestioned world leadership, after the collapse of Soviet power. Furthermore, George Bush, the American President, made skillful use of this fact, by lining up a wide alliance of both European and Middle Eastern states, under UN auspices, and immediately concentrating American forces to defend Saudi Arabia and its oil-fields against any further Iraqi thrust.

Saddam Hussein refused to withdraw from Kuwait, and the Gulf War became inevitable. An unprecedented build-up of men and matériel took place in Saudi Arabia during the closing months of 1990. About half of the soldiers were Americans, while the other half were British, French, Saudis, Egyptians, and Syrians, or were drawn from seventeen other countries. Bush side-stepped various diversionary diplomatic moves by the Soviets, France, Iran, and the UN. When a last ultimatum was refused by Hussein, Bush launched concentrated air strikes against Iraq on 17 January 1991. These air strikes continued for five weeks, effectively pulverizing most of Iraq's armed forces and its potential to wage war. Saddam Hussein's air force fled to Iran. His main counter-moves were to attack Saudi Arabia and neutral Israel with Scud missiles, to torch oil wells in Kuwait, and to pollute the Persian Gulf with oil.

Enthusiastic vocal support for Saddam Hussein in most Arab countries had little influence on events. In the end, the Allied ground forces needed but 100 hours (24 to 28 February) to defeat the Iraqi army. A naval feint from the east effectively immobilized many Iraqi troops; others were overrun by a frontal assault into Kuwait, mainly by US marines and Arab divisions. The main thrust came on the desert flank in the west, where American, British, and French armored forces, in a lightning advance through ideal tank country, encircled and cut off the Iraqi army fighting in Kuwait. The Iraqi soldiers surrendered by the thousands.

When Bush stopped the fighting, much (but not all) of the Iraqi army had been destroyed, and Kuwait had been liberated. America, Great Britain, and France were swept by euphoria. Mixed feelings were the lot of powers such as Germany and Japan, who had shown themselves to be but paper tigers in their support for the Western alliance.

Saddam Hussein successfully hangs on to power, in the process crushing, with much bloodshed, revolts in the Shi'ite south of Iraq and its Kurdish north. American forces had to be des-patched to save the lives of thousands of fleeing Kurds. Many Arabs continued to venerate Saddam Hussein, who stood up to America and the "hostile West," albeit unsuccessfully. In Kuwait hundreds of Iraqi collaborators (including many Palestinians) were executed.

The United States' Vietnam legacy of self-doubt and divisiveness was now overcome: Worldwide, America had shown that there was but one Superpower left. But it proved near-impossible to force Hussein to dispose of his nuclear potential, of his Scud missiles, and much of his other lethal weaponry.

80   The Rise of the States of the Pacific Rim

One of the most interesting recent world developments has been the rise of some of the states of the Far East to a position of economic affluence and importance. They rival the United States and western Europe as centers of industry and trading, and overshadow them as centers of banking. In an age in which economic strength has replaced military might, the Pacific Rim has become one of the most important centers of power in the world.

This development has been spearheaded by Japan. Between 1953 and 1965 Japan's gross national product grew by 10 percent yearly. In many areas, from shipbuilding to computer technology, she became the leading industrial power of the world. Nowadays her banks are the largest in the world and her millionaires the richest. The Japanese held in 1984 some 20 percent of international banking assets, and in 1990 their share had doubled, to 40 percent. Their bank deposits, measured in yen, had doubled in size between 1980 and 1988, and measured in dollars, doubled between 1986 and 1988. By 1990, Japanese banks owned four out of Californias's ten largest banks. In Hawaii people joke that the Japanese would not bomb Pearl Harbor again – they now own it.

The secret of Japan's success was twofold. Her workforce was very highly motivated. Some of the Confucian ethos inspired her white- and blue-collar workers to greater efforts than usual in America and Europe. They divined, quite correctly, that no strikes, but greater productivity, would lead to a higher standard of living. The second secret was the different structure of her industries. While America believes that free enterprise means a fight of everybody against everybody, and has anchored this concept in her anti-trust laws, Japan believes in close co-operation between government and big business. In an era when America is no longer economically pre-eminent, and different countries are competing for world markets, the American concept seems outdated and the Japanese concept much more effective. This sort of co-operation cannot, however, be achieved overnight by everybody who desires it, but has its roots deep in the Japanese past and social culture. Japanese firms have always tried to create a consensus inside the firm, and to build up loyalty to the firm. Americans prefer a dog-eat-dog system of "the best man wins." Job-hopping is a way of life for American managers. Already in school the American child is taught to compete and not to co-operate.

Japan has not remained alone. South Korea, Taiwan, and Singapore have also moved ahead, have expanded their industries and banking services, and increased both their exports and their standard of living dramatically. As wages in Japan became higher and less competitive, much of the actual production has been subcontracted to Taiwan and South Korea. This process continues today. Hong Kong is subcontracting some of its production to the nearby Chinese mainland province of Guangdong, where the standard of living is, as a result, much higher than in the rest of the country. Japan, Korea, Taiwan, and Australia pass business on to Indonesia, Thailand, and Malaysia, where labor is cheaper. The Philippines, under President [spelling, first name] Romos, are moving ahead as well.

Hong Kong and Singapore are now better off than their erstwhile British colonizers. Taiwan has an average income of $10 000 and foreign currency reserves as large as those of Japan. The average Taiwanese is twice as likely to go to university as his British peer. Life expectancy for women in China and Indonesia increased, respectively, from 59 and 45 years in 1965 to 71 and 63 years in 1989.

China occupies a special niche. With her 1250 million inhabitants she is potentially the most important country of the Far East. But the many ideological twists and reverses of policy under Mao Zedong have left her far behind the other countries. Under Deng Xiaoping a very different path was followed from that of Soviet Russia under Gorbachev. The economy was successfully freed from most ideological shackles, but the main attempt to achieve also political freedom was bloodily suppressed in the Tiananmen

Square massacre (1989). In spite of much criticism in the West, the results show Deng to have chosen well. While Soviet Russia has collapsed and cannot feed its population, China seems to be on the way to a much improved economic future.

81   The Collapse of the Soviet Empire

When Stalin died in 1953 Soviet Russia was thrown into some disarray. Nikita Khrushchev (1894–1971) denounced him at the Twentieth Congress of the Soviet Communist Party (1956), but when faced with the Hungarian revolt of that year, showed that he had the power and the will to maintain Russia's position in Eastern Europe. He did not have, however, Stalin's prestige, when it came to relations with the other great Communist power, China. The rift between them changed the character of the Soviet bloc, which was no longer united or monolithic. China became a third Superpower. This fact was skillfully played upon by Dr Henry Kissinger, in order to reduce the threat posed by the Soviet Union.

Khrushchev proved an erratic leader, on one hand making the Soviet regime less repressive at home, but on the other alternating peaceful gestures with threats abroad, and finally embarking on the frightening Cuban Missile Crisis. As a result he was replaced (1964) by the more conservative Brezhnev (1906–82), who steered a middle course between Stalin's excesses and Khrushchev's attempts at reform. Under him Soviet Russia reached the peak of its power, especially during Carter's weak presidency. Further satellites were added in Africa, and, seemingly, in the Middle East. The Soviet armed forces grew at a quicker pace than the American ones. It seemed at times that the Soviet Union was about to eclipse America as the prime Great Power.

Reagan's policy of strengthening America's armed forces reversed this trend. Under Brezhnev's two short-term successors, Russia's economic problems became more and more acute. There existed many points of basic weakness in the Soviet system. Collectivization had proved an abysmal failure. Central bureaucracies could not cope with the demands of markets and the problems of production and transportation of goods. The consumer sector was starved. The social equality promised by Lenin had produced in real life a *priveligentsia* of party members with special rights, shops, and dakhas, while the mass of the population spent much of their lives lining up in queues for scarce food and products.

In some of the Soviet satellites curious aberrations appeared. In Communist North Korea Kim Il Sung ruled like a feudal prince, with his son as heir apparent. In Cambodia Communist Prime Minister Pol Pot carried out a pointless genocide of his own people on an unprecedented scale. In Albania a complete isolation was imposed by the local Communist dictator, Hoxha, not only from the capitalist world, but also from the "deviationist" Communist world as well. As a result Albania has found it in recent years even more difficult than the other Balkan countries, to catch up with the rest of Europe.

When Mikhail Gorbachev (born 1931) took over as General Secretary of the Communist Party (March 1985) there seemed to be no other way but a complete overhaul of the Soviet system. Gorbachev launched a policy of "openness" (*glasnost*) and of economic reconstruction (*perestroika*). An unprecedented liberalization of the regime was followed by a complete reorganization of Russia's constitution and ruling structure. Gorbachev became very popular abroad, but much less so at home, because his economic reforms did not improve the critical situation of the country. Shops were emptier than ever.

In the political sphere, matters started to get out of hand when Gorbachev relieved the previous pressure on the satellites. This became evident first in Poland. The problem there went back to the visit of the Polish Pope John Paul II in 1979. It caused such widespread jubilation that the Poles became aware that they were still united by national and religious ties and had not completely sold out to Communism. These feelings were the background to the foundation in 1980 of the Solidarity movement, by Lech Walesa and others. Although repressed in 1981, it was far from forgotten and quickly revived in 1988, when the new wind began to blow from the Kremlin. One year later the ban was officially lifted. In the general elections of June 1989 Solidarity succeeded so spectacularly that one of its leaders had to be appointed Prime Minister.

Everybody in the Soviet bloc awaited Gorbachev's reaction. Would he act, as Khrushchev had done in 1956 in Hungary, or Brezhnev in 1968 in Czechoslovakia? When he did not intervene, there followed a rush to set up independent, increasingly non-Communist governments in all the other satellites, from Hungary to Mongolia. In Czechoslovakia, Vaclav Havel moved near-directly from prison to the presidency. Only in Romania a bloody revolution had to be staged before the local Communist strongman, Nicolae Ceauşescu, could be toppled and executed.

One of the least expected results was the reunification of Germany. When Hungary enabled East Germans in the summer of 1989 to move freely across its borders into Austria, a stampede ensued, first of holidaymakers already in Hungary, followed later also by others. East Germany's leadership was faced by a major crisis. Erich Honecker had to be replaced – but to no avail. On 9 November the Berlin Wall was rushed by ordinary people from both East and West and disappeared as an effective barrier.

Chancellor Kohl decided to push energetically for unification. The Soviet Union's desperate financial position enabled him to buy Gorbachev off, by substantial economic help. On 1 July 1990 currency union was achieved, and on 3 October of the same year the two Germanys were united.

The pay-off was Kohl's electoral victory – especially in East Germany. Later it was decided that Berlin would eventually be again the capital. But euphoria was short lived. West Germans started worrying about the severe financial drain on their economy. The position in the East was much worse: its economy practically collapsed and nearly a million became officially jobless, while more than double that number were being paid to do practically nothing.

The transition to a market economy has turned out not to be simply a matter of throwing switches and of spending money. Finding new managers and administrators for the East is a major problem. New machines had to be found for existing industries, people had to be trained in their use, other industries (such as shipbuilding, for instance) have had to be completely scratched.

The resulting economic recession and social foment have still not been overcome.

The lot of some other eastern European countries might be even less tractable.

Gorbachev had certainly not envisioned the far-reaching changes which followed. The Soviet Union itself collapsed, after an abortive Communist coup d'état (19 August 1991). Boris Yeltsin, the President of Russia, emerged as the central figure of the country. The Baltic countries had already demanded complete independence. Now Yeltsin encouraged the other republics of the Union to follow their example. Thus his way to the top would be smoothed. But it would be done at the expense of dissolving the Soviet Union. And this is the way it did happen. The Soviet Union, the Communist Party, and the central organs of the state were dissolved. Gorbachev retired into private life.

Attempts at radical economic cures made the situation only worse, especially in Russia itself. Lacking any capitalist tradition there seemed to be no alternative to central planning to fall back on. Mafia-type organizations, more than true private enterprise, started to fill the void.

During a short period the vast edifice of the Russian and Soviet Empires – built up over the centuries by Ivan the Terrible, Peter the Great, Catherine the Great, Lenin, and Stalin – has come crashing down.

Such new independent states as Ukraine, Belorus, Moldavia, and the Baltic countries appeared in Europe; Georgia, Armenia, and Azerbaijan in the Caucasus; and Kazakhstan, Turkmenistan, Uzbekistan, Kirigistan, and Tadjikistan in Central Asia. Some of them hope for great oil finds in the Caspian Sea; others, such as the Baltic states, have taken up old commercial relations with Central and Northern Europe. But in the central republics of Russia, Ukraine and Belorus, the economic situation has been going so far from bad to worse. The incapacitation of Yeltsin by sickness and age is weakening Russia ever more. Her separate regions are striving for more and more independence from the center. The catastrophic war in Chechnya has shown up the weakness of the Red Army and its inability to enforce the authority of Moscow.

Smaller wars developed elsewhere in the Caucasus, such as

between Armenia and Azerbaijan and between Georgia and Abhasia. But by far the bloodiest struggle occurred further west, in Yugoslavia. Tito's centralized semi-Communist state disintegrated. President Miloscovich's attempt to set up a strong Serbia at the expense of other minorities, caused Croatia and Slovenia to secede. A major war developed in Bosnia between Serbs, Croats, and Muslims. The Serbs initially occupied most of the country, but eventually, towards the end of the war, the Croats reoccupied parts of it. "Ethnic cleansing" caused the massacre of many thousands of men and women and the flight of millions of refugees. The European powers proved unable to stop the fighting and it took the intervention of the United States (1996) to impose peace.

Russia is being driven in the meantime farther and farther east, out of Europe. Such newly independent previous satellites as Poland, Czechoslovakia, and Hungary seem sure to join both NATO and the European Community. Further Balkan and Baltic states are likely to join later. Russia is putting up a bold front, but can actually do little to stop its rout and withdrawal. Five centuries of Russian advance westward have ended at one stroke, without any bloodshed, in débâcle and failure. The map of Europe and Asia has been drastically redrawn.

The United States and NATO find themselves suddenly without an adversary. The Cold War has come to its end. At first the very name "Communist" became a dirty word in Eastern Europe and Communist parties rushed to change their name. But after several years of economic disasters Communism has become popular again, and the Communists have gained substantially in free elections, even in Russia herself.

In some of the Balkan countries little difference could be found between the rulers and ways of government before the revolution and after. But by 1997 democratic ideas are seen to be advancing even in Serbia and Bulgaria. Worldwide, democracy seems at last to be on the move, though less so in the Islamic and African countries and certainly not yet in China.

No other revolution has, perhaps, been as sweeping and as far-reaching as this "Second" Russian Revolution. Where will it all lead?

Epilogue: On the Threshold of the Third Millennium

It can be argued that the 15th century was the Italian, the 16th the Spanish, the 17th the Dutch, the 18th the French, the 19th the British, and the 20th the American century. Just to show how changeable and uncertain human affairs are – whom should we nominate for the 21st century – the Japanese?, the Germans?, the Chinese?, the "Europeans"?, or once more the Americans? It would certainly be interesting to meet up in the year 2100 to compare notes.

But are we even certain that our descendants will still be around then? Might not pollution, or the greenhouse effect, or ozone depletion, or acid rain, or an atomic war, have wiped out the human race earlier than that?

On the other hand, human adaptability and initiative might have found solutions to these and other problems, just as solutions were found and implemented earlier – from the fashioning of stone tools to the discovery of antibiotics.

To make some sense out of the myriad events of human history, philosophies of history have been formulated over the centuries. St. Augustine regarded history as a struggle between good and evil, represented by church and state. To Hegel, history was the way to release the human spirit from its shackles, with human freedom as the goal, realized best in the law-abiding state. Karl Marx believed that history was motivated by economic, not spiritual, forces, and would lead, by necessity, from Capitalism to Socialism. More recently the cyclic theories of Oswald Spengler (1880–1936) and Arnold Toynbee (1899–1975) enjoyed considerable vogue, discussing the rise of civilizations and their decline. But in recent years historiography has become so specialized that the very formulation of theories is suspect.

It is easy to point out some possible scenarios for future conflict. The rich countries of the West and of the Pacific Rim face the abysmally backward and poor ones of sub-Saharan Africa and elsewhere. The many nations previously governed from Moscow have caused a Balkanization of all of eastern Europe, with each national splinter searching for a new identity. Civil war continues in many countries, as far apart as Sri Lanka, Colombia, and Rwanda. Such densely-populated countries as China and India have not yet solved some of their most pressing problems. The Islamic world is a powderkeg, about to explode. Nuclear proliferation is a constant danger, despite recent successful international agreements on decommissioning.

Other problems are of a different nature. About half of the world's population lives in urban centers and cities. But the biggest megacities are becoming unmanageable, face traffic strangulation, unbreathable air, and in some of the worst cases, the basic necessities of life are almost absent for most people. The poorer quarters of Mexico City, Cairo, Calcutta, Lagos, Tehran, and São Paolo are simply beyond any previous human experience. New epidemics spread like wildfire in the more backward countries. Man decimates the forests he cannot create. Pollution threatens the very roots of life. The West is swamped by hard drugs, grown mostly in the Golden Triangle of Southeast Asia, along the frontier of Afghanistan and Pakistan, and in the northwest of South America.

Thus, the young generations which will soon now enter into the third millennium need not fear that they will lack challenges. They should, however, heed George Santayana's warning:

Those who cannot remember the past are
condemned to repeat it.

Index